The Balzac Review / Revue Balzac

2025, n° 8

The Balzac Review / Revue Balzac

Écologies / *Ecologies*

Sous la direction de Göran Blix et Andrea Goulet

PARIS
CLASSIQUES GARNIER
2025

Université Roma Tre
Département de Sciences politiques
Via Gabriello Chiabrera, 199
I - 00145 Rome
Les articles spontanément soumis à la rédaction doivent être envoyés à :
thebalzacreview@gmail.com

Tous les textes reçus par *The Balzac Review / Revue Balzac* sont soumis à une double expertise anonyme (*double blind*).

ISBN 978-2-406-18771-4
ISSN 2646-2044

SOMMAIRE/*SUMMARY*

DOSSIER / *THEMATIC DOSSIER*
ÉCOLOGIES/*ECOLOGIES*

VARIA/*VARIA*

RUBRIQUES/*COLUMNS*

DOSSIER

ÉCOLOGIES/*ECOLOGIES*

ABRÉVIATIONS

Lov.	Bibliothèque Lovenjoul. Exemple : *Lov. A. 231, f° 19 v°*, Bibliothèque Lovenjoul, armoire A, cote 231, folio 19 verso.
CH	*La Comédie humaine*, édition publiée sous la direction de Pierre-Georges Castex, Paris, Gallimard, « Bibliothèque de la Pléiade », 1976-1981, 12 vol.
OD	*Œuvres diverses*, édition publiée sous la direction de Pierre-Georges Castex, Paris, Gallimard, « Bibliothèque de la Pléiade », 1990-1996, 2 vol.
PR	*Premiers romans*, édition établie par André Lorant, Paris, Robert Laffont, « Bouquins », 1999, 2 vol.
NC	*Nouvelles et contes*, édition établie, présentée et annotée par Isabelle Tournier, Paris, Gallimard, « Quarto », 2005-2006, 2 vol.
CHH	*Œuvres complètes*, édition nouvelle établie par la Société des Études balzaciennes [sous la direction de Maurice Bardèche], Paris, Club de l'Honnête Homme, 1955-1963, 28 vol.
BO	*Œuvres complètes illustrées*, édition inachevée, publiée sous la direction de Jean-A. Ducourneau, Paris, Les Bibliophiles de l'Originale, 1965-1976, 26 vol.
Corr.	*Correspondance*, édition établie, présentée et annotée par Roger Pierrot et Hervé Yon, Paris, Gallimard, « Bibliothèque de la Pléiade », 2006-2017, 3 vol.
LH	*Lettres à Madame Hanska*, édition établie par Roger Pierrot, Paris, Laffont, « Bouquins », 1990, 2 vol.
AB et millésime	*L'Année balzacienne*. Revue annuelle du Groupe d'Études Balzaciennes. Garnier (1960-1982) ; PUF (1983-).

PROLOGUE

On Balzac and All That Might Be Lost

In one of his most memorable anecdotes, the photographer Nadar speculated whether Balzac was actually afraid of the daguerreotype, that new, eerie device for extracting slices of life, or whether he was simply letting his imagination run free. Nadar gives this description of the novelist's disquiet:

> Balzac se sentit mal à l'aise devant le nouveau prodige: il ne se pouvait défendre d'une appréhension vague de l'opération Daguerrienne. [...] [S]elon Balzac, chaque corps dans la nature se trouve composé de séries de spectres, en couches superposées à l'infini, foliacées en pellicules infinitésimales, dans tous les sens où l'optique perçoit ce corps.
>
> L'homme à jamais ne pouvant créer, – c'est-à-dire d'une apparition, de l'impalpable, constituer une chose solide, ou de *rien* faire une *chose*, – chaque opération Daguerrienne venait donc surprendre, détachait et retenait en se l'appliquant une des couches du corps objecté.
>
> De là pour ledit corps, et à chaque opération renouvelée, perte évidente d'un de ses spectres, c'est-à-dire d'une part de son essence constitutive.[1]

Whether Balzac's fear was real or a mere thought experiment designed to produce a momentary *frisson*, I have been drawn again and again to this

1 Félix Nadar, "Balzac et le Daguerréotype", in *Quand j'étais photographe* (Paris: Flammarion, 1900), p. 5-6. "Balzac felt uneasy before the new marvel: he could not defend himself against a vague apprehension about the Daguerrian operation. [...] [A]ccording to Balzac, each body in nature is composed of a series of specters, in infinitely superimposed layers, foliated into infinitesimal pellicules, in all directions in which the optic perceives this body. Since man is unable to create — that is, to constitute from an apparition, from the impalpable, a solid thing, or to make a *thing* out of *nothing* —, every Daguerreian operation would catch, detach, and retain, by fixing onto itself, one of the layers of the photographed body. It follows that for that body, and with every repeated operation, there was an evident loss of one of its specters, which is to say, of a part of its constitutive essence." (Félix Nadar, "Balzac and the Daguerreotype", in *When I Was a Photographer*, trans. by Eduardo Cadava and Liana Theodoratou [Cambridge, MA: The MIT Press, 2015], p. 4)

theory, first because it accommodates both technophobia and mysticism — two personal favorite pastimes — and because it expresses that supremely human anguish at the prospect of losing something. To cede even one of the billions of flat ghosts that form our essence is to die a little bit.

That a journal devoted to Balzac would find a place for ecocriticism is not surprising. The theme accords perfectly with a general pattern in his novels and shorter works of people losing what they most prize: love, beauty, money, status, friendship, youth, ideals, property, political power, ways of life that can never be recovered. Balzac, a true man of the nineteenth century, bore witness to the phenomena to which we now attribute species loss, habitat loss, crop loss, Arctic and Antarctic ice loss, loss in the confidence of a future. That includes everything from industrialization and empire building, to urbanization, the ruthless hunger for progress, and the global lacemaking of ever more intricate transport networks to get people and goods from one place to another. He watched it all and wrote every bit of it down.

Our beloved "secrétaire de la Société" always took minutes at this meeting called Life. But why are minutes ever taken? So that a decision, a thought process, a series of administrative gestures and the presence of individuals receives a duration beyond its naturally fleeting one. Like early photographers, the realists were at least partly motivated by preservation, depositing in their novels the human types, figures of speech, silhouettes of dresses that season, or the current price lists of sugar or gold. We owe gratitude to these chroniclers who bequeathed to us high-resolution snapshots of the spirit of their age.

Balzac paused his fears long enough to let Louis-Auguste Bisson peel off one of his specters for that daguerreotype we all know from 1842. Shot in a studio, the proud man lives forever in a vacuum cut off from the natural world. He does not look at us but at something, at someone lost to our knowing. The word visionary might aptly describe his bearing and that far-off look on his face. The present volume highlights one aspect of Balzac's vision, namely his intuition about what is worth saving. As the contributors show, he understood that the high-velocity change of his era would mean the disappearance of cherished things that had to be preserved, if only in a story. He wrote and wrote, feeling the urgency to catch it all, burning the candle at both ends. In the end, he traded life for the need to record it.

When Victor Hugo returned from a visit to Balzac on his deathbed, he told those he encountered, "Messieurs, l'Europe va perdre un grand esprit".[2] Upon his death, there was a sprint to capture his likeness one last time. The artist Eugène Giraud managed to sketch a portrait, but the making of a death mask proved impossible, Hugo tells us: "On voulait faire mouler son masque, mais on ne le put, tant la décomposition fut rapide".[3] There would be no plaster glimpse of his repose. Nature had other plans. As the art historian Rosalind Krauss reminds us, "On the family tree of images [the photograph] is closer to palm prints, death masks, cast shadows, the Shroud of Turin, or the tracks of gulls on beaches."[4] That is, it is the index of a presence that is now an absence. While some of Balzac's indexes were lost to time, a healthy number have lasted and been made perennial in books and archives and in the cyber aether. This volume breathes life into Balzac's immense catalog of all that was and might be lost.

Christy WAMPOLE
Princeton University

2 "Gentlemen, Europe is losing a great spirit" (translation mine).
3 Victor Hugo, *Choses vues II*, in *Œuvres complètes* (Paris: Ollendorf, 1913), p. 69–70. "They wished to mold his death mask but could not; the decomposition was too rapid" (translation mine).
4 Rosalind Krauss, *L'Amour fou: Photography and Surrealism* (New York: Abbeville Publishers, 1985), p. 31.

INTRODUCTION

Balzac and New Critical Ecologies

How might a reading of Balzac's work contribute to contemporary ecological thought? And conversely, what light might ecocritical perspectives shed on *La Comédie humaine*? The risk of anachronism in posing such a question is of course considerable. But, as we hope to show in this special issue, the enterprise is at once timely, coherent, and fruitful. It is true that Balzac and his contemporaries possessed no proper word for *ecology*: the term was not coined until 1866, by Ernst Haeckel, one of Darwin's German disciples — and the science itself did not develop until well into the twentieth century, while what we now know as the environmental movement only emerged in the 1960s. Yet it would be myopic to think that, in the absence of our own terminology, Balzac and his contemporaries had no awareness or concern with the shifting, conflicted, and precarious place of humanity in the natural world.

The Industrial Revolution, after all, was already well underway; pollution and public health, especially in the growing cities, were becoming major concerns, as were cholera epidemics, miasma, insalubrious living conditions, and urban mortality rates (Villermé, 2008; Jarrige, 2017; Barnes, 2018; Finch-Race and Gosetti, 2019). Before Pasteur and the microbe, hygienists and demographers were already seriously studying public health. The imbalance between the city, the nation's major consumer, and the country, its major producer of foodstuffs, was acutely felt as the night-soil accumulated in the cities ceased being recycled to fertilize the land, giving rise to what Marx presciently termed a "metabolic rift" (Foster *et al*, 2010). Beyond the expansion of cities, the growing network of railways was rapidly and radically changing the face of the French countryside, imprinting on the landscape the rapid rhythms of commerce, travel, tourism, and resource extraction. In the meantime, a new scientific cosmology was emerging: the geology of deep time, ushered in by the works of Buffon, Hutton, Cuvier, and Lyell, was embedding what had so far been a strictly human history, with its periodic ruptures, battles, and coups, into a larger narrative of planetary cataclysms, giving birth to a new historical sublime but also setting the stage for our modern understanding of humanity as a geological agent. At the same time, the Promethean heritage of Renaissance humanism seemed to have delivered, at long last, on its euphoric early promises, since science and industry now seemed to be on track to tame and subjugate the natural world (Merchant, 1980). It was in this context, too, of course, that the Romantic reaction took place, valorizing anew a fragile natural world beset by growing industrial pressures and increasingly removed from city-dwellers. The *sentiment de la nature* was born, making its appearance in Bernardin de Saint-Pierre, Mme de Staël, Senancour, Sand, Maurice de Guérin, and many others, although this newly named ecological affect would only be fully conceptualized in Élisée Reclus's programmatic essay of 1866 (Guest, 2017; Blix, 2019). Human rapacity was increasingly bemoaned, and extinctions lamented, while a new concern for animal welfare entered the legal and public sphere.

It is thus a misconception that what we now call ecological awareness is somehow a strictly modern preoccupation. The misunderstanding may be due, at least in part, to what Christophe Bonneuil and Jean-Baptiste Fressoz, in *The Shock of the Anthropocene*, describe as a self-serving form of presentist amnesia. With the proposed coining of our new geological period the Anthropocene, by leading climate scientist Paul Crutzen, in 2000, a new word and discourse emerged into view, one that quickly acquired almost talismanic powers. Since scientists could name, measure, and discuss this new phenomenon, the implication went, they were also in an excellent position to counteract the very threat it posed. Thanks to their vigilance, the world was, if not entirely safe, at least in the benevolent hands of experts — never mind that it was techno-scientific capitalism that had provoked the climate crisis to begin with. In this new discourse, the *anthropos* of the Anthropocene was not, as one might have thought, a bumbling, accidental, and chastened agent that only now belatedly grasped its own outsize impact, but rather an ingenious and invincible creature so powerful that it was capable of reshaping the globe. On this reading, the new name merely reaffirmed centuries of Promethean pride, while repressing any shred of humility the term might have conveyed. Rightly opposing such amnesia — or what they call "a patronizing history that fail[s] to rescue the socio-environmental resistances to industrialism" (2016, p. 253) — Bonneuil and Fressoz suggest greater historical attention to the many symptoms, warnings, and alerts that have in fact been sounded since the outset of the Industrial Revolution.

To cite one significant illustration in this regard, Charles Fourier, in 1821, penned some pages of preparatory notes for his *Traité de l'association domestique agricole* that he entitled "Détérioration matérielle de la planète". Taking to task the modern period, which he pejoratively termed "la Civilisation", for its dismal resource management and "folle confiance" in its scientists, Fourier pointed prophetically to "la détérioration de la Planète qui périclite et décline à vue d'œil" (1847, p. 401–402). It was no use taking comfort in the alibi of innocence afforded by the supposed powerlessness of humanity to impact the planet: "ne voyons-nous pas le travail de l'homme opérer des modifications climatériques vraiment énormes?" (*Ibid.*, p. 403) Contrary to common belief, "le genre humain qui entoure partout et exploite le globe est réellement plus grand que la Planète même" (*ibid.*). With a single stroke, Fourier here underscores the tragic consequences of thoughtless human agency, upending the self-serving ambivalence of the Anthropocene. It is of course easy to dismiss Fourier's outlandish fantasies, for even if he were right to note "[que] l'on voit la température se vicier rapidement" and "[que] les saisons semblent travesties" — their natural order scrambled by human excesses (*ibid.*, p. 402) — he unfortunately also maintained that the planet was in fact cooling and for that reason threatening harvests and the food supply. In 1821, the planet was neither cooling nor heating, of course, at least not noticeably, but we can still understand Fourier's thought as the fantastic transposition of quite real and legitimate anxieties about the deleterious impact of industry on the globe. That impact, indeed, was felt on a much more mundane level, too, and by far less prophetic minds, as can easily be inferred from early French legislation against urban pollution, at a time when small industries were still often sited in densely settled areas. Responding to an outpouring of complaints by town dwellers in 1810, the Empire passed a "Décret relatif aux Manufactures et Ateliers qui répandent une odeur insalubre ou incommode" (Barles, 1999; Fressoz, 2012; Jarrige and Le Roux, 2017).

This was the historical context in which Balzac wrote. That does not make him, automatically, an ecological writer, a pastoral poet, or an advocate for preservation, care, *Naturphilosophie*, degrowth, beauty, or biocentrism —far from it. But we do suggest that Balzac's work responds to the creeping crisis eventually known as the Anthropocene: it records attitudes, affects, tropes, concepts, forces, fantasies, energies, and ideologies operative in the early industrializing world and which, to a surprising degree, continue to shape attitudes today. As the deepening environmental crisis urges scholars across the humanities to approach their fields afresh, bringing to them a new set of questions concerned with modes of dwelling in, relating to, exploiting, and imagining the natural world, it seems imperative to interrogate anew the literature of the nineteenth century, both to illuminate the prehistory of our present predicament and to shed new light on the ecologies found — sometimes implicitly — in the Balzacian universe.

If ecology can be understood simply as the study of relationships between living organisms and their physical environment, our choice to pluralize the term in this special issue's title is meant, rather, to evoke the multiple ways in which ecologies of the human and non-human have been articulated beyond biological science. Building on a relational turn in critical theory exemplified by the work of Donna Haraway and Bruno Latour, the editors of a recent issue of *Victorian Literature and Culture* propose a wide-ranging set of "Open Ecologies" that recognize the mutual entanglements of society and nature without reinscribing an organicist harmony upon them (Griffiths and Kreisel, 2020, p. 6). If we widen the lens to contemporary studies in environmental humanities, we find a proliferation of terms: material ecocriticism, affective ecocriticism, anthropocene ecocriticism, bioregional ecocriticism, queer ecocriticism, postcolonial ecocriticism, temporalised ecocriticism (Ryan, 2019; Finch-Race and Gosseti, 2019; Albrecht, 2019; DeLoughrey, 2011). But of course not all of these categories resonate equally with the Balzacian œuvre. The contributors to this special issue explore *La Comédie humaine* through new avenues of inquiry that have been opened by recent ecocritical approaches, engaging with them in the spirit of open ecologies without losing sight of the specificity of the author to whose work this journal is devoted.

In our Call for Papers, we asked how the plots, themes, and imagery, the poetics and politics, the milieus and the landscapes, the theories and ideologies, the human and animal figures, the energetics and economics of *La Comédie humaine* might speak to concerns raised by the 21st century notion of the Anthropocene. Are there ways, for example, to articulate studies of land and landscape in *La Comédie humaine* (Mitterand, 2004; Spandri, 2019) with larger scale geo-temporalities and the kinds of global concerns that Serres and Latour bring to the fore with their reflections on Gaia (Serres, 1990; Latour 2017; Aït-Touati *et al*, 2021)? What picture, we wondered, does Balzac paint of human terraforming agency and large-scale landscape engineering in *Le Curé de campagne*, in which an effervescent graduate of the École Polytechnique is tasked with reanimating a barren and backward village, Montégnac, hemmed in and held back by somber forests and infertile rocks? Is this already a form of geoengineering (Hamilton, 2013), or just Saint-Simonian optimism — or rather a prescient recipe for reconciling, as Reclus felt was possible, natural beauty with productivity? What impact do geographic isolation, and, conversely, the advent of roads, commerce, and the integration of the nation have on public health, local cultures, and patterns of travel and exile for Balzac's characters? New roads amplify commerce and change, rapidly altering both the land and the culture, or, when absent, condemning regions and towns to remain frozen in time, as happens with Guérande in *Béatrix*, "[une ville] complètement en dehors du mouvement social qui donne au dix-neuvième siècle sa physionomie." Even a modest row of poplars planted there in 1820 to make a "promenade" shocks the inhabitants (*CH*, II, p. 637–639). How do the competing logics of commerce and aesthetics shape Balzac's practice of representing nature? Do the ecological affects that underpin romantic reveries in Balzac, and, before him, the meditations of Rousseau, Senancour, and Lamartine, constitute a kind of commerce in themselves? If Balzac invents capitalism, essentially, by mapping the endless circulation and transformation of forms of energy (such as money, goods, affects, intelligence, magnetism, vital fluids, electricity, geological forces, and so on — *l'or et le plaisir*), where does this energy come from and is it ultimately something renewable — capable of endless growth and accumulation — or is its fate rather to shrink, like the *peau de chagrin*, with every careless act of exploitation? How are fortunes made, and how might economic logic, in the narrow sense, be related more broadly to Félix Guattari's "three ecologies" of mind, society, and nature? What shadow does the plantationocene cast on the accumulation of wealth in France? (Ferdinand, 2019) Crimes, in Balzac, routinely mark the origins of fortunes, but Vautrin's strange plan for future respectability, which has him settling in the American south as a "planteur" and *esclavagiste* in *Le Père Goriot*, would presumably fail to launder his ill-begotten money and whitewash his new profile (*CH*, III, p. 141). How far does Vautrin's cynicism unmask the capitalist enterprise itself? What relationships does Balzac establish between health, atmosphere, and the larger social and natural environment? Aside from the insalubrity of cities, Balzac also took a keen interest in pathogenic landscapes, such as the damp and sunless valleys allegedly responsible for the scourge of Alpine *crétinisme*, a condition that increasingly vexed health experts, and which Benassis sets out to remedy in Balzac's philanthropic utopia, *Le Médecin de campagne*, at least a decade before Guggenbühl founded his pioneering clinic at the Abendberg in 1841 (Kanner, 1959). How are social species shaped by their urban and natural milieux and to what extent do they also fabricate, transform, and even constitute that very mileu in turn? If there is only one animal, variously modified, to recall Balzac's adoption of Geoffroy de Saint-Hilaire's transformism in the *Avant-propos*, does his famous analogy between "animality" and "humanity" also imply a form of biological continuity, an implicit anticipation of post-humanism? What links, more broadly, weather and mood, climate and character, ecology and ideology in Balzac's work?

The resulting contributions to this special issue take up a number of these questions, while also extending them into new realms of *La Comédie humaine*'s engagement with the nature-culture spectrum. What emerges is an *eco-Balzac* — or even more playfully: a green Balzac, whose writings span the *vert*iginous scalar depths of deep time (Bauer), the green prairies and *buissons verts* of provincial landscapes (Fields, Carrico), the conversion of silviculture into currency (Forfert) and the *chiffons verts* of counter-industrial papermaking (Quandt), the unity of composition between *vert*ebrates and non-human beings (Robison), the vegetal miasmas of urban space (Berkery), and the *herbe verte* underlying both textual and pictorial art in a botanical unconscious (Duzer). A short prefatory reflection by Christy Wampole reminds us that for all of his attempts to fix the present, our *secrétaire de la Société française* shared a visionary, proto-ecological sense of fleetingness, futurity, and the threat of loss.

Balzac's own birth at the start of the nineteenth century coincides with two contexts that have inspired constellations of recent ecocritical thought: the rise of the natural sciences, with their discovery of geological timescales leading to the Anthropocene; and the early onset of a Western industrial revolution that would reconfigure relations between city and nature, labor and resources, wealth and land, production and consumption, and therefore also between the scenes representing *la vie de Paris* and *la vie de province*. Our special issue begins with a reflection on how the recent discovery of a deep, geological past disrupts aesthetic and temporal continuities in Balzac. The Cuvierian geochronologies of the early nineteenth century paved the way for new conceptions of global time and human history that emphasize fragment over whole, cataclysm over harmony (see Heringman, 2015; Morgan, 2017; Goulet, 2021; Lloyd and Mortimer, 2024). In her essay "Deep Time in an Age of Traces. Modern Temporality in Balzac's *Le Colonel Chabert*", Dominique Bauer contextualizes the human "fossil" that Chabert's life layers within the incoherent stratigraphy of deep pasts and apocalyptic futures. By tracing gestures of re-enactment and an aesthetics of poetic reconstruction, she shows how the Balzacian text aims to restore a lost wholeness to a present modernity marked by ruins and debris.

The scalar shifts introduced by early nineteenth-century geological science led to a radical de-centering of humankind, heralding the advent, in our own time, of the Anthropocene as an era in which, paradoxically, the *anthropos* both dominates the globe (by making irreversible changes to it) and submits to its unsuspected constraints (the non-human telluric or biological forces that go by the name of Gaia). The ecocritical quest to find alternatives to this anthropocentric framework has spurred thinkers to redefine the rapport between the human and the non-human in terms of interconnectedness, entanglement, networked agency, or "making kin" (Haraway, 2016), supplanting the type of strict categorical separation that would seem to inform the broad zoological analogy in Balzac's *Avant-propos* between *espèces sociales* and *espèces animales*. A number of authors in our special issue explore, in *La Comédie humaine*, a more complex engagement with the non-human other, whether animal (Robison, Fields) or botanical (Quandt, Forfert, Duzer).

Balzac's Swedenborgian angel-spirits commune with all forms of the non-human, including those of the mineral world: "ils peuvent interroger le minéral, et le minéral répond à leurs pensées." (*CH*, XI, p. 781) But if those exceptional beings share what Jeffrey Jerome Cohen (2015) would call an "affective enmeshment" with metal or stone (p. 65), it is with the botanical other — and in particular, trees — that *La Comédie humaine*'s wider ecological stakes emerge. Both Karen Quandt, in her essay "Leaves of Thistle: Paper Ecologies in Balzac's *Illusions perdues*" and Pierre Forfert, in "Balzac's Poplar Trees: The Economy of Timber in *Eugénie Grandet*", explore the "material interconnectedness of human and arboreal lives" that Giulia Pacini (2016) has theorized in relation to late eighteenth-century and early nineteenth-century mesmerist vitalism and horticultural practices (p. 177). Quandt's reading of David Séchard's quest for local fibrous plant materials in an increasingly mechanized age of paper production uncovers a Balzacian botanical *poesis* rooted in ancient Chinese papermaking. Bucking the shift from artisanal practice to assembly-line industry, Balzac and his literary inventor attempt to reconcile vitalist natural ecosystems with France's mechanistic future. Forfert's analysis of a silvicultural economy in *Eugénie Grandet* also situates Balzacian botany in a transitional age between late eighteenth-century agronomy and burgeoning capitalist modernity. While monocultural tree plantations might seem to hark back to retrograde models of land exploitation out of step with the modern speculative market, Forfert shows that Grandet's cultivation of poplars is in fact deeply intertwined with new profit modes, tracing the material entanglement between *terre* and *argent* that registers itself in the very language of the Balzacian text.

In her essay "Peasants v. Pastoral: Some Uses of Animality in Balzac's *Les Paysans*", Abigail Fields distinguishes nineteenth-century notions of *terre* and *argent* according to class positionality, with Parisian urbanites projecting romantic pastoral fantasies not only onto the idealized landscape, but also onto peasant laborers, figured here as animal others. With an eye to the economic counter-discourses embedded in the Balzacian text, Fields suggests that the material realities of the beast-like land worker disrupts the bucolic aesthetics of the Parisian spectator through a form of non-human environmental agency. The Animal Other takes a more literal form in Balzac's "Une passion dans le désert", which Christopher Robison puts into dialogue with *Séraphîta* in his essay "Panthers and Pantheism: Animal Sympathy and Balzac's Mystical Biology". By staging fictional encounters of the human with the non-human, whether in the form of desert panther or androgynous angel, Balzac tests the bounds of anthropocentrism implied by transformist theories of the *échelle des êtres*; Robison's readings of interspecies (non)linguistic communication reveals a dialectics of alterity and kinship more commonly associated with today's critical work in animal studies (Haraway, 2008; Kohn, 2013; Weil, 2012; Simon, 2021; Despret, 2021).

Affective responses to the non-human world turn out to span *La Comédie humaine.* Although the field of Green Romanticism has primarily taken up anglophone writers like Wordsworth, Shelley, and Thoreau (Coupe, 2000; McKusick, 2000; Hunt, 2011; Ottum and Reno, 2016), the questions it raises about human sympathies with nature also resonate with French writers grappling with regionality and landscape in an age of early industrialization (Finch-Race and Gosetti, 2019). In her essay "The Ecology of Emotions: Exploitation of Nature in Balzac's *Le lys dans la vallée*", Abbey Carrico asks whether the natural world can exist as pure escape or radical non-human other, beyond the social networks that subject it to rhetorical projection and agricultural exploitation. Félix de Vandenesse's triangulated affective relations to the Touraine weave an "ecology of emotions" that bypasses the city-country dichotomy through its anthropocentric investment in the *paysage.* Charlotte Berkery's "Night Air: Miasma Theory and *La Cousine Bette*" takes us into the fetid urban *quartiers* of nocturnal Paris. Despite the July Monarchy's hygienist efforts and the invasive rhythm of capitalist production during the workday, the microclimates of Paris at night remain surprisingly steeped in vegetal nature, whether through damp dankness or metaphorical miasma. Nature also appears as a return of the repressed in Virginie Duzer's "*Le Chef-d'œuvre inconnu*, ou la disparition de l'herbe verte", an essay that draws on *critique génétique* to explore a realm of eco-poetics that reveals deep tensions between art(ifice) and nature. Duzer's "diagonal" reading of two artistic creations — Frenhofer's painting and Balzac's own text — identifies, through ellipses and substitutions, a doomed attempt to banish the environment (and perhaps environmental concerns) to the limits of the human.

In this spirit of recovering *La Comédie humaine*'s green substratum, we conclude this introduction with a reflection of our own on how Balzac might be reframed as a prescient ecological writer. His work deserves far more scrutiny from environmental criticism, we believe, and still has many crucial insights in store for the modern attempt to rethink the world in more ecological terms. The dominant social science, at least since Smith, Ricardo, and Marx, has unquestionably been economics, and it has proven easy to interpret Balzac as a pioneering observer of economic life, concerned with commerce, speculation, social mobility, property, money, class, publicity, credit, commodification, and so on. Thomas Piketty, indeed, invokes Balzac as a key informant at the outset of his seminal work *Capital in the Twenty-First Century*, and before him Marx and Engels found much to flesh out their vision of capitalism in *La Comédie humaine*. But economics, notoriously, abstracts human production from the natural world, or recognizes the latter only insofar as its parts can be extracted and priced out in the market. Natural resources either have no intrinsic value (and acquire it only through the cost and labor of extraction, processing, and exchange), or derive that value, paradoxically, from their own scarcity and subsequent capacity to be treated as property (as in the case of land and minerals, but also, increasingly, water and fresh air).

The notion that nature itself — the precondition of all production, starting with sunlight — might itself be valuable, never enters the economic picture, except in strictly negative terms, insofar as scarcity sparks human competition for limited resources. Free and abundant resources, such as air, have no monetary value, even when life itself depends on them. Environmental economics has tried to overcome this blind spot by arguing that it is indeed possible to put a price on nature's invisible *gifts* by factoring in so-called ecosystem services the calculating, say, the hypothetical value of a wetland, rainforest, or watershed, in terms of how much value would be lost if this free gift were eliminated or destroyed. But aside from the fact that much of nature, perhaps most of it, inevitably escapes such utilitarian math — how can a value be placed on the extinction of the Panamanian golden frog? (Kolbert, 2014) — and that much that people value (aesthetically, spiritually, morally or scientifically) cannot be properly priced, this model also disregards the possibility of nature's value to itself. This is a value that might be glossed — still invoking utilitarian logic — as the interest of living things in their own unimpeded existence and flourishing. Reflecting on the inscrutable purpose of the blind, useless energy raging in the seas and winds, Victor Hugo, in *Les Travailleurs de la mer*, coins an apposite phrase to name the forms of value that have failed to receive human recognition so far: "c'est de l'utilité inconnue" (1980, p. 245). Balzac, we would argue, is clearly an economic thinker, but his overall conception of value, like Hugo's, stands out as refreshingly broad, agnostic, and cosmic, so much so that it escapes the pitfalls of economic reductionism. Price, for Balzac, is merely one manifestation of value, but value itself, reframed in ontological terms, takes on multiple, fluid forms, and operates like a cryptic, vital currency running through the substance of the world, traversing minds, bodies, plants, animals, landscapes, products, machines, roads, gazes, sounds, words, and images.

Marx famously drew attention to the "theological niceties" of the commodity (1990, p. 163), but largely to denounce a mystification: the eerie and seductive twinkling of the alienated labor trapped within the product. Balzac's insight is similar: to his observing gaze — far more visionary than empirical, as Baudelaire famously noted — much of the world possesses a kind of auto-luminescent radiance. Objects in Balzac's world, like the vibrant debris that Raphaël de Valentin encounters in the antique store in *La Peau de chagrin*, seem to shine in the dark, beckon, speak, beam, whisper, and interpellate the viewer. As with stars in daylight, however, the subcurrent that animates them remains largely elusive, at least to an untrained and inattentive observer. And Balzac's interest, unlike Marx's, does not seem to lie so much in debunking a pernicious illusion as in detecting and tracing the vibrant forces, whatever their origin, that run beneath the outward texture of things, and in mapping their transformations. While the metaphysical substrate of Marx's vision, *labor*, only ever takes an anthropocentric form (since animals, in his view, did not labor, and much less nature), Balzac's metaphysics of *energy* is at once more nebulous and capacious, more imprecise and inclusive, pointing to a deep kinship among the various forms of force at work in the world, whether they appear to us as sunlight, energy, electricity, magnetism, will, desire, heat, movement, affect, gaze, spirit, or thought. Neither labor, the sole source of value for Marx, nor money, his universal equivalent, can be said to possess any real privilege in Balzac's much more comprehensive algebra of energetic transformations.

The novelist's calculus, then, is necessarily vaguer than the economist's, and more resistant to quantification (although money clearly plays a significant part in many of Balzac's plots). But in focusing on energy as the occult currency of the world, Balzac's vision also excludes nothing, rejects the truncated math of *le grand partage*, and points beyond the anthropocentric reduction of value to price. We suggest, then, that Balzac's economic thought, when seen through the lens of energy, grows richer and acquires a more ambitious, holistic, and ecological form. Future readings of Balzac that adopt some form of this heuristic are likely to make surprising discoveries. Approaching *La Comédie humaine* in this way is also timely because it promises to broaden the scope of the energy humanities, well established in Anglo-American criticism already, to the French domain, following the lead being taken by Anne O'Neil-Henry and Cary Hollinshead-Strick in their pioneering volume of *Nineteenth-Century French Studies* entitled "Fueling the Nineteenth Century: Energy and Nineteenth-Century French Studies."

To offer, finally, some illustrations of how Balzac's work might lend itself to a broader economic reading — indeed, to an ecological one, grounded in energy — we explore a few significant scenes that suggest how Balzac's realist gaze implies a theory of energy and value that links mind, body, world, and meaning in a single field. To begin with, then, when Grandet *le père*, in *Eugénie Grandet*, muses out loud how much profit he stands to gain from planting a field with poplars, and Eugénie, his daughter, at the same time "regardait le sublime paysage de la Loire sans écouter les calculs de son père" (*CH*, III, p. 1081), Balzac purposely contrasts two incompatible attitudes to the land. There is little surprise, perhaps, in discovering this contrast between the utilitarian and the aesthetic gaze. It crops up everywhere in this period, and has long since hardened into a dogma, one which has come to seem by now almost natural, transparent, and eternal to our eyes. But that is precisely the point: Balzac and his contemporaries register the event of this epochal dissociation. Rousseau had been aware of no such stark opposition in the rural landscapes of the Valais. Even a century later, Élisée Reclus could still make the case that these increasingly distinct functions — beauty and utility, farming and scenery, exploitation and contemplation — could and should be reconciled once more, since they presented no insuperable contradiction that required them to be split apart and zoned into distinct spheres: sacred nature reserve, on the one hand, and industrial wasteland, on the other, or aesthetic landscape and productive soil (1866). "Heureusement", Reclus could still claim, whether naïvely or clairvoyantly, "le beau et l'utile peuvent s'allier de la manière la plus complète", adding with a certain optimism that it was in fact in places where "l'industrie agricole est le plus avancée [...] que les exploiteurs du sol savent lui faire rendre les plus larges produits tout en respectant le charme des paysages" (p. 379). Care and productivity, yield and embellishment, were by no means conflicting imperatives, and it was fully in the farmer's power to "exploiter la terre à son profit tout en la rendant plus belle" (*ibid.*).

An interesting confirmation of this outlook comes from a modern environmental historian who has grappled with the long-term transformation of the Columbia River in the American Pacific Northwest. Richard White had first taken for granted the outlook of what we might term deep ecology, which sacralized all of nature, making its use by humans — any kind of use, be it extractive or sustainable — antithetical to the acquisition of true "knowledge" about it (1995, p. x). But in studying the pre-industrial rapport of the Nisqually to the Columbia River, on which this indigenous tribe depended for the salmon sustaining their form of life, White quickly came to reject the superficial equation between disinterested contemplation and genuine knowledge, arguing that "it is our work that ultimately links us, for better or worse, to nature" (*ibid.*, p. x). He came to see that knowledge of nature — which is itself a form of relation — arises chiefly in the process of using it: "The Nisqually knew salmon by catching them. They taught me, although I was too dim to recognize it then, how nature can be known through labor" (*ibid.*). Contemplation, in this view, is just one form of use, made possible by spinning off and isolating beauty from other kinds of use (industrial, scientific, religious, military, territorial, recreational, transportational, memorial, identitarian, etc.). To bring this insight back to Balzac, Eugénie and her father would both *know* nature, then, but by using it in very distinct ways, each use being an increasingly partial view made possible only by suppressing rival approaches. As an antidote to the historical reification of such narrow and specialized ways of looking, White instead understands work in a way that seems, in retrospect, remarkably congruous with Balzac's poetics, in which such antinomies as values and feelings, *affaires* and sentiments, love and business, city and country, spirit and matter, repeatedly prove inseparable.

In fact, the key operative term knitting the world together in Balzac's cosmic vision may well be energy. Electricity, magnetism, money, willpower, vitality, genius, authority, power, "l'or et le plaisir" — these are among the names of the endlessly multiplying forces (or rather Force), simultaneously ideal and material, seemingly distinct but also deeply unified, that ripple through Balzac's world, shaping it into an inextricable whole that resists facile attempts to distinguish them by recourse to rationalizing sub-disciplines such as psychology, aesthetics, politics, economics, and ethics. It might be said that there are not only "three ecologies" in Balzac, to allude to Félix Guattari's model, in which mind, society, and nature together constitute three distinct but interconnected ecological spheres (Guattari, 1989), but rather dozens, all of which are united by Balzac's nebulous metaphorical regime of energy. Or perhaps it should be called work: indeed, for Richard White, work is energy, and the world is entirely made of it: sunshine, wind, rivers, dams, the power of plants, animal protein, salmon, labor, food, metabolism, and the expenditure of force. "Like us, rivers work. They absorb and emit energy; they rearrange the world" (1995, p. 3).

If the world is work, then, or rather energy, as Balzac might put it, the best way to understand it would indeed be to study the endless, complex transformations of energy across seemingly discontinuous domains. We would argue here that Balzac, perhaps more so than any other contemporary author, envisaged the world ecologically, in the sense that his main subject, the invisible object his writing tracks, more so than individual persons, places, or entities, was the circulation and metamorphosis of energy throughout the world — along with its capture, concentration, investment, dissipation, and dispersal. But this is also to say that Balzac's major work, *La Comédie humaine*, constitutes an ambitious ecology *avant la lettre*, a quixotic attempt to map the world holistically as an inextricable network of forces and flows. It is of course true that Balzac's focus, unlike Buffon's, is almost entirely restricted to the human world, but the apparent dichotomy implicit in Balzac's strategic appropriation of Buffon — the famous *grand partage* (Descola, 2005, p. 91–131) — is as much reinforced as it is undercut by his heuristic appeal to natural history in the *Avant-propos*. "Il n'y a qu'un animal" (*CH*, I, p. 8). This means that humans, too, are animals, and that Balzac's famous "social species" do not just mirror "natural" ones, analogically, but also share a single, unified *scala naturae* with them. Just so, we could claim, there is also only nature, or rather energy, a single universal equivalent, however varied its forms, which governs the process of the world in Balzac's proto-ecological metaphysics. The sublime and the profitable may appear to be at odds, then, in any concrete situation, as it is for Eugénie and her father, but both values ultimately find their roots in a unified ecological vision of the cosmos as energetic flow — which is not necessarily an environmentalist vision.

One way to think about how Balzac's realism might itself be indebted to an energetic vision of the world is to reflect on the idiosyncratic use he makes of one of his key concepts, *physionomie*, ostensibly used to designate the outward appearance of a person (as opposed to *physiologie*, pointing to its secret anatomy). Why does *physionomie* occupy such a privileged place in Balzac's poetics? There is Lavater's pseudo-science, of course, and Gall's phrenology, both claiming to infer moral traits from facial and cranial features — a correlation that Balzac extends beyond persons and onto buildings, streets, scenes, offices, landscapes, cities, and environments. It becomes, in fact, the very principle of legibility of Balzac's world: through *physionomie*, the entire visible world acquires meaning, character, and significance; it becomes legible, in human terms, as a form of moral force — in other words, through a sort of systematic anthropomorphism that endows it with the semblance of a human face. Consider, for instance, the incipit of *Ferragus*, where Balzac reflects on the visual impact of Parisian streets on the curious observer. There are, he writes, "[des] rues déshonorées", "des rues nobles", "des rues simplement honnêtes", "de jeunes rues", "des rues assassines", and so on — the list includes streets that are old, clean, respectable, dirty, working-class, commercial, etc. — a fact that Balzac goes on to gloss as follows: "Enfin, les rues de Paris ont des qualités humaines, et nous impriment par leur physionomie certaines idées contre lesquelles nous sommes sans défense" (*CH*, V, p. 793). The symbolic extension of human "physionomie" to the streets seems obvious enough; the urban scenery even acquires facial blemishes — "une verrue, un bouton, une rougeur" (*CH*, V, p. 795) — and a collective global personality: Paris is a "[m]onstre complet" (*CH*, V, p. 794). It is tempting to reduce this figuration to a fantastic expression of human agency, since it is the presence of criminals, presumably, who make criminal streets, and merchants who make commercial streets, and so on. Indeed, a Durkheimian reading of the force of the setting would be entirely appropriate. The milieu that Balzac deciphers could then be seen as a collective projection into the cityscape of the human agents who inhabit it, much as God (in Durkheim's religious sociology) is simply the unconscious power of Society writ large (Durkheim, 1912). But we should not forget that such projection generally goes both ways in Balzac, with the setting retroacting on its occupants as well, as is famously the case with Mme Vauquer in *Le Père Goriot*: "toute sa personne explique la pension, comme la pension implique sa personne" (*CH*, III, p. 54). Similarly, Balzac's observer, in the *Ferragus* passage, doesn't just decipher the streets like a scientist, aloof and immune to their impact, but also registers the eerie force of their *physionomie*: "[elles] nous impriment [des] idées contre lesquelles nous sommes sans défense" (*CH*, V, p. 793). The rapport is an energetic one. Face-to-face with the street — or with the landscape, building, or setting — the spectator is inscribed in a continuous exchange with his or her environment: a current passes both ways. That commerce entails gain and loss, simultaneously, and the balance between them is always uncertain. The nameless observer in *Ferragus* is first classed with "ces hommes d'étude et de pensée, de poésie et de plaisir qui savent récolter, en flânant dans Paris, la masse de jouissances flottantes, à toute heure, entre ses murailles » (*CH*, V, p. 794). But pleasure tends to be an ambivalent harvest in Balzac, usually entailing some form of expenditure — if only in the form of attention — so a few lines later the flâneur's bill arrives: "Voyager dans Paris est, pour ces poètes, un luxe coûteux. Comment ne pas dépenser quelques minutes devant les drames, les désastres, les figures [...] qui vous assaillent au milieu de cette mouvante reine des cités [...]!" (*CH*, V, p. 795).

What this passage illustrates for an ecological approach to Balzac is two key propositions: the first is the pivotal place of energetics, which governs the reciprocal impact that beings and their environment exercise on each other. The second is the central role played by *physionomie* in mapping this circular economy. Energy itself is of course a largely invisible quantity for a strictly empirical gaze, but Balzac's unique brand of realism is demonstrably organized around overcoming that blindness. As Frenhofer impatiently exclaims to Porbus in *Le Chef-d'œuvre inconnu*: "La mission de l'art n'est pas de copier la nature, mais de l'exprimer!", a cryptic precept he glosses, significantly, by insisting that it is the artist's task to capture the *physionomie* of things: "Nous avons à saisir l'esprit, l'âme, la physionomie des choses et des êtres" (*CH*, X, p. 418).

Les choses et les êtres: both of these, then, possess *physionomie*, and consequently, we might add, agency. No visible surface is inert, passively photographic, or exposed submissively to neutral observation, but each influences the spectator and also serves as a flashing screen on which the occult play of forces animating the world becomes legible. The art of *physionomie* is thus the art of detecting the way that force courses through matter, and therefore of mapping the world as an intricate network of influences. This is an outlook that embeds human agency in a much larger field of forces, rendered visible by Balzac's broad application of *physionomie* to the entire world: buildings, streets, cities, landscapes, atmospheres, persons, animals, things, even substances. The picture of Paris, once more, in *Ferragus*, confirms the sheer hybridity of Balzac's urban assemblage, irreducible to the self-satisfied machinations of a few powerful human actors (be they the "treize rois inconnus", the self-serving conspirators invoked in the novel's preface [*CH*, V, p. 792]): "Paris est [une] monstrueuse merveille, étonnant assemblage de mouvements, de machines et de pensées." The image of this hybrid constellation is followed by an even stranger assemblage of flesh and stone: "Paris est une créature; chaque homme, chaque fraction de maison est un lobe du tissu cellulaire de cette grande courtisane" (*CH*, V, p. 795). For the poet's gaze, it is the entire network, the seamless tissue of an integrated world, that swims into focus, rather than the misleading and inflated perspective of discrete human agents.

What is true of Paris is true also of the larger world beyond: the non-human world of meadows, forests, lakes, seasons, and skies. It too has *physionomie* and can become the vehicle of a latent signifying force that we may not always register but to which we nonetheless remain receptive. From an anthropocentric viewpoint, the notion that nature might in some way *signify* (and perhaps even influence us outside the bounds of coded language) must sound like an absurd heresy. Ruskin named it the "pathetic fallacy", suggesting that only second-rate poets succumbed to the irritating habit of projecting their feelings on inanimate nature (Ruskin, 1856). To this day, that charge has stuck as a blanket allegation periodically leveled by critics at Romantic writing in general. Baudelaire was one of its first spokespeople, noting in his acerbic critique of landscape painting in the *Salon de 1859* that "si tel assemblage d'arbres, de montagnes, d'eaux et de maisons, que nous appelons un paysage, est beau, ce n'est pas par lui-même, mais par moi, par ma grâce propre, par l'idée ou le sentiment que j'y attache" (p. 320). The pathetic fallacy is unquestionably a real thing; but whether it should be invoked to dismiss every attribution of meaning (a term taken here to exceed its linguistic sense) to the non-human world is another matter. The charge of narcissism carried by the pathetic fallacy might in that case bounce right back against the anthropocentrism of the critique itself, for how plausible is it to claim that we always remain resolutely immune — safely barricaded within language — to the non-human world beyond our symbolic structures?

That world, too, exists for Balzac, even if Paris, a largely built environment, perhaps illustrates that point poorly. But consider instead Balzac's extended foray into the fields in *Le Lys dans la vallée*, where an idyllic landscape mediates the illicit passion that flowers between Félix de Vandenesse and Mme de Mortsauf. One can see the landscape here as a simple *adjuvant*, or passive screen reflecting and amplifying the human romance. But that is to miss the subtle part it plays in inciting and framing this passion, which, outside this context, might have remained mute and inaudible even to the main actors, and perhaps even required the complicity of the elements. As much as their passion is projected, then, it is also deeply modeled on the landscape, which suggests and supplies the wordless meanings that cannot find verbal expression. When their souls mingle on the terrace — "Quand les mots manquaient, le silence servait fidèlement nos âmes qui pour ainsi dire entraient l'une chez l'autre sans obstacles" (*CH*, IX, p. 1051-1052) — this chaste embrace seems at first to occur in a kind of spiritual ether. But their communion is in fact subtly induced by and silently patterned on the disinhibiting force of the landscape they behold together. Their "souls" require its sensuous mediation: "[nos âmes] s'engagaient dans les ondulations d'une même rêverie, se plongeaient ensemble dans la rivière, en sortaient rafraîchies comme deux nymphes aussi parfaitement unies que la jalousie le peut désirer" (*CH*, IX, p. 1052). Their *rêverie*, in other words, is shaped by a *rivière*, a non-human natural feature, which gives it imaginative shape and sustenance, sensation and force, even supplying it with a kind of kinetic frequency ("les ondulations") and sensory meaning ("rafraîchies").

When Félix then proceeds to woo Henriette with flowers that he gathers in the surrounding meadows, alluding to the existence of a floral symbolism, or complex botanical code, to express his illicit feelings for her, it is tempting, once again, to dismiss this floral rhetoric as an instance of the pathetic fallacy. Indeed, Henriette's "soul", or rather Félix's affect for it, seems to color his perception of the landscape, since the "fugitives allégories où pour moi se peignaient les phases les plus contrastantes de la vie humaine" turn out to be colored, retrospectively at least, by "le souvenir de l'âme alors épandue sur la nature" (*CH*, IX, p. 1055). All that Félix sees out there would be Henriette. But this turns out to be misleading. Looked at more closely, the flowers do in fact have an independent power to signify; they speak to the human observer in an obscure and uncoded language, making Félix quite powerless to make them mean what he happens to be feeling. Their language, while natural, resembles that of music, which, if obviously conventional, also possesses no clear semantic meaning: "je pensai que les couleurs et les feuillages avaient une harmonie, une poésie qui se faisait jour dans l'entendement en charmant le regard, comme les phrases musicales réveillent mille souvenirs au fond des cœurs aimants et aimés" (*CH*, IX, p. 1053). Félix's earlier experiences in life ("mille souvenirs") pattern his reception, but it is inevitably the specific forms and colors he sees (or sounds he hears) that determine what affects will be triggered. The flowers, then, read him, rather than the reverse. Their meanings are perhaps indeterminate, but they are not, for that reason, empty signifying screens; rather, they constitute a series of mute appeals to the viewer to translate their implicit injunctions: "Il est dans la nature des effets dont les signifiances sont sans bornes, et qui s'élèvent à la hauteur des plus grandes conceptions morales" (*CH*, IX, p. 1054).

And these floral meanings, moreover, may not be fully arbitrary (unlike the linguistic sign): "Si la couleur est la lumière organisée, ne doit-elle pas avoir un sens comme les combinaisons de l'air ont le leur?" (*CH*, IX, p. 1053) The euphonic sonority of this particular sentence (*couleur*, *lumière*, *l'air*, *leur*) strongly suggests a cryptic form of motivation. It is also the case that a natural analogy predisposes the flowers to mimic human affects; love is the human equivalent of sunlight: "Quel charme que de faire exprimer ses sensations par ces filles du soleil, les sœurs des fleurs écloses sous les rayons de l'amour!" (*CH*, IX, p. 1054) There is a telling suggestion that more than mere analogy might be at stake in this kinship, since Félix hints at a kind of ontological continuity between plants and the people enveloped in their sensory embrace; invoking the proverbial renewal of spring (with all its floral eroticism), he mentions "ce parfum qui communique à tous les êtres l'ivresse de la fécondation" and under whose spell "vos pensées reverdissent comme les touffes forestières" (*CH*, IX, p. 1056). Félix here becomes, we might say, a thinking plant, finding more fertile ground in which to grow than he had as a child, when his "racines tendres" had been bruised by "[les] durs cailloux dans le sol domestique" (*CH*, IX, p. 970). It is significant, too, that the floral messages are cryptic, even resistant, and that Félix has to make a genuine hermeneutic effort to decipher the flora correctly before assembling his bouquets. For "toutes les variétés des graminées [...] je fis [donc] une étude approfondie, moins en botaniste qu'en poète, étudiant plus leur esprit que leur forme" (*CH*, IX, p. 1054). To assemble his floral *billets doux*, he also has to travel far and wide across the landscape, combing it to find the right botanical figures. It is quite plausible to argue that their presumed referent, Félix's emerging feelings, do not even pre-exist their fortuitous embodiment in the flowers that interpret them. In other words, the floral dictionary gives him a tool to explore, decipher, and amplify his own feelings. "Pour trouver une fleur là où elle venait, j'allais souvent à d'énormes distances, au bord des eaux, dans les vallons, au sommet des rochers, en pleines landes, butinant des pensées au sein des bois et des bruyères" (*CH*, IX, p. 1054). Needless to say, this is not how narcissistic projection works, nor does it usually claim to have "retrouv[é] [...] une science perdue en Europe" (*CH*, IX, p. 1054). The thoughts that make up Félix's amorous discourse have to be gleaned, quite literally, in the fields, and it is as if they had no verifiable existence outside the landscape that first incubates them and endows them with sensible form.

It is important to note here that Balzac stresses the role, as he does throughout the *Comédie humaine*, of the gifted observer capable of sensing and transcribing the cryptic *physionomie* of the world. This might be termed seeing ecologically, since it is also a way of tracking the infinite porosity of life — the endless imbrication of figures and landscapes, signs and forces, meanings and textures, affects and things — and seems to require a special kind of gaze, one which varies in Balzac from one context to the next (his observer may be a poet, an archeologist, a natural historian, a flâneur, or something else). This ritual inscription of the observer in Balzac's work is no mere tic, on this account, but rather a trace of his enduring concern with seeing in depth, beneath the empirical surface of things, into the maelstrom of forces that give rise to the visible world. For such seeing, it turns out, there is also no fixed recipe, no pre-constituted scientific protocol that would identify the pertinent variables. Félix has to operate blind: "dans ces courses, je m'initiai moi-même à des plaisirs inconnus au savant qui vit dans la méditation, à l'agriculteur occupé de spécialités, à l'artisan cloué dans les villes, au commerçant attaché à son comptoir" (*CH*, IX, p. 1054). Specialized knowledge of such kinds offers no compelling models — one thinks here of Goriot's narrow genius in the flower trade, applicable nowhere else. All Félix tells us is that such seeing and its attendant pleasures are "connus de quelques forestiers, de quelques bûcherons, de quelques rêveurs" (*CH*, IX, p. 1054). These hints are, of course, rather unhelpful, unless their point, precisely, is to draw attention to a form of solitary, unmapped, and pre-symbolic engagement with the world's wilderness. More illuminating as an attribute of such seeing may be the unique pleasure it yields — "des plaisirs inconnus au savant" — a kind of pleasure due, perhaps, to the unexpected insights it offers, which are new, fresh, and sensational, but perhaps also to their form, which is experiential rather than just cognitive, plunging the observer into a transformative adventure. In so doing, such seeing also annuls the safe and sheltering isolation of the observer figure, immersing her into the invigorating and exhausting current of universal life, much like the gifted observers in *Ferragus*, "qui savent récolter [...] la masse de jouissances flottantes" in the streets "[et] qui ne marchent jamais en écervelés, [mais] dégustent leur Paris" (*CH*, V, p. 794-795). Ecology knows no separation, and to see and write ecologically, as we think Balzac does, is to be in permanent commerce with the always enigmatic *physionomie* of an animate world.

Göran BLIX
Princeton University

Andrea GOULET
University of Pennsylvania

WORKS CITED

Aït-Touati Frédérique, and Coccia Emanuele (eds.), 2021, *Le cri de Gaïa. Penser la terre avec Bruno Latour* (Paris: Éditions la Découverte).

Albrecht Glenn A., 2019, *Earth Emotions: New Words for a New World* (Ithaca: Cornell University Press).

Barles Sabine, 1999, *La Ville délétère: médecins et ingénieurs dans l'espace urbain, XVIII*[e]*–XIX*[e] siècle (Seyssel: Champ Vallon).

Barnes David, 2018, *The Great Stink of Paris and the Nineteenth-Century Struggle against Filth and Germs* (Baltimore: John Hopkins University Press).

Baudelaire Charles, 1992, "Salon de 1859", *Critique d'art* (Paris: Gallimard).

Blix Göran, 2019, "Natura Magistra Vitae: Natural Pedagogy in Élisée Reclus's *Histoire d'un ruisseau*", *Dix-Neuf*, vol. 23, no. 3–4, p. 220–230.

Bonneuil Christophe, and Fressoz Jean-Baptiste, 2013, *L'évènement anthropocène. La Terre, l'histoire et nous* (Paris: Seuil).

Bonneuil Christophe, and Fressoz Jean-Baptiste, 2016, *The Shock of the Anthropocene* (London and New York: Verso).

Cohen Jeffrey Jerome, 2015, *Stone: An Ecology of the Inhuman* (Minneapolis: University of Minnesota Press).

Coupe Laurence (ed.), 2000, *The Green Studies Reader: From Romanticism to Ecocriticism* (London: Routledge).

DeLoughrey Elizabeth and Handley George B. (eds.), 2011, *Postcolonial Ecologies: Literatures of the Environment* (Oxford University Press).

Descola Philippe, 2005, *Par-delà culture et nature* (Paris: Gallimard).

Despret Vinciane, 2021, *Autobiographie d'un poulpe et autres récits d'anticipation* (Arles: Actes Sud).

Durkheim Émile, 1912, *Les Formes élémentaires de la vie religieuse: le système totémique en Australie* (Paris: F. Alcan).

Ferdinand Malcom, 2019, *Une écologie décoloniale. Penser l'écologie depuis le monde caribéen* (Paris: Seuil).

Finch-Race Daniel A. and Posthumus Stephanie (eds.), 2017, *French Ecocriticism: From the Early Modern Period to the Twenty-First Century* (Frankfurt am Main: Peter Lang).

Finch-Race Daniel A. and Weber Julien (eds.), 2017, "French Ecocriticism / L'Écocritique française", *L'Esprit Créateur*, 57.1, p. 1–8.

Finch-Race Daniel A. and Gosetti Valentina, 2019, "Editorial: Discovering Industrial-Era Francophone Ecoregions", *Dix-Neuf: Journal of the Society of Dix-Neuviémistes*, 23.3–4, p. 151–162.

Foster John Bellamy, Brett Clark, and Richard York, 2010, *The Ecological Rift: Capitalism's War on the Earth* (New York: Monthly Review Press).
Fourier Charles, 1847, "Manuscrits de Fourier. Détérioration matérielle de la planète", in *La Phalange: journal de la science sociale: politique, industrie, sciences, art et littérature*, XVIe Année, 1re Série, Tome VI (Paris: Bureaux de la Phalange), p. 401–440.
Fressoz, Jean-Baptiste, 2012, *L'Apocalypse joyeuse. Une histoire du risque technologique* (Paris: Seuil).
Goulet Andrea, 2021, "Anthropocene Under Paris? Rethinking the Quarries and Catacombs", *Dix-Neuf: Journal of the Society of Dix-Neuviémistes*, 25:3–4, p. 225–241.
Goulet Andrea, forthcoming, "Balzac géologue, ou Horace de Saint-Aubin à l'aube de l'anthropocène", *Actes du colloque de Cerisy, Balzac et les disciplines du savoir*, Bordas Éric, Del Lungo Andrea, and Glaudes Pierre, eds.
Griffiths Devin, and Kreisel Deanna K., 2020, "Introduction: Open Ecologies", *Victorian Literature and Culture*, 48.1, p. 1–28.
Guattari Félix, 1989, *The Three Ecologies* (New York: Bloomsbury Revelations).
Guest Bertrand, 2017, *Révolutions dans le cosmos. Essais de libération géographique: Humboldt, Thoreau, Reclus* (Paris: Classiques Garnier).
Haeckel Ernst, 1866, *Generelle Morphologie der Organismen. Allgemeine Grundzüge der organischen Formen-Wissenschaft*, 2 vols. (Berlin: Georg Reimer).
Hamilton Clive, 2013, *Earthmasters: the Dawn of the Age of Climate Engineering* (Yale University Press).
Haraway Donna, 2008, *When Species Meet* (Minneapolis: University of Minnesota Press).
Haraway Donna, 2016, *Staying with the Trouble: Making Kin in the Chthulucene* (Durham: Duke University Press).
Heringman Noah, 2015, "Deep Time at the Dawn of the Anthropocene", *Representations*, 129.1, p. 56–85.
Hugo Victor, 1980, *Les Travailleurs de la mer* (Paris: Gallimard).
Hunt Stephen E., 2011, *Green Romanticism: the Natural World and Human Well-Being, 1775–1900* (Saarbrücken: VDM Verlag Dr. Müller).
Jarrige Francois, and Le Roux Thomas, 2017, *La Contamination du monde: une histoire des pollutions à l'âge industriel* (Paris: Seuil).
Kanner Leo, 1959, "Johann Jakob Guggenbühl and the Abendberg", *Bulletin of the History of Medicine*, vol. 33, no. 6, p. 489–502.
Kohn Eduardo, 2013, *How Forests Think: Toward an Anthropology beyond the Human* (Berkeley, University of California Press).
Kolbert Elizabeth, 2014, *The Sixth Extinction: An Unnatural History* (New York: Henry Holt).

Latour Bruno, 2017, *Facing Gaia: Eight Lectures on the New Climactic Regime* (Cambridge, UK: Polity).

Lloyd Declan, and Mortimer Warren, 2024, *Digressions in Deep Time: Ecocritical Approaches to Literature and the Arts* (Lanham: MD Rowman and Littlefield).

Marx Karl, 1990, *Capital*, vol. I (London: Penguin).

McKusick James C., 2000, *Green Writing: Romanticism and Ecology* (New York: Palgrave Macmillan).

Merchant Carolyn, 1980, *The Death of Nature: Women, Ecology and the Scientific Revolution* (New York: HarperCollins).

Mitterrand Henri, 2004, "Terre, terrain, territoire. Variations géocritiques balzaciennes", in Dufour Philippe, and Mozet Nicole (eds.), *Balzac géographe: territoires* (Saint-Cyr-sur-Loire: Christian Pirot.

Morgan Benjamin, 2017, "Scale as Form: Thomas Hardy's Rocks and Stars," in Tobias Menely and Taylor Jesse Oak (eds.), *Anthropocene Reading: Literary History in Geological Times* (Pennsylvania: Penn State University Press).

Nordhaus William, 2013, *The Climate Casino: Risk, Uncertainty, and Economics for a Warming World* (New Haven: Yale University Press).

O'Neal-Henry Anne and Hollinshead-Strick Cary, eds., forthcoming, "Fueling the Nineteenth Century: Energy and Nineteenth-Century French Studies", *Nineteenth-Century French Studies*, 53:3–4.

Ottum Lisa and Reno Seth T., eds., 2016, *Wordsworth and the Green Romantics: Affect and Ecology in the Nineteenth Century: Affect and Ecology in the Nineteenth Century* (Durham: University of New Hampshire Press).

Pacini Giulia, 2016, "Arboreal Attachments: Interacting with Trees in Early Nineteeth-Century France", *Configurations*, 24:2, p. 173–195.

Piketty Thomas, 2014, *Capital in the Twenty-First Century* (Cambridge, MA: Harvard University Press).

Posthumus Stephanie, 2017, *French 'Écocritique': Reading Contemporary French Theory and Fiction Ecologically* (University of Toronto Press).

Reclus Élisée, 15 mai 1866, "Du sentiment de la nature dans les sociétés modernes", *Revues des Deux Mondes*, p. 352–381.

Ruskin John, "Of the Pathetic Fallacy", 1856-1860, *Modern Painters*, vol. III, p. 157–172 (London: Smith, Elder and Co).

Ryan John Charles, 2019, "Foreword: Ecocriticism in the Age of Dislocation?", *Dix-Neuf: Journal of the Society of Dix-neuvièmistes*, 23.3–4, p. 163–170.

Serres Michel, 1990, *Le Contrat naturel* (Paris: François Bourin).

Simon Anne, 2021, *Une bête entre les lignes. Essai de zoopoétique* (Marseille: Wildproject).

Spandri Francesco, 2019, "Balzac et le non-sens de la terre", *French Studies*, 73.4, p. 513–524.

Villermé Louis-René, [1830] 2008, *La Mortalité dans les divers quartiers de Paris* (Paris: La Fabrique).
Weil Kari, 2012, *Thinking Animals: Why Animal Studies Now?* (New York: Columbia University Press).
White Richard, 1995, *The Organic Machine: The Remaking of the Columbia River* (New York: Hill and Wang).

DEEP TIME IN AN AGE OF TRACES

Modern Temporality in Balzac's *Le Colonel Chabert* and *La Peau de chagrin*

> Vous êtes-vous jamais lancé dans l'immensité de l'espace et du temps, en lisant les œuvres géologiques de Cuvier ? [...] En découvrant de tranche en tranche [...] ces animaux [...] l'âme est effrayée d'entrevoir des milliards d'années.
> *CH*, X, p. 74–75.

Deep time is generally thought of as the overwhelming, unimaginable vastness of geographical time that dwarfs human history and experience (Heringman, 2015, on the historiography of the term). Deep time opens a window onto the vertiginous origins of the earth, while it also has the end of historical time in sight. As the geological sublime, deep time embodies creation, origin, the preservation of pre-human history in a vast stratigraphy of layers, as well as the revelation of the future destruction of historical, human time. Deep time in this sense constitutes a framework for critically scrutinizing the destructive, human-centred effects of modern culture. In the framework of *New Nature Writing* for example, a movement that explores a new experience and observation of nature that is not instrumental, deep time emerges as a critical backdrop for examining the time of modernity. As Alexander Hampton argues, in *New Nature Writing*, nature is "something irreducible, that cannot be exhausted by a disenchanted, subject-centred immanent narrative" (Hampton, 2018, p. 465). In a post-secular context, in which instrumental narratives of modernity are critically assessed without returning to any religious or sacred framework, deep time discloses new ways of enchantment of nature, and of releasing the incomprehensible sublime in nature. Referring to Benjamin's *The Storyteller*, Menely and Taylor foreground "the amplitude of time" of the earth's vastness and distance as epic form against the modern novel that offers fast, immediately accessible information (Menely and Taylor, 2017, p. 1–2). Against this human time, deep time is marked by an "irreducible alterity" that both comforts and unsettles, since it is disconnected from human desires (Reno, 2022, p. 21).

Deep time is described in its intimate connection with a human present that points forward to its future demolition. Deep time is a future past (Huggan, 2018, p. IX ; Marland, 2021, p. 299). Regarding *New Nature Writing*, Pippa Marland, quoting from Robert Macfarlane's *Underland* (2019), points out that "the Anthropocene compels us to think forward in deep time, and to imagine ourselves as ancestors". Deep time, as the time of origin and a precondition of existence itself, is an apocalyptic leap back and forward in time. In David Gange's *Frayed Atlantic Edge*, "the geological freaks of deep time, felt like the imaginary future ruins of a civilisation lost to the rising seas of the Anthropocene". *New Nature Writing* has the ability, Marland argues, "both to think forward to the lives of generations to come and, ultimately, to imagine a time when the human species will no longer exist" (Marland, 2021, p. 299). The idea of a future past is what is referred to as "the prevalence of the future anterior, or future perfect tense, which is oriented towards an eschatological future which is always already looking back" (Marland, 2021, p. 301, referring to Huggan, 2018, p. VIII–IX).[1] As pioneering eco-critic Lawrence Buell already phrased it : "Apocalypse is the single most powerful master metaphor that the contemporary environmental imagination has at its disposal" (Buell, 1995, p. 285). In deep time, the "other" time of a radical, vertiginous origin joins that of an apocalyptic ending, a coincidence that acts out the dynamic of an ephemeral historical present : in the now we are "ancestors", we are traces of the future in a present that is always already tumbling into the past.

In this essay, it is argued that fundamental elements of the contemporary ecocritical understanding of deep time echo important aspects of the nineteenth-century awareness of time and history. These

1 See also in this respect Huggan, 2018, p. 90, on industrial slaughter and the association of whales with myths about human origin and apocalyptic presentiments.

concern its sense of future pasts, its overlapping end-time and time of origin dimensions in human history, and its search for new historical continuities and wholeness. This issue is addressed by turning to the work of Balzac, and in particular to the imagery of deep time in two complementary novels, *Le Colonel Chabert* and *La Peau de chagrin*. In *Le Colonel Chabert*, the modern present of future pasts is the time of the surface, "la couche de terre" (*CH*, III, p. 325), on top of an "other" violent, and forgotten time of origin. From this threshold, and from this underlying past, Chabert is resurrected as both an inanimate, mannequin-like relic and a supernatural spectacle, as both fragmented and whole. In *La Peau de chagrin*, the vast spaces of the *magasin d'antiquités*, filled with objects from all the ages of the world, visualise the vast layers and timespan of antediluvian deep time through human history. This timespan connects Cuvier's resurrected animals from bone fragments, lost civilisations, and objects, like for example a cameo on which one can see the conquests of Alexander the Great (*CH*, X, p. 71). As a chain of ruins, an "Apocalypse rétrograde" (*CH*, X, p. 75) of future pasts, they crush the pettiness of the subject amid the fragmentation and confusion of human history. As a grid of the sublime geological in the hands of the poet Cuvier, "whole worlds" in it are saved from the grip of "le néant" (*CH*, X, p. 75). In both novels, Balzac eventually weaves deep time into the aesthetic-literary experience of wholeness, preservation and vivification. This experience overlaps with and emerges in tandem with an encompassing scientific and geological understanding, as if it were taking part in the wholeness of a mystic, mysterious, infinite time and space (see also *CH*, I, p. 7).

DEEP TIME HISTORICAL TIME AND A WORLD OF TRACES

When the first geologists interpreted fossils, rocks, or mountains, the earth became the spatial archive that materialised the history of nature, of which the vast expanses of pre-human deep time were a part. As Martin Rudwick argued, "nature has had a history of its own" (Rudwick, 2014, p. 10). Historical time became space and spatial layers and vice versa. Interestingly, in works like Buffon's *Époques de la nature*, a sober, historical approach to the earth's history — that was not any different from "civil history" for example — yet served to fix "quelques points dans l'immensité de l'espace" and "sur la route éternelle du tems" (Buffon, 1780, p. 1–2). Buffon thus expressed a sense of the geological sublime, like also in James Hutton's *Theory of the Earth* (1788/1795) or in Charles Lyell's *Principles of Geology* (1830–1833), that seamlessly connected with the history of the world.

In Balzac's literary transformation, deep time as this sublime geological, foundational time, reached far and deep, materialized in the imagery of the Parisian catacombs (Goulet, 2021, p. 235), or, hyperbolized in the "milliards d'années" in the *magasin d'antiquités* in *La Peau de chagrin* (*CH*, X, p. 75). In the latter novel, deep time became an essential, original full time, an absolute memory-collection serving as a counterweight to oblivion, a transcendent depot of all that ever existed. As Gautier also wrote in *Arria Marcella*, on the resurrection of a woman from the imprint of her breast in the ashes of Pompei : "Rien ne meurt, tout continue à exister ; nulle force ne peut annéantir ce qui fut une fois." (Gautier, 1990, p. 45) The past remained present in its own realm (Nelson, 1972, p. 825), as an "indestructible" archive (Blix, 2008, p. 113, 115). Or, in art, it was retrievable as an unaltered past, or as a universal archetype through déjà vue, as if one involuntarily recalled past events or experiences that were therefore not really absent, disconnected or alien (Girard, 2013, p. 39 ; Poulet, 1950, p. 280 ; Brix, 1996, p. 227). Similarly, Georges Cuvier (1769–1832), awakened the remains of animals from "le néant", having "repeuplé mille forêts de tous les mystères de la zoologie avec quelques fragments de houille" (*CH*, X, p. 75). The past, "le commencement du monde et les événements d'hier" (*CH*, X, p. 69), thus including petty human history and its fantasmagoric panorma of the past (*CH*, X, p. 76), was re-enacted : it was restored and experienced in its whole and immediate presence.

This latter perspective, as well as the problematic, even destructive inclusion of human history in this process, immediately connected with the broader concerns of the age to hold past and present together. This sensitivity voiced the problem of lost historical continuities. As Koselleck, Habermas, Fritzsche and Hartog have shown, the present time of modernity, catalysed by the shock of the French Revolution, was singular and elusive, caught up in what Habermas called "the new experience of an advancing and acceleration of historical events [...] A present that understands itself from the horizon of the modern age as the actuality of the most recent period has to recapitulate the break brought about with the past as a *continuous renewal*" (Habermas, 1990, p. 6–7, italics in text). Against this "régime d'historicité" of newness, an irrevocably alien past could no longer serve as *exemplum* or *magistra vitæ* for the present (Koselleck, 1988, p. 58–59 ; Habermas, 1988, p. 15 ; Fritzsche, 2004, p. 15–54 and Hartog, 2012, p. 124). This context of actualisation necessitated new ways of looking at a past that needed deciphering and unmuting. New strategies were needed to connect a disconnected past with a modern present that "made fragments" for its museums and collections (Kirshenblatt-Gimblett, 1998, p. 18–19 and Bauer, 2018, p. 35–52).

The modern present as this newness, as this process of immediate actualisation, including its strategies of re-enactment, created however an opposite world of traces and debris of things that were absent. This world was critically echoed in Balzac's phantasmagoric vastness and re-enactment of human history. Actualisation constituted historical time as a succession of future pasts, characterised by imminent disappearance. They were therefore essentially traces — as Derrida beautifully argued, "an ineffaceable trace would not be a trace at all, but pure presence" (Derrida, 1967, p. 339). Every layer, every era, ultimately pointed forward to the next one and eventually to the apocalyptic ending of time and of the world. Many examples demonstrate this nineteenth-century interest in an eschatological future and the end of time. This future articulated a world in which the present-as-trace constantly pointed to its own coming annihilation and that of the world as the very precondition of existence itself. As Léo Clarétie wrote in his 1886 novel *Paris depuis ses origines jusqu'en l'an 3000* : "Paris n'est plus. Ses ruines elles-mêmes auront bientôt péri" (quoted in Bernard, 2001, p. 56).[2]

Balzac's sensitivity fits the more general image of the layered, future past city as an iconic image of modern temporality, where, as Gautier phrased it, "le présent [...] marche sur le passé" (Gautier, 1856, p. 39–40). Balzac perceives a built environment that is continuously re-arranged,

2 See also the destruction of "the ruins of the ruins" in Flaubert's *Salammbô* : Flaubert, 1970, p. 434 ; see also Bancquart, 1979, *passim*, for many other examples.

demolished, re-used, and reassigned in a rapidly changing social environment, driven by the market. Balzac's work offers many examples of places and their entwinement with traces, debris, and fragments. The antiques shop in *La Peau de chagrin* is again a good example. Jan-Henrik Witthaus argues that in the shop, ruin and fragment were taken as a point of departure and therefore "the present crumbled under the weight of the past" (Witthaus, 2013, p. 234–235). One can also refer to the numerous collections, like that of Pons or of abbé Troubert in *Le Curé de Tours*, or, to the court-turned-hôtel (d'Estrignon) in *Le Cabinet des Antiques* with its corresponding out of place women, "desséchées et noires comme des momies" (*CH*, IV, p. 976).

The awareness of the present as this future past was an intrinsic part of critical subtexts in literature regarding the modern world and its production of historical debris, its logic of demolition and oblivion. Throughout the century, remains of the past emerged from the destruction of original historical contexts. The culture of the moribund Ancien Régime and the post-revolutionary French world filled up with disconnected fragments, from objects to buildings in ruins. Objects and places had become incomprehensible, had become waste, trinkets, knick-knacks, or commodities. They were reset, actualised in an ephemeral *now*, where they could be *à la mode*, or not, as curios reduced to economic value. Debris of the past in this sense abounds in Balzac's work. In *Le Cousin Pons*, for example, Pons exclaims that "le mérite du collectionneur est de devancer la mode" (*CH*, VII, p. 511). Collecting things and being ahead of fashion were the two sides of the same coin of a modern present and a disconnected, alien past. When Pons in the same passage explains the history and origins of "les porcelaines de Frankenthal" to Mme de Marville and her daughter Cécile, the women, unsurprisingly, remain utterly clueless : "la mère et la fille se regardaient comme si Pons leur eût parlé chinois" (*CH*, VII, p. 511). Pons loves the past, but also needs to explain it, while its value is determined by fashion and the thrill of the *aujourd'hui*. Jeannine Guichardet argues that as an "archaeologist", Balzac studied the ephemeral present precisely in terms of its "reliques domestiques", a world already past, as a memory to be constructed for future generations (Guichardet, 1986, p. 147).

Balzac's take on the world of superposed trace-layers was rooted in the awareness and the regret that the present was a time of demolition.

It was founded by the need to create a collective memory as an act of restoration in a world of mutilated buildings or dispersed furniture (Lochmann, 2007, p. 20). In Balzac's world, things would soon become incomprehensible and out of place, like "bientôt" the "marchand de coco" in *Ce qui disparaît de Paris* (Balzac, 1845–1846, p. 179). So would the ruined old "piliers des Halles" in *Le Martyr calviniste* : "dans quelques jours, ce reste du sombre dédale de l'ancien Paris sera-t-il démoli" (*CH*, XI, p. 209). When discussing the incipit of *Les Petits Bourgeois*, Aude Déruelle calls buildings in Balzac's novel therefore very aptly a "feuilleté temporel [qui] se donne à lire dans une superposition spatiale" (Déruelle, 2007, p. 12). Apart from various other examples, in the 1842 "Avant-propos", Balzac presented his project as one that readers would wish had been written about lost civilisations such as Rome or Athens. This passage illustrates again the perspective from a future past in which things have disappeared (*CH*, I, p. 11), a time filled with waste of the past and fashionable collectibles that necessitated new strategies of wholeness.

In this context, it must be asked in what sense deep time, as an "other" time, critically tackled the shallow time of modern presentism and the ephemeral moment. It must also be asked how deep time could operate as a viable strategy of wholeness and continuity as an answer to the challenges of living in constant newness. In order to answer these questions, we will first turn in what follows to the clashing temporalities and deep time in *Le Colonel Chabert.*

LE COLONEL CHABERT

Le Colonel Chabert tells the tragic story of the "défunt" colonel Hyacinthe Chabert. Left for dead in a gruesome soldiers' grave after the bloody battle of Eylau in Poland (1807), he miraculously survives and makes his way back to the surface, to "la couche de terre" that is thrown on top of the corpses (*CH*, III, p. 325). He eventually returns to France to reclaim his life, his marriage, his fortune and, above all, his identity. He fails to do so, however, and remains buried, under the living, under bureaucracy, and under the whole of society (*CH*, III, p. 328).

From the threshold moment of his resurrection onward, Chabert's existence comes across as peculiarly hybrid. On the one hand, his appearance is static and inanimate, "aussi parfaitement immobile que peut l'être une figure en cire de ce cabinet de Curtius" (*CH*, III, p. 321). Chabert's mannequin-likeness articulates the anaemia, the virtual non-being or loss of being of a man who belongs to an alien, even unwanted past, and who is supposed to be dead. On the other hand, Chabert's existence cannot be reduced to this near-non-being. As a whole, Chabert's appearance also offers an intriguing "spectacle surnaturel" that completes the effect he has on his onlookers : "Cette immobilité n'aurait peut-être pas été un sujet d'étonnement, si elle n'eût complété le spectacle surnaturel que présentait l'ensemble du personnage" (*CH*, III, p. 321). The sight of this supernatural spectacle cannot be absorbed into his waning existence. As a "spectacle surnaturel", Chabert's appearance displays a wholeness that transcends the fragmentation of his mutilated body. In this way, neither does he solely display the fragmentation of time and things, nor does he fit the fragmenting linearity of future pasts. His time is that of a constant reference and return to the absolute moment of his resurrection and the time beneath the surface of the present. It is interesting, in this respect, that his name, Hyacinthe, refers to the mythical Hyacinthe, whom Apollo, after his accidental death, turned into a flower that was reborn every spring.

Through his wax figure-likeness, Chabert represents the anaemia of a fragile trace-like present that produces debris and fragments of a lost past. At the same time, he bears the dimension of a time that escapes historical time and opposes the shallowness of an era that was present and newness-centred, as Balzac's take on the fashionable will illustrate. Chabert's wax figure-likeness, and his decrepit dwelling that literally consists of the waste of demolished buildings, embody a critical subtext of the modern era's mentioned obsession with the immediate, new present. The latter presentness refers to the awareness of time as "the current state of affairs," the time of fast perception, the time of the journalist, the clockwork time of passing on paperwork, and the time that allows things to be *à la mode*. It is the time of the modern world with its increasing speed, experiential fragmentation, and bombardment of mental stimuli. This preoccupation with the moment was sometimes also ridiculed. Balzac opposed what Diaz called the deleterious effects of the "journalisation accélérée du vécu contemporain" (Diaz, 2008, p. 5). In the introduction to *Mademoiselle de Maupin* (1830), Théophile Gautier takes the logic of this "journalisation" to the point of absurdity : "Le livre qui sera beau et qu'on louera est le livre qui n'a pas encore paru. [...] Celui de demain sera superbe ; mais c'est toujours aujourd'hui" (Gautier, 1973, p. 64).

In *Le Colonel Chabert*, the ambiguities of presentness come into the picture through Curtius' wax figure cabinet, and through the presence of Chabert's widow/wife, la comtesse de Ferraud. Both are very much exponents of reality as actuality, and of the realm of all things fashionable. Curtius' cabinet, very tellingly, thrived on the fashion of the moment. In 1770 the Swiss physician Philippe Curtius (1737-1794) had opened a cabinet of wax figures of celebrities on the Boulevard du Temple in Paris. The collection was publicized in touristic guides, and adapted, every day, to the taste of the public and the fashion of the moment, in order to give the audience a "sensation d'actualité" (a term coined by Gabriel Tarde), a sense of participation in lost worlds that were re-enacted in front of their eyes, as Jennifer Ruimi argues (Ruimi, 2017, p. 327–333). Chabert is also such alien piece of a past one could re-connect with through the entertainment of an as-really-here experience. In addition, the fact that Balzac also describes Chabert's appearance in terms of a painting, echoes the modern gaze of the museumgoer who pastes his or her own aesthetic experience and transportation upon objects or art in museums or period rooms : "Qu'un homme d'imagination aurait pu prendre cette vieille tête [...] pour un portrait de Rembrandt" (*CH*, III, p. 321).

Also the comtesse de Ferraud effortlessly incarnates the temporality of presentness : "Encore jeune et belle, Madame Ferraud joua le rôle d'une femme à la mode" (*CH*, III, 349), contrary to the anaemic Chabert. As Eileen Sivert argues, madame Ferraud's lack of identity, psychological depth and consistency make her into a "modern non-character", that bears nothing behind the mask she wears in company, other than being "other". Moreover, she seems forever new (Sivert, 1988, p. 221). In contrast, Chabert is negatively affected by the fact that he is old and decrepit, lacks a name and suffers from a mutilated, non-unified body, something that is reflected in the state of his new home and in the fact that his "real" home has been demolished ; in his absence, other houses have been built in its garden and the name of the street has been changed.

Chabert's anaemia and loss of subjectivity and coherence are thus expressed through an imagery of shallow presentness, reflecting the moral shallowness of the Restauration, fashion, and the thrill of the moment. The hybridity of the seemingly animated wax figure, in which the subject appears as a mere contentless other, masks a fundamental ephemerality, absence, and anaemia, instead of performing the re-enactment and the radical presence with which modernity is obsessed. The latter is most poignantly expressed in Chabert's eventual dementia, or mental "absence" at the end of the novel, when he has actually given up any connection between the past and a present where he has become a mere number : "Pas Chabert ! Pas Chabert ! je me nomme Hyacinthe [...] je ne suis plus un homme, je suis le numéro 164" (*CH*, III, p. 372).

There is nothing behind the mask. Actuality is in fact a contradictory reality. The temporality of modernity is a Chimera. Like the other side of the same coin, the modern temporality of presentness paradoxically implies an existence that is fundamentally trace or debris-like. It implies an environment that is always already past and that is conceived and experienced from the angle of its future demolition or disappearance. Hence the anaemia, debris-likeness, and utter ephemerality of the present and the present culture as a future past.

In *Le Colonel Chabert*, the future past is especially the time of buildings that are being destroyed "journellement" (*CH*, III, p. 337). As has been mentioned, the undermining of modern presentness draws the attention to an often apocalyptic fear of the present time as a succession of mere traces. This fear is radically ecocritical, as it hinges upon a kind of premonition of the utter destruction of the environment itself, not just of things in the environment, and on the idea that this destruction takes the shape of major urban developments. As traces, things only spuriously "exist". They exist in a state of imminent disappearance. Things become waste and debris, which in Balzac's literary universe betoken, as has been mentioned, the anaemia of modernity's radical presentness. The modern age as an age of traces is reflected as much in Balzac's own post-factum account of the culture of the Restoration in the novel as in Chabert's mentioned peripheral, decrepit dwelling, or in the logic of constant demolition that pervades the modern city. Interestingly, Chabert's dwelling breathes a spatial lack of determination and out-of-placeness : "Aucun des matériaux n'y avait eu sa vraie destination, ils provenaient tous des démolitions qui se font journellement dans Paris" (*CH*, III, p. 337). The lodging, made up of rubble of demolished houses, literally materialises this logic. Ironically, like a brilliant subtextual pun, one of the shutters of the house is made of a board that once belonged to a shop and has the words "Magasin de nouveautés" on it. In this sense, *Le Colonel Chabert* very much resonates with Balzac's disappearing professions and buildings amidst the futility of newness in the moment.

DEEP TIME AND THE COHERENCE OF THE WORLD

Chabert cannot be reduced to a straightforward anaemic figure, and neither does he succumb to a complete loss of cohesion of his body and his dwelling. A particular value resides in the sheer indeterminacy, confusion and fragmentation of his appearance and dwelling. This indeterminacy connects with a sense of coherence in a fragmented and ephemeral world, rooted in aesthetic experience. As mentioned, Chabert resembled a Rembrandt portrait. His dwelling, situated on the fringes of the urban world and in the margins of society, out of place and time, displays characteristics that define the realm of aesthetic and literary creation, in the suburban margins between the city and countryside, or as indeterminate or ill-defined spaces. Huysmans' later suburban Fontenay is also such example. Des Esseintes' aesthetical home, no matter how much this over-the-top aestheticist place differs from Chabert's masure, is also an attempt to ward off the modern world's presentness beneath a sheltering literary construct (Bauer, 2024). Additionally, the "Magasin de nouveautés" shutter is text, a metatextual pun that escapes the very fragmentation of the modern world to which it draws attention simply by being about it.

In order to understand the aesthetic coherence of a mythical figure who opposes modern shallow time, its fragmented debris, and the role of deep time in this construction, it is helpful to return to *La Peau de chagrin*. The confrontation between the critical reflection of modern temporality and deep time is poignantly explored in the antiques shop passage. There, traces and fragments are set in a total, palaeontology-inspired, all-inclusive time that is materialised in a seemingly endless space and collection characterised by "l'absence des limites" (Mozet, 2007, p. 86). Opposed to this, in the world outside its walls, time swiftly diminishes with the shrinking of the magical skin. Willy Jung called Raphaël de Valentin "un avare du temps", who has the eyes of a young man, already "sous la marque d'un vieillard" (Jung, 2007, p. 110). Outside, Raphaël's being is that of a future past.

As "les palais enchantés de l'Extase" (*CH*, X, p. 70), the spatial and experiential translation of deep time as the realm of the sublime, the antiques shop provokes sensations that are dangerously overwhelming and enchanting. They overstretch an imagination perched on the thin line between aesthetic enchantment (*CH*, X, p. 73) and depression and confusion (*CH*, X, p. 76). In so doing, the shop materialises the dramatic state of despair with which Raphaël had first entered it. The vertiginous state of the shop echoes Raphaël's vertiginous state of mind and imagination : "Il retomba bientôt dans ses vertiges, et continua d'apercevoir les choses sous d'étranges couleurs" (*CH*, X, p. 68). In this context, Cuvier's resurrection of animals from "l'abîme sans bornes du passé" (*CH*, X, p. 75), comes across as a hyperbolic re-enactment, presenting itself as a critical, ironic echo of modern life's excessive re-enactments of what ultimately remain ruins. Casted into a mental vertigo, Raphaël comes to doubt his own existence, appearing to himself, much like the surrounding debris of the past, as neither really dead nor alive (*CH*, X, p. 73).

However, the vastness of deep time in the antiques shop does not play a merely subtextual role exposing modernity's obsession with presentness, any more than it does in *Le Colonel Chabert.* As a "supernatural spectacle" and as a portrait, Chabert gained wholeness in the aesthetic receptivity he inspired. This saved him from the complete anaemia that would have absorbed him if he were only a critical reflection of modern time's debris of the future past. Echoing the often troubling emotional experience of museumgoers of his time,[3] Balzac also presents the experience of the overwhelming spectacle in the "magasin d'antiquités" in

3 For example, Thomas Jessop mentioned in his 1820 *Journal d'un voyage à Paris* : "La vue se perd dans cette vaste et originale perspective, les sens s'égarent [...] les idées se bousculent" (quoted in Poulot, 1997, p. 350).

terms of aesthetic receptivity. The traces of past worlds, for example, come to life by being admired aesthetically ("admirant" : *CH*, X, p. 72), an experience to which furthermore "d'étranges couleurs" and "les formes les plus étranges" add vividness (*CH*, X, p. 73).

In human history we, too, like Chabert, remain "écrasés [...] sous tant d'univers en ruine" (*CH*, III, p. 75). Balzac's re-enactment did not do away with the deleterious state of ruin of the successive ages of human time, and despite being an "poème sans fin" it did not offer wholeness (*CH*, X, p. 71). This is unlike Cuvier's "whole worlds" snatched from "le néant" in pre-human deep time, unaffected by the pettiness of mankind (*CH*, X, p. 75), modernity, and its retrograde Apocalypse that falls back endlessly into a past of growing ruins. Cuvier, with his wide, encompassing perspective of a literary-aesthetic nature offers a way out of the ravages of actualisation. In salvaging the past from nothingness, Cuvier was "le plus grand poète de notre siècle" (*CH*, X, p. 75). Cuvier created, shaped continuity, like a writer or an artist, "a peculiar kind of antiquarian", as he called himself, who restored those past "monuments" (Cuvier, 1812, p. 2).

Like the palaeontologist, the archaeologist-writer also performed a restoration, albeit a textual one, in which human history, its objects, and its buildings had become "documents" (Hamon, 1989, p. 56 on buildings). They were preserved and existed as text and as literary constructs. Text was able to hold together the disappearing city. As textual-literary traces, they exemplified what Priscilla P. Ferguson called "the conjunction of literature and the city" as a means "to make the city whole" (Ferguson, 1997, p. 66).[4] While stressing the fragmentation of the actual city, the city as text is able to integrate its fragments as metonymic figures, as "traces typographiques" (Ferguson, 1997, p. 67 and Guichardet, 1986, p. 186), like Cuvier's bones in the vastness of deep time are able to evoke a whole world, and not just the endless poem of human history where "rien de complet ne s'offrait à l'âme" (*CH*, X, p. 71–72). As metonymical traces, they are preserved in the untainted present of literature. As textual building blocks, they persist. In modernity, the weight of ruins keeps on crushing us, but amid the smallness of our present in the face of the geological sublime of millions of years,

4 See also Citron's "vue synoptique", 1961, p. 256–257 and Guichardet's "ville-texte", 1986, p. 19.

the past lives. For better or for worse, as an "épouvantable résurrection" in our modern time (*CH*, X, p. 75), the past remains sheltered in our aesthetical receptivity and experience.

Balzac's deep time constituted a critical subtext of the modern present as a future past and its production of fragments, debris, commodities, or trinkets that were prone to destruction and oblivion. However, deep time was not a straightforward reversal of this modern present. Though opposed to the ephemerality of shallow time and distinguished from human, historical time, as also a mystic time of mystery, deep time was both in and above history. With the geological sublime, earth became a spatial archive of historical developments that preceded human history. Time materialised in the spatial layers of the earth and space became time. Through this spatial entwinement with the past as a historical succession of layers, deep time did not just transcend contingent, human time. As a container in which every present was preserved in its own timespan, it represented a spatial and material grid of continuity and possibility of re-enactment that met the need and the search for historical continuity in the modern world. As a strategy of re-enactment, it also catalysed the eschatological dynamic of modern temporality and its logic of future pasts, having modernity bite its own tail. For, the strategies of re-enactment that were meant to save the past from complete absence and alienation, only catalysed the latter process. This paradox is made explicit in Balzac's devastating, retrograde Apocalypse in *La Peau de chagrin*, that, as a logic of future pasts, runs back in human time. This paradox of modernity also persists in contemporary ecocritical thought, when, from the perspective of an apocalyptic Anthropocene, one looks back or forward, and the present takes on the shape of a future past echoing the end-time dimension of deep time.

These complexities of deep time are followed through in the hybridity of Colonel Chabert, shattered between a time of origin and shallow surface time, and in the seemingly endless spaces and eras in the "magasin d'antiquités" in *La Peau de chagrin*. This spatio-temporal imagery develops critical subtexts of modern presentness. Both the mannequin-like Chabert and his decrepit dwelling, and Raphaël, who resembles the objects that surround him and succumbs to too many ruinous re-enactments, lose being and become thing-like. Such are the implications of a perpetually new present that is always tumbling into a disconnected past of traces.

Neither Chabert, nor Raphaël, however, were ever totally absorbed into this critical dimension or the logic of future pasts. Chabert became whole through his aesthetic effect as a portrait and as a supernatural spectacle that transcended the fragmentation in modernity. In *La Peau de chagrin*, Cuvier's scientific restoration of the past in the realm of deep time was an act of poetry in which metonymic fragments made present once more a lost wholeness that persisted in words.

Dominique BAUER
KU Leuven

WORKS CITED

Balzac Honoré de, 1845, *Ce qui disparaît de Paris*, in *Le Diable à Paris* (Paris : Hertzel), p. 170–179.

Bancquart Marie-Claire, 1979, *Images littéraires du Paris "Fin-de-siècle"* (Paris : Éditions de la Différence).

Bauer Dominique, 2025, "The artist's Studio as a Memory Space. The Case of Villa Khnopff", in *Spaces of Belgian Culture*, ed. by Dominique Bauer, Marjan Sterckx and Ilja Van Damme (Amsterdam : Amsterdam University Press), forthcoming.

Bauer Dominique, 2018, *Place-Text-Trace. The Fragility of the Spatial Image* (Leuven : Peeters).

Bernard Jean-Pierre A., 2001, *Les deux Paris. Essai sur les représentations de Paris dans la seconde moitié du* XIXe *siècle* (Paris : Champ Vallon).

Blix Göran, 2009, *From Paris to Pompeii. French Romanticism and Cultural Politics of Archaeology* (Philadelphia : University of Pennsylvania Press).

Brix Michel, 1996, "Résurrection du passé et création romantique à propos d'*Arria Marcella*", *Bulletin de la Société Théophile Gautier*, 18, p. 227–237.

Brossat Alain, 2007, "Colonel Chabert ou le revenant intempestif", *Intermédialités/Intermedialities*, 10, p. 61–75.

Buell Lawrence, 1995, *The Environmental Imagination. Thoreau, Nature Writing, and the Formation of American Culture* (Cambridge, MA : Harvard University Press).

Buffon, Georges-Louis Leclerc, comte de, 1780, *Les Époques de la nature*, tome premier (Paris : L'Imprimerie Royale).

Citron Pierre, 1961, *La Poésie de Paris de Rousseau à Baudelaire*, vol. II (Paris : Éditions de Minuit).

Claretie Léo, 1886, *Paris depuis ses origines jusqu'en l'an 3000* (Paris : Charavay frères).

Cuvier Georges, 1812, *Recherches sur les ossemens fossiles de quadrupèdes*, vol. 1 (Paris : Deterville).

Derrida Jacques, 1967, *L'écriture et la différence* (Paris : Éditions du Seuil).

Déruelle Aude, 2007, "Le roman balzacien entre histoire et mémoire", *AB*, p. 33–48.

Diaz José Luis, 2008, "Balzac face aux révolutions de la littérature", *AB*, p. 25–42.

Ferguson Priscilla Parkhurst, 1997, *Paris as Revolution : Writing the Nineteenth-Century City* (Berkely ; Los Angeles : University of California Press).

Flaubert Gustave, 1970, *Salammbô* (Paris : Gallimard).
Fritzsche Peter, 2004, *Stranded in the Present. Modern Time and the Melancholy of History* (Cambridge, MA : Harvard University Press).
Gautier Théophile, 1856, *Mosaïque de ruines*, in Alexandre Dumas, Théophile Gautier *et al.*, *Paris et les Parisiens au* XIXe *siècle* (Paris : Morizot), p. 38–41.
Gautier Théophile, 1973, *Mademoiselle de Maupin* (Paris : Gallimard).
Gautier Théophile, 1990, *Arria Marcella*, in Théophile Gautier, *Contes et récits fantastiques* (Paris : Le Livre de Poche), p. 292–323.
Girard Marie-Hélène, 2013, "Théophile Gautier et le Musée imaginaire", *Revue de l'art*, 182, p. 35–42.
Goulet Andrea, 2021, "Anthropocene under Paris ? Rethinking the Quarries and Catacombs", *Dix-Neuf*, 25 (3–4), p. 225–241.
Guichardet Jeannine, 1986, *Balzac archéologue de Paris* (Paris : Sedes).
Habermas Jürgen, 1990, *The Philosophical Discourse of Modernity. Twelve Lectures*, Translated by Frederick G. Lawrence (Cambridge, MA : The MIT Press).
Hamon Philippe, 1989, *Expositions. Littérature et architecture au* XIXe *siècle* (Paris : José Corti).
Hampton Alexander J. B., 2018, "Post-Secular Nature and the New Nature Writing", *Christianity and Literature*, 67 (3), p. 454–471.
Hartog François, 2012, *Régimes d'historicité. Présentisme et expériences du temps* (Paris : Éditions du Seuil).
Heringman Noah, "Deep Time at the Dawn of the Anthropocene," *Representations*, 129 (1), p. 56-85.
Huggan Graham, 2018, *Colonialism, Culture, Whales : The Cetacean Quartet* (London : Bloomsbury).
Jung Willy, 2007, "*La Peau de chagrin* : une théorie romantique du temps", *AB*, p. 105–115.
Kirshenblatt-Gimblett Barbara, 1998, *Destination Culture. Tourism, Museums, and Heritage* (Berkeley, CA : University of California Press).
Koselleck Reinhardt, 1988, *Vergangene Zukunft. Zur Semantik geschichtlicher* Zeiten (Frankfurt am Main : Suhrkamp).
Lochmann Blanche, 2007, "Mémoire des lieux, lieux de mémoire dans *La Comédie humaine*", *AB*, p. 131–147.
Marland Pippa, 2021, "Deep Time Visible", in *The Cambridge Companion to Literature and the Anthropocene*, ed. by John Parham (Cambridge : Cambridge University Press), p. 289–303.
Menely Tobias and Jesse Oak Taylor (ed. by), 2017, *Anthropocene Reading. Literary History in Geological Times* (University Park : Penn State University Press).
Michel Arlette, 2000, "Chateaubriand, Balzac et le temps aboli", *AB*, p. 249–264.

Mozet Nicole, 2001, "Le passé au présent. Balzac ou l'esprit de la collection", *Romantisme*, 112, p. 83–94.

Nelson Hilda, 1972, "Théophile Gautier : The Invisible and Impalpable World : *A Demi Conviction*", *The French Review*, 45 (4), p. 819–830.

Poulet Jean, 1950, *Études sur le temps humain* (Paris : Plon).

Poulot Dominique, 1997, *Musée, nation, patrimoine 1789-1815* (Paris : Gallimard).

Reno Seth T. (ed. by), 2022, *The Anthropocene. Approaches and Contexts for Literature and the Humanities* (London : Routledge).

Rudwick Martin, 2014, *Earth's Deep History. How it was Discovered and Why it Matters* (Chicago : The University of Chicago Press).

Ruimi Jennifer, 2017, "Spectacles de cire. Le cabinet de Curtius", *Dix-huitième siècle*, 49 (1), p. 319–334.

Simpson Thomas, 2018, "Historicizing Human in Colonial India", in *Historicizing Humans. Deep Time, Evolution and Race in Nineteenth-Century British Sciences*, ed. by Efram Sera-Shrirar (Pittsburgh : University of Pittsburgh press), p. 113–137.

Sivert Eileen B., 1988, "Who's Who : Non-Characters in *Le Colonel Chabert*", *French Forum*, 13 (2), p. 217–228.

Witthaus Jan-Henrik, 2013, "Raum der Überreste. Zur literarischen Inszenierung des Zeit-Raums bei Balzac", in *Die Neuvermessung romantischer Räume : Raumkonzepte der französischen Romantik vor dem Hintergrund des Spatial turn*, ed. by Maria O. Hertrampf and Dagmar Schmelzer (Berlin : Frank & Timme), p. 221–243.

LEAVES OF THISTLE

Paper Ecologies in Balzac's *Illusions perdues*[1]

While the socioeconomic, literary, and even existential implications of the printing industry drive the intense tragedy that is Balzac's *Illusions perdues* (1837–1843),[2] a botanical history lurks in the novel. Seeking to redress this "plant blindness" (Gagliano, Ryan, and Vieira, 2017, p. 6), the present essay offers a fuller ecology of *La Comédie humaine* by shifting to a botanical Balzac. As the narrator of *Illusions perdues* remarks at the outset, the novel is due as much to the "existence matérielle" of paper as it is to the Press that churns it out (*CH*, V, p. 218). The fate of the botanically named protagonist Lucien *Chardon* (thistle), though heavily determined by his reckless ambition and the crippling capitalist machinations of Parisian society, ultimately depends on his brother-in-law's stymied quest to invent a cheap but excellent quality plant-based paper.

The undercurrent of botanical vitalism in Balzac's *Illusions perdues* invites a reexamination of his turn to the fabrication of plant-based paper within the context of industrialization and the mass production of books. As his character David Séchard crafts paper pulp from the nettles and thistles of nearby swamps, Balzac roots his novel in a paper ecology that, in its emulation of ancient Chinese practices, recycles the practice of exploiting local plants to produce writing and printing surfaces.

---

1 This article was written in memory of Alain Toumayan, who first introduced me to Balzac. I am indebted to the anonymous readers of my initial manuscript for their insightful suggestions and generous attention to polishing my prose.

2 *Illusions perdues* in its final form consists of three novels that Balzac published separately: *Illusions perdues* in 1837, *Un grand homme de province à Paris* in 1839, and *Ève et David* in 1843. The three were merged into one novel in the 8th volume of the Furne edition of *La Comédie humaine* in 1843.

BOTANICAL BALZAC

With his detailed portraits of interiors and urban life, Balzac might not seem to have much in the way of the archetypal botanist: "Botaniste très fantaisiste que Balzac, qui avoue [...] ne pas 'savoir comment s'organisent les herbiers'" (Mozet, 2017, p. 22). As a mesh of dramas and protagonists from all strata of society, the *Comédie humaine* suggests an animate and even frenetic zoo more than a mute herbarium of motionless leaves and flowers. Yet, the demarcation between zoology and botany was hardly distinguishable when biology was emerging as a distinct field at the start of the July Monarchy. If "the life science of biology [served] as [Balzac's] model and most direct inspiration", it was in the more general sense of a universal energy and movement that connected all forms of life: "Suddenly, life was perceived to be everywhere, from infinitesimal entities to colossal creatures in an immemorial past, and was being defined in terms of energy and movement rather than of static form" (Gerwin, 2017, p. 20–21). It was less a specialized science and more the evocative movement of a "morphologie transcendentale", inspired by German *Naturphilosophie* and appropriated by natural historians as a unifying force between all living beings, that offered a sense of structure and vitality to Balzac's vast literary project (Cohen, 2007, p. 58).[3]

Naturalists' ties with plant life invite a less anthropomorphic reading of the *Comédie humaine*: "Buffon's descriptive writings were mainly concerned with animals, [but] his influence on botany was no less far reaching than on zoology" (Morton, 1981, p. 294). The dialectic that Balzac presents with his weaving of Cuvier and Geoffroy Saint-Hilaire in the "Avant-Propos" can be extended to the ongoing debate throughout the "golden age" of botany — which spanned the immediate wake of Linnaeus to Darwin (1790–1850) (Dayrat, 2003)[4] — as to whether the science of plants was a

3 Georges Gusdorf traces the development of *Naturphilosophie* and its numerous epistemic strands (Schelling, Schlegel, Novalis, Goethe, etc.) throughout the early nineteenth century and claims that the "souffle romantique" of *Naturphilosophie* was most saliently represented in France by the Cuvier / Geoffroy Saint-Hilaire debate (1985, p. 277–278).

4 The Revolution was the "grande chance de l'histoire naturelle" due to the opening of the Muséum national d'histoire naturelle in 1793, the establishment of university chairs in botany, and the creation of botanical gardens across France (Dayrat, 2003).

taxonomical practice of naming based only on the sexual parts of plants or a synthesizing science that considered a fuller morphology of plants as well as their evolving processes and ongoing adaptations to their *milieux* (natural method). Embracing an entanglement of both models as a catalyst for his fiction, Balzac presents a literary cosmos that analyses differences within and homologies between social microcosms and the human types that inhabit them. Reconciling synthesis with analysis, "He used the nascent science of biology as well as the taxonomic tradition of natural history, arguably for the first time, as categories for understanding of the world" (Thiher, 2001, p. 46).[5] In its attention to material properties, plant behavior, and milieu, the science of botany reflects the practices of a novelist who aims to capture the developing history and material minutiae of early 19th-century France. Botany, in other words, informed the realist novel. Working against traditional views of Rousseau's *Rêveries du promeneur solitaire* (1782) as solipsistic and inward-facing retreats into nature, Célia Abele reads Balzac's botanizing as anticipating realism in its attention to details and the discourses on society that they yield: "Rousseau's epistemology works primarily through how the herbarium [...] acts as a formal double for the *Rêveries* as a text and points to the wider world while being imbricated in its social and natural networks" (2022, p. 202). Abele shows the extent to which botany — a practice that involves cataloging, interacting with a network of scientists, and creating books — underpins the *Comédie humaine*: "Rereading Rousseau's *Rêveries* with its conjoined structure of diary and herbarium as well as the Île Saint-Pierre's employment of realist procedures allows us to revalue Balzac's claims about the relationship between literature and natural history" (*ibid.*, p. 216). Plants provide nuances that inspire the literary imagination and capture the various microcosms of post-Revolutionary French society.

Beyond the genre of the realist novel, plants came to evoke the creative imagination itself. In view of botany's ever-elusive project of naming and classifying all vegetation, plant science exemplified an alluring model for a distinct poesis: "As a material, literary, and cultural practice, romantic era botany foregrounds what Linnaeus and later taxonomists put aside and Foucault cannot: that plant nature

5 Balzac does not fully embrace Geoffroy Saint-Hilaire's evolutionary model of life forms since he often notes the categorical differences between species (*CH*, I, p. 1116, n. 8).

occupies the disputed middle kingdom of nature, neither fully mineral nor fully animal but disturbingly in between" (Kelley, 2012, p. 4). Botanical treatises such as Johann Wolfgang von Goethe's *Metamorphose der Pflanzen* (1790) — later published in the form of a lyric elegy in 1798 — and Alexander von Humboldt's *Essai sur la Géographie des Plantes* (1804) "mark profound transitions away from plants as objects of the classifying imagination and toward vegetal beings' capacities for endless growth, inciting revolutionary thinking about questions of representation" (McHugh, 2021, p. 3). What Kelley refers to as the "resilient hiddenness" (2012, p. 5) of plants as a fertile source for the Romantic imagination lies in their evocation of "difference and permutation" (*ibid.*, p. 19). The Swiss botanist Augustin-Pyramus de Candolle (1778–1841) emphasized this force in vegetal life when he published *Physiologie végétale ou exposition des forces et des fonctions vitales des végétaux* in 1832 — shortly before Balzac visited him during a sojourn in Geneva in 1833 to inform his representation of Nordic flora in *Séraphîta* (1834) (*Corr.*, I, p. 912–913) — in which he probes not only the characteristics of plants but their movements in all forms: "Contrairement aux corps bruts, identiques entre eux, les végétaux sont différents les uns des autres, non seulement sur le plan des espèces mais jusque sur le plan des individus" (Oghină-Pavie, 2024, p. 41). Likewise, Balzac's *Comédie humaine* is an animate and interacting network of unique and complicated physiologies that constantly develop and morph in reaction to ongoing history, an emerging capitalist democracy, and the attendant drives of societal mores and expectations.[6] A "cultural ecology" that responds to the fracture between culture and nature, the series of novels reflect "a special sensibility for the ecopsychological and ecocultural impoverishment caused by conformist, standardized structures of a one-sided economic and technocentric modernization" (Zapf, 2014, p. 57). Considering the overlooked role of plants in Balzac is a way to read his flowering of novels as an ecosystem that constantly grows, adapts, and

6 In his history of botany, Morton notes this merging of natural history and how Hegel's "profoundly advanced understanding of the nature of developmental processes, and of the causal interconnections and inner dialectic of progressive change" was reflected in "the actual course of botanical investigation" in the 1830s, "with its decisive turn towards the processes of plant development, the relations between development and environment, and the integration of different levels of structure and activity within the plant body" (1981, p. 380).

intertwines: "Les petits limbes verts qui peuplent la planète et capturent l'énergie du soleil sont le tissu connectif cosmique qui permet, depuis des millions d'années, aux vies les plus disparates de s'entrecroiser et de se mélanger sans se fondre réciproquement l'une dans l'autre" (Coccia, 2016, p. 42). Paying attention to the movement of plants allows the young and creative printer David Séchard to emulate their "poéticité", their capacity to "faire monde (au sens du *poiesis*, comme fabriquer) en nouant les relations avec d'autres organismes, avec le sol et les éléments comme l'air, l'eau et le soleil" (Bouvet and Posthumus, 2024, p. 7). Through the character of David, Balzac presents a vitalist ecosystem that resists mechanistic approaches: "La plante est constituée d'un assemblage de matières, mais elle est un organisme fonctionnel parce que doté de la vie. La physiologie est l'étude des mouvements propres à l'état vivant et s'intéresse donc à ce qui distingue les phénomènes de la vie du fonctionnement d'une machine" (Oghină-Pavie, 2024, p. 26). In *Illusions perdues*, it is particularly the ancient practice of crafting paper out of bamboo within the lush landscapes of China that inspires Balzac's poetic inventor to turn to local plants for a natural material that can withstand industrialized machines.

CHIFFONS VERTS[7]

Since landscapes and vegetation do not play outsized roles in *Illusions perdues*, botany only seems to apply in analogical form in how the novel presents a morphology of the 19th-century Restoration book: an exhaustive study of all its parts and materials, its habitats, all aspects of its history over time, and how this history relates to the evolution of civilization more generally and post-Revolutionary French society more specifically. But vegetation lurks in *Illusions perdues* through Balzac's focus on the materiality of paper. David Séchard and his quest for plant paper foregrounds a pursuit of the life sciences, a slow act of botanizing and experimentation, within the throes of a mechanical age.

7 *CH*, V, p. 628.

The basic paper-making process — which consists of breaking down plant cellulose fibers with water, collecting the remnants with a screen, and forming the remaining substance into molds — was more or less the same in Balzac's France as it had been in ancient China (Kurlansky, 2016, p. 205). The stuff of the book is its paper, and paper is derived from plants: "The first Chinese papers [...] were made from a blend of bast — the soft, fibrous material scooped out of the inner bark of trees — and old fishnets, cloth scraps, and hemp gathered from frayed rope" (Basbanes, 2013, p. 9). First recorded in China in 105 CE, paper's origin in the southwestern province of Yunnan was due to the area's wide variety of vegetation and the water flowing through its gorges:

> The high terrain of the fertile Yungui Plateau on which most of the province lies is crossed by three major river systems — the Yangtze, the Mekong, and the Salween — each running through deep gorges that in places are several thousand feet below the nearby peaks. With an abundance of limestone-filtered mountain water, the region is ideally suited to the making of paper; the other core ingredient, cellulose fiber, is provided by a cornucopia of vegetation. (*Ibid.*, p. 13)

The intimate connection between paper and nature in ancient China appeared in the forms of calligraphy, poetry, and painting:

> Chinese painting and the poetry that accompanied it were deeply rooted in the spiritual beliefs of Taoism, which dates back to the fourth century BCE and extolls a love of nature and of finding the natural balance inherent in all things, as well as more abstract concepts such as embracing nothingness. Both the poetry and the painting, therefore, were largely, though not exclusively, focused on landscapes. (Kurlansky, 2016, p. 46)

The series of 18th-century gouaches from the album *Art de faire le papier à la Chine*, sent by French Jesuit missionaries to the printer and book seller Jean-François Delatour (Drège, 2019), vividly illustrate the extent to which paper pertains to a lush environment (Fig. 1).

Fig. 1 – "On coupe les Bambous", gouache, *Art de faire le papier à la Chine*, 18th cen., Bibliothèque nationale de France, Département estampes et photographie, EST OE-110, gallica.bnf.fr / BnF [accessed 13 January 2025].

Even if Balzac's *Illusions perdues* is set squarely in the industrialized context of Restoration France, the rich history of paper that the novel traces has its roots in the fibers of an ancient art.[8]

8 Balzac was familiar with both P. du Halde's and abbé Grosier's *Descriptions* of China (published in 1735 and 1787), which each include a chapter on paper (Chollet, 1977, p. 95).

Balzac's first-hand experience with printing and publishing, along with his particularly dynamic process of working on manuscripts and editing proofs, led him to a close relationship with the medium of paper:

> À travers ce dialogue constant de l'inscription manuscrite et de la mise en forme imprimée, l'œuvre entière est vouée à la mobilité, aux transferts d'un support à un autre, à une matérialité perpétuellement remodelable — vue sous cet angle, la "cathédrale de papier" balzacienne trahit non pas une différence, mais bien au contraire une préoccupation constante à l'égard des diverses possibilités offertes par ce matériau fascinant, tantôt "plâtre", tantôt "marbre": le papier. (Bustarret, 1995, p. 83)[9]

Heightening this feverish interaction with the writer's medium were the rapid developments in paper-making and the printing industry in the first decades of the nineteenth century. As Balzac churned out manuscripts, he faced the perilous commercial tactics and predatory publishing agglomerations that maintained a grip on the publishing market: "le fonctionnement de cette lourde machine qu'on appelle globalement, à l'époque, la librairie" (Berthier, 1999, p. 8). The metaphorical "lourde machine" of publishing was fueled by the development of the Fourdrinier continuous paper machine, as patented in 1799, assembled in England in 1803 and in France in 1816: "La première conséquence de l'invention concerne la baisse du prix de revient (environ 45 % pour le papier d'imprimerie courant), tandis que l'éventail des formats est très simplifié" (Barbier, 2020, p. 319). As Balzac would lament in ["De l'état actuel de la librairie"] (*Le Feuilleton des journaux politiques*, 3 and 10 Mar. 1830), the rapid production of paper ushered in serial novels printed on low-quality paper and a severe devaluation of literature along with it: "Or, il est bon de dire ici que le commerce de la librairie peut se formuler en peu de mots. Une rame de papier blanc vaut quinze francs; noircie, elle se vend cent sous ou cent francs: cent francs si l'ouvrage réussit, cent sous s'il tombe" (Berthier, 1999, p. 51–52). On the cusp of the July Monarchy, paper had become more valuable than literature. As an aficionado of all forms of high-quality paper (Bustarret, 1995, p. 83–85), Balzac put up a form of

---

Chollet gives a thorough account of Balzac's knowledge of paper and the bibliographical sources that would have informed *Illusions perdues* (*ibid.*, p. 91–97).

9 The exhibition catalog *Balzac, imprimeur et défenseur du livre* (1995), which includes Bustarret's chapter on Balzac and paper, is an essential resource for all things related to Balzac and the printing industry.

resistance against machine-made paper that traded quality for efficiency and cost-effectiveness. Scouting inexpensive yet good-quality paper for his never realized *Société d'abonnement*, Balzac searched in Angoulême, Besançon, and Paris for a feasible printing support in 1833, but "il semble [...] que la production mécanique française n'ait pas été assez sophistiquée pour répondre aux besoins formulés par Balzac" (*ibid.*, p. 90).

Balzac's effort to reconcile traditional high-quality paper with increasingly sophisticated technology anticipates the dissonance that plays out in *Illusions perdues* between old modes of paper production and a changing society that was adapting to a new economy: "Il se veut le poète du temps qui meurt [...]; ou plutôt, il est fasciné par ce qui disparaît, par ce qui va disparaître, par l'effondrement, le craquement qui annoncent les temps nouveaux" (Chollet, 1977, p. 94). The answer for an ideal paper lay not in machines — "L'aventure de l'industrie l'intéresse peu" (*ibid.*) — but in its material. In exploring the possibilities of plant-based paper, Balzac's novel brings out a central preoccupation of 18th-century naturalists in a 19th-century industrialized context. The scarcity of rag stocks and the expense that resulted from their use prompted a reexamination of ancient Chinese practices. As the natural sciences flourished, experimenters and entrepreneurs were keen to identify natural resources for paper production to circumvent increasingly "desperate" demands for rag stocks (Kurlansky, 2016, p. 220). The French entomologist Réaumur looked to wasp nests, the German botanist Jacob Christian Schäffer experimented with a wide variety of vegetable fibers, and in England Matthias Koops published a book with paper made of straw and tree bark (*ibid.*, p. 214–226). This spirit of botanical ingenuity continued in the nineteenth century; during the Second Bourbon Restoration alone, patents were sought for paper made from hemp, esparto grass, licorice bark or root, straw, thistle, hop, corn, hay, and beet pulp (Chollet, 1977, p. 93).

The *Encyclopédie*'s entry on "Papier" warned that using plants to produce paper involved high production costs:

> En un mot, on est parvenu à faire du papier de toutes sortes de matières végétables, & d'une infinité de substances que nous rejettons comme inutiles; je ne doute pas qu'on n'en pût faire encore de boyaux & de tripes d'animaux, même de matieres minerals cotonneuses, puisqu'on en fait de l'amianthe ou de l'asbeste; mais l'important seroit d'en faire qui coûtât moins que le *papier* de chiffons, sans quoi toutes les recherches en ce genre ne sont que de pure curiosité. (Jaucourt, 1765, p. 847)

The lengthy account cautions against pursuing the "prétendue ressource" of plant material: plants located near the paper manufacturer would be hard to find and of limited supply, and the fibrous vegetable material would have to be supplemented with rag stocks to achieve the proper consistency (Desmarest, 1788, p. 384). Rendering plants into paper amounted to an amusing pastime and had no place in an increasingly "serious" industrialized setting. Whereas the paper industry in 18th-century China remained indelibly associated with natural scenery and vegetation (Fig. 2) —

Fig. 2 – "On coupe les Bambous en petits morceaux", gouache, *Art de faire le papier à la Chine*, 18th cen., Bibliothèque nationale de France, Département estampes et photographie, EST OE-110, gallica.bnf.fr / BnF [accessed 13 January 2025].

— the *Encyclopédie*'s showcasing of paper production in France emphasized the stark interiors of factories and the geometric forms of mechanical tools (Fig. 3).

FIG. 3 – "Papetterie, Dérompoir". *Encyclopédie, ou dictionnaire raisonné des sciences, des arts et des métiers, etc.*, Planches, vol. 5, 1751–1780, Bibliothèque nationale de France, gallica.bnf.fr / BnF [accessed 13 January 2025].

Concerns about the speed and cost of production outweighed concerns over quality: "With the increased use of machines, chemicals, wood pulp, and bleaching agents, papermaking became less of a craft and more of an assembly-line industry, and the quality of the product itself suffered a significant decline" (Basbanes, 2013, p. 69). Paper had shifted from an artisanal and even poetic pursuit into a race for the bottom line.

From the outset of *Illusions perdues* in "Une imprimerie en province", Balzac captures this sense of the correlation between papermakers' distancing from plants and the deteriorating quality of paper. As the closing instalment of *Scènes de la vie de province* and thus a segue to *Scènes de la vie parisienne*, the novel sets up the contrast between the new technology of the cast-iron Stanhope mechanical printing press primarily used in Paris and the old wooden presses of Angoulême that the parsimonious Séchard *père* refuses to abandon.[10] Despite Balzac's portrait of Séchard as a drunken and miserly "bear" who has no qualms taking advantage of his son David's meek and generous nature, the father's resistance to "Les dévorantes presses mécaniques" belies the narrator's sense of nostalgia as he evokes the high-quality (if flawed) books of the past:

> Les dévorantes presses mécaniques ont aujourd'hui si bien fait oublier ce mécanisme, auquel nous devons, malgré ses imperfections, les beaux livres des Elzévir, des Plantin, des Alde et des Didot, qu'il est nécessaire de mentionner les vieux outils auxquels Jérôme-Nicolas Séchard portait une superstitieuse affection; car ils jouent leur rôle dans cette grande petite histoire. (*CH*, V, p. 124)[11]

When David, apprenticed in Paris at the renowned Didot printing house (which played a role in bringing the Fourdrinier machine to France),[12] weakly protests as his father insists on keeping the old wooden presses, Séchard *père* warns that the unforgiving metal of the new Stanhope machine will deform type characters:

> Ah! vous avez voulu des Stanhope! merci de vos Stanhope qui coûtent chacune deux mille cinq cents francs, presque deux fois plus que valent mes trois bijoux ensemble, et qui vous échinent la lettre par leur défaut d'élasticité.

10 Lord Charles Stanhope invented the cast-iron printing press in England at the end of the 18th century, but it did not arrive in France until 1814.

11 Chollet (1977, p. 94) points out that, although Balzac had Stanhope presses in his print-shop during the Restoration, "c'est les *sabots* du père Séchard qu'il décrit".

12 Nicolas-Louis Robert, who worked for the Parisian printer Pierre-François Didot, invented the continuous paper machine. Didot had it patented in London. The papermakers Henry and Sealy Fourdrinier then built prototypes of the machine but went bankrupt in the process. The industrialist Bryan Donkin financed the first successful machine in 1804 (Kurlansky, 2016, p. 213–215).

> Je ne suis pas instruit comme toi, mais retiens bien ceci: la vie des Stanhope est la mort du caractère. (*CH*, V, p. 132)

The near extinct "elasticity" of the natural material of the wooden press is what had helped to produce the "beaux livres" of the past. Even if it produced imperfections, the wooden press created centuries of beautiful books of excellent quality that stand as monuments to craftsmanship and a more intimate human relationship to natural resources. *Illusions perdues* is dedicated to Victor Hugo and resonates with *Notre-Dame de Paris* (1831): just as the printing press killed off cathedrals, cheap paper will kill off well-made books.

The narrator turns to the closely intertwined friends David Séchard (printing apprentice, though a poet by nature) and Lucien Chardon (son of a pharmacist and an aspiring poet, though swayed by the allure of fame and material luxuries). Their respective pursuits of economic stability and social acclaim prompt Lucien to pass down to David his father's plan to reduce the price of paper by looking to America for "certaines matières végétales analogues à celles dont se servent les Chinois et qui coûtaient peu" (*CH*, V, p. 143). David is eager to marry Lucien's sister Ève and find a way to support her and his printing house. His quest for inventing an effective modern plant paper seems to be a get-rich-quick scheme. However, he is the only character in *Illusions perdues* who demonstrates a genuine sensitivity toward Nature: "Il y a pour les gens aimants un plaisir infini à trouver dans les accidents d'un paysage, dans la transparence de l'air, dans les parfums de la terre, la poésie qu'ils ont dans l'âme", he confides to Ève as they walk along the Charente River and contemplate a sunset (*CH*, V, p. 212). His botanical exploits evoke traditional practices that have been lost to mechanical modes of production. This unique wooing scene culminates with David regaling Ève with a history of paper going back to ancient China: "toutes les grandes acquisitions de l'industrie et de l'intelligence se sont faites avec une excessive lenteur et par des agrégations inaperçues, absolument comme procède la Nature" (*CH*, V, p. 219). Having apprenticed with Didot in Paris, David understands the most pressing need in the paper industry: due to the limited availability of rag stocks and the redistribution of wealth in postrevolutionary society, inexpensive paper needed to be developed to satisfy the bourgeois market for cheap books:

> Nous arrivons à un temps où, les fortunes diminuant par leur égalisation, tout s'appauvrira: nous voudrons du linge et des livres à bon marché [...]. Les chemises et les livres ne dureront pas, voilà tout. La solidité des produits s'en va de toutes parts. Aussi le problème à résoudre est-il de la plus haute importance pour la littérature, pour les sciences et pour la politique. (*CH*, V, p. 220–221)

The movement and energy of plants would infuse a modern botanical paper with fiber and substance.

David appropriates a botanical lexicon when conveying to Ève his epiphany upon learning that abbé Grosier, a specialist in Chinese history and culture and an administrator at the Arsenal, claimed that the Chinese made their "perfect" paper out of bamboo pulp. A Chinese book of illustrations in Grosier's possession confirmed it:

> Le papier de Chine ne se fabrique ni avec de la soie ni avec le *broussonatia*; sa pâte provient des fibres du bambou triturées. L'abbé Grosier possédait un livre chinois [...] où se trouvaient de nombreuses figures représentant la fabrication du papier dans toutes ses phases, et il nous montra les tiges de bambou peintes en tas dans le coin d'un atelier à papier supérieurement dessiné. Quand Lucien m'a dit que ton père [...] avait entrevu le moyen de remplacer les débris du linge par une matière végétale excessivement commune, immédiatement prise à la production territoriale, comme font les Chinois en se servant de tiges fibreuses, [...] je me suis mis enfin à étudier la question. Le bambou est un roseau: j'ai naturellement pensé aux roseaux de notre pays. (*CH*, V, p. 221–222)

Balzac seems to allude to the 18th-century album *Art de faire le papier à la Chine*, where bamboo at one point is stacked in bundles to the side of a production station (Fig. 4):[13]

13 Berthier deems David to be referencing Grosier's *Description générale de la Chine* (Berthier, 2006, p. 161, n. 4). However, Balzac's specific reference to iconography, the superior quality of the drawing, and the emphasis on "toutes phases" of bamboo paper production make it likely that he was referring to the album of gouaches sent from China that was housed at the Arsenal. Chollet notes that Balzac was frequenting the Arsenal during Grosier's time as an administrator (*CH*, V, p. 221, n. 4). The album is entered in the BNF catalog as *Art de faire le papier en Chine*, but the handwritten title within the album is *Art de faire le papier à la Chine*.

FIG. 4 – "On tare les Bambous", gouache, *Art de faire le papier à la Chine*, 18th cen., Bibliothèque nationale de France, Département estampes et photographie, EST OE-110, gallica.bnf.fr / BnF [accessed 13 January 2025].

The question was how to reconcile the surrounding flora with the new technology of continuous paper machines.

In the third and final section of *Illusions perdues*, *Les Souffrances de l'inventeur*, David looks to his local landscape to find his own version of Chinese bamboo. Handing Ève samples of paper that he has successfully produced out of reeds, he continues to consider other plant possibilities that might be even more cost-effective:

> Notre roseau commun, *l'arundo phragmitis*, a fourni les feuilles de papier que tu tiens. Mais je vais employer les orties, les chardons; car, pour maintenir le bon marché de la première matière, il faut s'adresser à des substances végétales qui puissent venir dans les marécages et dans les mauvais terrains: elles seront à vil prix. Le secret gît tout entier dans une préparation à donner à ces tiges. (*CH*, V, p. 583)

Later, as his father and the Cointet brothers connive to discover his secret, David continues undeterred with his experiments as he adds artichoke stems, asparagus stems, and stinging nettles that can be cut by the river (*CH*, V, p. 627). After months of experimentation, David creates a "seconde nature des substances" out of humble local plants:

> Il épiait avec une sagacité merveilleuse les effets si bizarres des substances transformées par l'homme en produits à sa convenance, où la nature est en quelque sorte domptée dans ses résistances secrètes, et il en déduisit de belles lois d'industrie, en observant qu'on ne pouvait obtenir ces sortes de créations qu'en obéissant aux rapports ultérieurs des choses, à ce qu'il appelle la seconde nature des substances. (*CH*, V, p. 727)

Though he has succeeded in creating a suitable paper for the continuous paper machine, it lacks the "perfection" of the Chinese paper that had been David's primary objective. While the Cointet dynasty quickly amasses wealth by spitting out David's newly invented paper on his Fourdrinier machine — "La découverte de David Séchard a passé dans la fabrication française comme la nourriture dans un grand corps. Grâce à l'introduction de manières autres que le chiffon, la France peut fabriquer le papier à meilleur marché qu'en aucun pays de l'Europe." (*CH*, V, p. 732) —, David retreats to his countryside home, "accompagnée de trois arpents de jardin et d'un clos de vignes" with a "rangée de grenadiers, d'orangers et de plantes rares" (*CH*, V, p. 729). He takes up other pursuits: "il s'est bravement rangé dans la classe des rêveurs et des collectionneurs; il s'adonne à l'entomologie, et recherche les transformations jusqu'à present si secrètes des insectes que la science ne connaît que dans leur dernier état" (*CH*, V, p. 732). David embodies Balzac's sense of heroism, with his slow "botanizing" of old modes of production and materials butting against the forces of the Industrial Revolution and insatiable drive for profit.

PLANTS, PAPER, *POÉTICITÉ*

Balzac's focus on the materiality of paper in *Illusions perdues* is an *éloge de la plante* that recognizes the vital force of flora even in an industrial age: "Mises dans des conditions franchement défavorables, les plantes peuvent évidemment mourir; mais si vivre reste possible, elles surmontent les difficultés avec une opiniâtreté qui force l'admiration" (Hallé, 1999, p. 202). By presenting a paper page as the nexus of Nature and human ingenuity, David makes the connection between science and art explicit: "Pour arriver à leur perfection, l'écriture, le langage peut-être [...] ont eu les mêmes tâtonnements que la typographie et la papeterie" (*CH*, V, p. 219–220). Turning to plants and the natural world is a way to elude machines, instead encouraging "tâtonnements" of enterprising research as a way to resist the violent forces of a bourgeoning capitalist state and the cheapening of products: "Dans notre monde de frime, de fric, de pub, de bruit, de pollution et de brutalité, quel meilleur témoignage que celui des plantes, belles et utiles, discrètes et autonomes, silencieuses et d'une totale non-violence?" (Hallé, 1999, p. 328) The steady energy of plants is a counterpoint to the ephemeral whims and damaging effects of industrial production.

The energy and ingenuity involved in botanical papermaking turn books into living monuments that reaffirm the writer's commitment to his art. *Illusions perdues* thus anticipates the luxurious use of Japanese paper by modernist poets and artists such as Manet and Mallarmé. David Séchard's patient quest for a perfect botanical paper heeds Mme de Bargeton's admonition to Lucien, a "Chardon" from Nouvelle-Aquitaine who tries to uproot and graft himself onto Parisian high society: "Il n'y a pas de gloire à bon marché."

Karen QUANDT
Wabash College

WORKS CITED

Abele Célia, 2022, "Rousseau on the Île Saint-Pierre: Realism as Circumscription", *Romanic Review*, 113, p. 199–221.

Berthier Patrick, 2006, "Préface", in Balzac, *Illusions perdues* (Paris: Librairie Générale française, « Le Livre de poche classiques »), p. 7-28.

Balzac: imprimeur et défenseur du livre, 1995 (Paris: Paris-Musées).

Barbier Frédéric, 2020, *Histoire du livre en Occident* (Malakoff: Armand Colin).

Basbanes Nicholas A., 2013, *On Paper: The Everything of Its Two-Thousand-Year History* (New York: Alfred A. Knopf).

Berthier Patrick, 1999, *Balzac et l'imprimerie: anthologie* (Paris: Imprimerie nationale).

Bouvet Rachel and Posthumus Stephanie, 2024, "Introduction", in *Mouvantes et émouvantes: Les Plantes à travers le récit*, ed. by Rachel Bouvet and Stephanie Posthumus (Les Presses de l'Université de Montréal), p. 7–20.

Bustarret Claire, 1995, "Balzac et le papier: de la Société d'abonnement général à *Illusions perdues*", in *Balzac: imprimeur et défenseur du livre* (Paris: Paris-Musées) p. 81–104.

Chollet Roland, 1977, "Introduction" à *Illusions perdues*, *CH*, V, p. 3–108.

Coccia Emanuele, 2016, *La vie des plantes: Une métaphysique du mélange* (Paris: Payot & Rivages).

Cohen Claudine, 2007, "De la biologie au roman: le modèle morphologique et ses variations", *Romantisme*, 138, p. 47–59.

Dayrat Benoît, 2003, *Botanistes et la flore de France. Trois siècles de découvertes* (Paris: Publications scientifiques du Museum), <http://books.openedition.org/mnhn/1905> [accessed 30 July 2024].

Desmarest M., 1788, "Papier", *Encyclopédie méthodique: Arts et métiers mécaniques*, vol. 5, (Paris: Panckoucke), p. 463–592, <https://gallica.bnf.fr/ark:/12148/bpt6k5838654v> [accessed 4 September 2024].

Drège Jean-Pierre, 2019, "Le papier", France-Chine, Bibliothèque nationale de France, <https://heritage.bnf.fr/france-chine/fr/le-papier-article> [accessed 30 August 2024].

Gagliano Monica, John C. Ryan and Patrícia Vieira, 2017, "Introduction", in *The Language of Plants: Science, Philosophy, and Literature*, ed. by Monica Gagliano, John C. Ryan, and Patrícia Vieira (Minneapolis: University of Minnesota Press), p. vii–xxxiii.

Gerwin Elisabeth, 2017, "Balzac: A Portrait of the Novelist as Social Historian and Scientist", in *The Cambridge Companion to Balzac*, ed. Owen Heathcote and Andrew Watts, (Cambridge: Cambridge University Press), p. 11–26.

Gusdorf Georges, 1985, *Le Savoir romantique de la nature* (Paris: Payot).
Hallé Francis, 1999, *Éloge de la plante: pour une nouvelle biologie* (Paris: Seuil).
Jaucourt Louis de, 1765, “Papier”, in *Encyclopédie, ou dictionnaire raisonné des sciences, des arts et des métiers, etc.*, ed. by Denis Diderot and Jean le Rond d’Alembert, ARTFL Encyclopédie Project, ed. by Robert Morrissey and Glenn Roe (University of Chicago), <https://encyclopedie.uchicago.edu> [accessed 1 August 2024]
Kelley Theresa, 2012, *Clandestine Marriage: Botany and Romantic Culture* (Baltimore: The Johns Hopkins University Press).
Kurlansky Mark, 2016, *Paper: Paging through History* (New York and London: W. W. Norton & Company).
McHugh Susan, 2021, “Plants and Literature”, in *Oxford Research Encyclopedia of Literature* (Oxford: Oxford University Press), <https://oxfordre.com/literature/view/10.1093/acrefore/9780190201098.001.0001/acrefore-9780190201098-e-1267> [accessed 15 December 2024].
Morton Alan G., 1981, *History of Botanical Science* (London, Academic Press)
Mozet Nicole, 2017, “Balzac (Honoré de): Symbolique des jardins”, in *Dictionnaire littéraire des fleurs et des jardins (XVIIIe et XIXe siècles)*, ed. by Pascale Auraix-Jonchière and Simone Bernard-Griffiths (Paris: Honoré Champion), p. 22–28.
Oghină-Pavie Cristiana, 2024, “Les mouvements de la vie immobile. Le végétal chez Augustin-Pyramus de Candolle”, in *Mouvantes et émouvantes: Les Plantes à travers le récit*, ed. by Rachel Bouvet and Stephanie Posthumus (Les Presses de l’Université de Montréal), p. 23–43.
Thiher Allen, 2001, *Fiction Rivals Science: The French Novel from Balzac to Proust* (Columbia: University of Missouri Press).
Zapf Hubert, 2014, “Creative Matter and Creative Mind: Cultural Ecology and Literary Creativity”, *Material Ecocriticism*, ed. by Serenella Iovino and Serpil Oppermann (Bloomington: Indiana University Press), p. 51–66.

BALZAC'S POPLAR TREES

The Economy of Timber in *Eugénie Grandet*

Money grows on trees in *La Comédie humaine*. Among Balzac's herbarium, poplars provide a particularly coveted source of income for landed characters eager to transform their plots into profitable woodlots. In *Pierrette*, the felling of "cinq cents peupliers" finances Vinet's acquisition of "plusieurs enclaves" (*CH*, IV, p. 90), while the newly-planted trees along the canals of Montégnac considerably increase the value of Véronique Graslin's estate in *Le Curé de village*. Similarly, M. de Bourbonne from *Madame Firmiani* lovingly watches his "rangées de peupliers s'embellir" as he turns to tree farming to secure his beloved nephew's inheritance (*CH*, II, p. 147). But the Balzacian poplar-farmer comes into full bloom in *Eugénie Grandet*. In 1793, hoping to profit from fields recently purchased through the State auction of confiscated Church-owned lands, notorious miser Félix Grandet decides to plant "trois mille peupliers" on his "cent vingt-sept arpents de prairies" (*CH*, III, p. 1032). Monoculture tree plantations prove to be very lucrative operations at a time when severe timber shortages induced an upsurge in lumber prices.[1] Grandet's arboreal flair pays off: the clearcutting of his plantations (*peupleraies*) around 1819 yields the considerable sum of 60,000 francs. Alongside vines and wheat crops, silviculture strategically fits into a land-focused economic model that relies on the productive exploitation of arable land and environmental resources.

Yet the sale of white wood pales in comparison to the millions Grandet later earns through the speculative market. The slow growth and meticulous management of poplars run parallel to the revelation of a new economic model that holds the promise of a quicker, larger, and effortless horizon of profitability. These new investment strategies

---

1 For more on the rising cost of timber throughout the 18th and 19th centuries, see Corvol, 1987, p. 49–50.

have long been analyzed by critics as manifestations of Grandet's *début* in a modern economy. Georg Lukács sees the decision to profit from government bonds and lend money at exorbitant interest rates as a "partie intégrante de l'évolution capitaliste du début du XIXe siècle" (1967, p. 45). Lukács's interpretation teaches us not to read the Balzacian miser as a trans-historic type, but rather as the successful product of a shifting economic reality reconfigured under the *Premier Empire* and the *Restauration*. Furthering this claim, Pierre-Georges Castex sees in Grandet "un homme [...] qui pendant trente-cinq ans, a pris le vent de l'histoire", and whose financial decisions highlight "par quels mécanismes ont pu se constituer, d'un siècle à l'autre, les grandes fortunes de la bourgeoisie nouvelle" (1965, p. LVIII). This equation frames the mastermind's spectacular ascension as a linear trajectory: that of an insatiable greed, unsatisfied with the acquisition and exploitation of landed property, turning to the appealing prospects of the speculative market. But limiting Grandet's success to a sequential transition from tangible to intangible assets runs the risk of undercutting the complexity of his "système d'existence méthodiquement *cultivé*" (*ibid.*, p. LIX, my emphasis).

Taking Castex at his word, I ponder what it means to "cultivate" wealth in *Eugénie Grandet*. In what follows, I propose to view Balzac's depictions of wood management practices as investigations of the exponential and uncontrollable growth of this new market economy. Examining the "morphological variations" of capital in *La Comédie humaine*, Francesco Spandri notes how the novels explore the contact zone of two interlocking "hémisphères qui communiquent entre eux [...]: *terre* et *argent*" (2020, p. 262). Caught in the inescapable interaction of these intersecting systems, characters like Grandet oscillate between "le calcul des risques et le calcul des ressources" (*ibid.*, p. 263) — a dynamic interplay that fundamentally renegotiates the traditional partition between "richesse naturelle et richesse monétaire" (*ibid.*, p. 266). Challenging a reading that understands Grandet's mutable wealth as a schematic shift from "older" to "newer" patterns of investment, I investigate the discursive potential of poplars for apprehending stories of colliding economic ideologies. What happens if we start reading plants not simply as commodities, but as sense-making cues of a burgeoning economic modernity?

Even our understanding of the most famous poplars of 19th century French art would benefit from this critical inquiry. More than capturing atmospheric shifts through contrasting palettes of blues and yellows, Claude Monet's *Poplars* series surreptitiously paints the fleeting picture of the Limetz village economic climate and shows how timber markets might intersect with artistic creation. After the trees were sold at a town auction in 1891, Monet had to pay a "local lumber merchant to ensure that the [poplars] remained standing until he finished his work" (MET, 2024, online). I suggest reading Balzac's poplars in the same light — cases where the realist novel carves into the treescape an ephemeral economic reality that could otherwise pass as mere background "detail".

Against the received idea that trees are static entities aimed for long-term investments, Balzac's poplars expose the instability and transience of the economic markets Grandet navigates. That the description of Grandet's speculative feats relies on an arboreal lexicon requires critical attention. I propose to examine the way Balzac mobilizes knowledge about wood management to structure and flesh out practices of usury and bond investment. Reading *Eugénie Grandet* in conversation with horticultural literature, I contend that Grandet's silvicultural endeavors reflect contemporary debates among agronomists and landowners on the merits of intensive poplar farming. A product of rampant capitalism, the newly designed *peupleraie* model — a geometrically organized grove where every inch is optimized for maximum yield — significantly reconfigured the use of wooden resources. In addition to furnishing wood, timber farms became reliable assets that could easily be exploited and reinvested into the speculative market.

LAY OF THE LAND

Grandet certainly knows his way around wood: a cooper by trade, he married the daughter of a wealthy "marchand de planches" through his connections with the woodworking professions, and purchased a significant amount of "superbes prairies", several of which he turned into tree farms (*CH*, III, p. 1030, 1031). That a wood connoisseur like Grandet chooses to plant 3,000 poplars across his estate is not surprising. By the early 1800s, the poplar tree was deemed as one of the most profitable species to grow commercially.[2] Taking "only" twenty-five to thirty years to mature to harvestable size, its fast growth rates and resilience ensured greater financial returns compared to other tree species. Calling this exponential growth a "prodige de végétation", François-Antoine Rauch argues that black poplars should be "digne de la plus avide préférence" for landowners hoping to rapidly establish woodlots and produce timber (1818, p. 414–415).

While thorough descriptions of poplar-sowing techniques for plant nurseries already appear in Pliny the Elder's *Histoire naturelle*, Paul Arnould dates the standardization of the "peupleraie linéaire" to the second half of the 18th century, following the introduction of the Italian poplar on French soil in the 1740s (2003, p. 18–19). With its even faster growth and picturesque pyramidal shape, the Italian tree rapidly became one of the most widely planted species in fields and ornamental gardens — leading to such widespread acclaim that Pelée de Saint-Maurice published the first monograph solely dedicated to poplar farming.[3] With their "géométrie rigoureuse aux espacements strictement définis" (*ibid.*, p. 16), poplar groves offered, Sophie Le Floch and Daniel Terrasson explain, an uncharted agribusiness system at the crossroads between "agriculture et foresterie" (1999, p. 604).[4]

The proliferation of *peupleraies* throughout late 18th century France was further bolstered by the importation of numerous foreign species from the *populus* genus; the taxonomy established in Auguste-Denis Fougeroux de Bondaroy's *Mémoires d'agriculture* (1786) features no less than eleven different entries.[5] Besides endemic European species, the introduction of species fit to grow in France's climates considerably increased cultivation options for burgeoning tree farmers like Grandet. Examining the mechanisms of the plantation model, Donna Haraway

2 See for instance Rougier de la Bergerie, 1831, p. 49–68.

3 See Pelée de Saint-Maurice, 1762, *L'art de cultiver des peupliers d'Italie, avec des observations sur le choix, la disposition des pépinières, leur culture, & sur celle des arbres plantés à demeure.*

4 See also Arnould, 2004, p. 265–266.

5 This exhaustive taxonomy goes as follows: *Peuplier noir, Peuplier de Lombardie, Peuplier de Virginie, Peuplier de Caroline, Peuplier Tacamahaca, Peuplier Liard, Peupliers hétérophiles, Peuplier blanc de Hollande, Peuplier blanc à petites feuilles, Peuplier Tremble, Peuplier de l'Amérique.* See Fougeroux de Bondaroy, 1786, p. 75–106.

and Anna Tsing stress how the "transportation of genomes, [...] is crucial" to grasp the "kinds of long-distance simplification of landscapes" (2016, p. 556–557). Predicated on the "systematic practice of relocation for extraction", the rise of *populiculture* is symptomatic of the geological epoch Haraway defines as "Plantationocene" — a radical "transformation of human-tended farms, pastures, and forests into extractive and enclosed plantations" (2015, p. 162). The importation of non-endemic poplars as a result of imperial expansion quenched the capitalist thirst for industrial farming in metropolitan France; Rauch claims that the *peuplier de Caroline*'s recent introduction in Europe is rich with promising financial (and aesthetic) opportunities:

> Ce bel arbre, arrivé des mêmes rives américaines que les peupliers baumiers, mérite aussi notre prédilection, nos recherches et la propagation la plus infatigable. [...] Combien nos prairies, nos ruisseaux, nos étangs et nos fleuves, se trouveroient noblement décorés, enrichis et enorgueillis de sa possession!... (1818, p. 415)

The environmental and economic costs of deracination resonate in the exploitative nature of Grandet's *peupleraies*, where plants — whose exact species remain unclear, hinting at the rich diversity of potentially cultivated species — are similarly "abstracted in order to become resources that can be used for investment".[6]

The trees became so widespread among French plantations that a letter from M. Léorier published in the 1830 *Recueil agronomique* identifies poplar farming as a specifically French obsession: "la croissance rapide de cet arbre flatte les spéculateurs ou les propriétaires avides de jouir: on le voit partout; [...] aussi l'a-t-on surnommé, par raillerie sans doute, l'arbre français, l'arbre du siècle" (1830, p. 9). The ironic designation of the poplar as the "French tree" *par excellence* reads as an offspring of its revolutionary past. It qualified, indeed, among the sixty-six wood species chosen to embody the liberty trees and was therefore extensively planted across France in the aftermath of the Revolution.[7] Twisting these patriotic tendencies to his own advantage, Grandet exploits the national need for primary resources as an opportunistic window to increase his landed

6 See Haraway *et al.*, 2016, p. 556.

7 For more on poplar farming during and after the Revolution, see Arnould, 2003, p. 21. See also Pacini, 2018, p. 413.

capital. His acquisition of "les plus beaux vignobles de l'arrondissement" — purchased at a state auction "pour un morceau de pain" (*CH*, III, p. 1030) — later allows him to sell wine to the Republican army in exchange for several "superbes prairies dépendant d'une communauté de femmes" (*CH*, III, p. 1031) as form of payment in kind. Presumedly converted into tree farms on which Grandet establishes his *peupleraies*, the tree's Latin etymology *Populus* — which translates both as "poplar" and "the people" — reads as a symbolic evocation of the acquisition of private properties by new landowners. In a literal sense, *populus* farming emphasizes how Grandet rises to prominence by swindling the agents of the Revolution.

If Grandet falls prey to this poplar fever, it is also because the trees strategically complement his two main streams of income: cooperage and viticulture. Poplars and wine production, as it turns out, have a longstanding affinity. The *Populus tremula*, Duhamel du Monceau explains, is often used by barrel-makers "[qui] en font des barres pour affermir les fonds de leur futailles" (1780, p. 46); while Fougeroux de Bondaroy notes that poplars are commonly planted on the edges of vineyards to allow easy access to malleable branches "pour attacher la vigne à l'échalas" (1786, p. 80–81). Farming his own wood, Grandet avoids being subject to fluctuating lumber prices and significantly lowers the cost of production from his auxiliary businesses. Lukács' reading of the miser type as a character "concerned with scraping and saving" certainly holds true (1973, p. 45). Still, the case of tree farming complicates the nature of Grandet's misery — suggesting he simultaneously relies on spending strategies to achieve financial autonomy and self-sustainability. Entering the tree farming business at a time when *populiculture* emerged as a subcategory of silviculture in its own right, Grandet's timely decisions echo and draw inspiration from broader contemporary botanical discourses on tree planning. Balzac does not make him an isolated hoarder, but a horticulturally conscious investor actively taking part in France's changing economy.

HEDGE FUNDS

Grandet chops his poplars around the year 1819. Estimating that haystacks would resell for "1,100 francs", he argues that poplar plantations have become less lucrative than wheat fields:

> Eh bien, ca… ca.. ca… calculez ce que que que dou… ouze cents francs par an pen… pen… pendant quarante ans do… donnent a… a… avec les in… in… intérêts com… com… composés que que que vouous saaavez. […] ça ne ne ne fera que que que soixante mille francs. Eh bien, reprit le vigneron sans bégayer, deux mille peupliers de quarante ans ne me donneraient pas cinquante mille francs. Il y a perte. (*CH*, III, p. 1081)

The syncopated wordflow from Grandet's (pretend) stuttering makes this *demonstratio* deceptively confusing. The final return to a coherently articulated language deliberately confuses the reader, compelling us to subscribe to the calculations without fully understanding them. Stylistically, it tricks us into taking the paradoxically simple conclusion to this agricultural lesson at face value: "les peupliers ne doivent se planter que sur les terres maigres" (*CH*, III, p. 1081). A pastiche of contemporary horticultural treatises, the reasoning makes an otherwise compelling claim: poplars have the power to make profit sprout out of the poorest soils. While agronomists agreed that poplars thrive in soils with high moisture levels, classifying the poplar as an "aquatic tree", Duhamel du Monceau stresses its remarkable adaptability to grounds with variable water concentration: "Les peupliers se plaisent dans les terres fort abreuvées. Le tremble aime l'argile; mais le Peuplier blanc, qui [réussit] très bien dans les terreins marécageux, [fait] de belles productions dans les terres sèches" (1780, p. 73). M. Datty also promotes poplars's sanitizing power to planters interested in converting swampy areas infested with wetland plants into arable fields:

> Les racines de tous ces arbres, gourmandes de nature, […] étouffant nécessairement les roseaux et le genre des plantes qui se trouvoient à leurs places. Vous serez étonné, au bout de quelques années, de voir un bois, là où il n'y avait qu'un marécage infect. (1805, p. 40–41)

Despite his previous recommendations, Grandet asks his workman to replant poplars near the Loire, on the edges of his fields: "Jean, reprit-il, tu combleras les trous, excepté du côté de la Loire, où tu planteras les peupliers que j'ai achetés" (*CH*, III, p. 1081). Contradicting his own verbose lesson on the profitable shift from silviculture to agriculture, this seemingly paradoxical decision bespeaks a form of arboricultural *bon sens*: "Il faut", the 1826 *Recueil agronomique* notes, "pour la belle végétation du peuplier, que ses racines puisent une partie de leur nourriture dans une eau courante et sans cesse renouvelée" (1826, p. 40). The presence of hedgerow trees along the riverbanks not only maximizes profits by exploiting the very last inches of the field but also ensures ideal growth conditions.

That we usually skim through this passage without realizing its incoherence speaks to our tendency to relegate vegetal components to the novel's textual margins — to view plants not as meaningful signifiers, but as background details intended to enhance the realistic quality of the story. What happens if we redirect our attention to the plants that now purposefully grow on the outskirts of the field and on the edges of the text? The horticultural knowledge underlying Grandet's pragmatic deduction encodes a more significant economic realization: in this modern economic climate, minimal investments can easily fructify and generate substantial wealth with very little effort.

LANGUE DE BOIS

What initially appears as a meticulous application of farming recommendations turns out to be an investment lesson in disguise. The establishment of newly farmed strips of land on river banks might indeed read as an oblique projection of Grandet's future speculative endeavors. Alexandre Péraud has pointed out the aesthetic challenges the Balzacian novel faces in transcribing a newly theorized economic language "qui manie sans arrêt le chiffre, convoque le vocabulaire complexe et, surtout, exige une évacuation de la subjectivité si peu en rapport avec la langue littéraire" (2012, p. 6). Péraud refers to this problematic inscription as "une langue de bois", that Balzac incorporates into the novel to expose a newly coined "sociolecte économique [...] qui ne parvient pas à définir son rapport au réel" (*ibid.*, p. 13–16). Whether seamlessly woven into the narrative through interconnected metaphors and double entendres, or abruptly isolated within the text through dizzying calculations and technical logorrheas, realist depictions push economic language to a breaking point that highlights the "spectaculaire propension romanesque consistant à tordre la langue économique, à la prendre en défaut, à la soumettre à différents procédés d'ironisation" (*ibid.*, p. 15).

Inspired by these observations on the novelistic "distortion des signifiants" (*ibid.*, p. 12) that allows Balzac to reveal the duplicity of this "economic sociolect", I suggest reading what Péraud terms *langue de bois* in a more literal sense — a wooden tongue that relies on vegetal tropes to metaphorically capture the changing economy. After all, poplars are money trees *par excellence*. If the name of the shimmering *peuplier argenté* refers to the silvery color of its leaves, its onomastics simultaneously evokes potential monetary gain. Similarly in Balzac, the technical expression of financial growth and profitability borrows from arboreal terminology to the point where the two become semantically intertwined. After ordering the replanting of poplars near the Loire, Grandet explains his reasoning to his notary Maître Cruchot: "En les mettant dans la rivière, ils se nourriront aux frais du gouvernement, ajouta-t-il en [...] imprimant à la loupe de son nez un léger mouvement qui valait le plus ironique des sourires." (*CH*, III, p. 1081) Grandet refers here to the decree that made the edges of navigable waterways the property of the French state. Since poplars thrive near water, planting them by the river ensures their easy growth without the need for additional irrigation.[8] Upon closer inspection, however, this parasitic profitability belies his spectacular *coup* when he invests in government securities at an extraordinarily low rate. Poplar farming exposes the duplicity of Grandet's financial schemes. We, readers, have been played: what we initially interpreted as a clear case of land-focused economy turns out to be the opposite — a concealed lesson on how to succeed on the speculative market.

Silvan and agricultural practices provide a lexicon to capture the mechanisms of what Allan Pasco summarizes as the costless "manœuvring [of] his dead brother's debt through Parisian financiers, so as to erase it" at no cost (2017, p. 74). Under the pretense of rescuing the family's

8 See the *Recueil agronomique*, 1826, p. 40–41.

honor, Grandet offers to become the liquidator of his brother's fortune and takes on the task of reimbursing his creditors. If the liquidation from "valeurs, possessions, biens [...] appartenant à feu Guillaume Grandet" allows the redistribution of "quarante-sept pour cent à chaque créancier", Félix then postpones all payments and keeps the creditors waiting in hope that their impatience will make them withdraw from the process (*CH*, III, p. 1143). Using Charles' extended trip to India and time-consuming notarial procedures as excuses to justify belated payments, Grandet succeeds in discouraging most creditors and dies without spending another dime, leaving it to Charles (and Eugénie) to pay off Guillaume's debt. As shrewd liquidation tactics are expressed through weather terminology, the tree farmer's sensitivity to climatic variations highlights how profits can be derived from receivables. The way Grandet patiently observes "les variations atmosphériques des créanciers" (*CH*, III, p. 1144) lexically feeds from his previous silvicultural knowledge: "Dans ce pays, comme en Touraine, les vicissitudes de l'atmosphère dominent la vie commerciale. Vignerons, propriétaires, marchands de bois, tonneliers [...] sont tous à l'affût d'un rayon de soleil." (*CH*, III, p. 1029) Used to describe both meteorological shifts as well as the uncertainties of the economic climate, the permutability of atmospheric terms illustrates how a prior farming background provides linguistic frameworks to sharpen Grandet's speculative acumen. Beyond vocabulary overlap, familiarity with deep dendrological time fosters the patience necessary to expose and exploit the blind spots of capitalist haste: "Le tonnelier avait calculé sur la puissance du temps, qui, disait-il, est un bon diable" (*CH*, III, p. 1144).

Poplars' potential to capture mechanisms of usury and speculation is also reflected through noticeable shifts in the way Grandet invests the money derived from timber sales. Exploitation of wood resources originally serves as a way of replenishing his coffers after the purchase of the Froidfond estate for "trois millions": "pour remplir de nouveau son trésor presque vide, il décida de couper à blanc ses bois, ses forêts, et d'exploiter les peupliers de ses prairies" (*CH*, III, p. 1038–1039). The enumeration of varied kinds of woodlots takes the form of a tree census that assesses the quantity of timber required to offset land investments. In converting timber into a form of currency, Grandet sees tree farms as promising reserve funds to consolidate personal wealth and subsidize occasional purchases — a popular savings tactic that incurred the wrath of contemporary agronomists like Nicolas Douette-Richardot:

> Un autre abus bien plus éversif des forêts, c'était l'arrachement que s'en permettaient des propriétaires particuliers; ils trouvaient un avantage dans cette spéculation qui leur était toute personnelle, en réduisant leurs bois en culture [...] pour satisfaire l'intérêt du moment [...] afin de se créer des capitaux. (1806, p. 340)

Yet, over time, the money from Grandet's groves goes from being a source of savings and investment in landed capital to a means of financing his foray into the speculative market. Upon realizing the foreseeable profits to be made from public securities, he decides to fell his remaining poplars to secure the necessary resources for his speculative ventures:

> il monta promptement à son cabinet pour y méditer un placement dans les fonds publics. Ses deux mille arpents de forêt coupés à blanc lui avaient donné six cent mille francs; en joignant à cette somme l'argent de ses peupliers, ses revenus de l'année dernière et de l'année courante, outre les deux mille francs du marché qu'il venait de conclure, il pouvait faire une masse de neuf cent mille francs. (*CH*, III, p. 1099)

Striking a profitable deal from the uneven balance between the high price of wood and low cost of government securities, the exploitation of timber generates immediate liquid capital, which is then converted into intangible assets.

OVERGROWTH

Remnants of this poplar fever are still observable today. With nearly 200,000 hectares of poplars nationwide, France is the third largest poplar-farming country in the world — after China and India.[9] Yet in the past decades, measures have been passed to regulate poplar farming. The tree's invasive root system has proven to be an important cause

9 This poplar census was established by the Observatoire de la Biodiversité des Hauts-de-France. See: <https://www.observatoire-biodiversite-hdf.fr/sites/default/files/documents/medias/fiches-indicateurs/surface_peupleraies_2011.pdf> [accessed 2 August 2024].

of bank erosion, and prevents the implantation of other species whose rootstocks are more suited to stabilizing watercourses (willows, alders) — a harmful impact already described in Rougier de la Bergerie's *Cours d'agriculture pratique*: "leurs racines se multiplient et [...] s'opposent indéfiniment au tassement parfait des terres nouvelles" (1820, p. 526–527). As one detractor of many, la Bergerie denounced the irresponsibility of profit-driven agronomists, whose lack of interest in long-term land health and sustainable farming practices influenced greedy lot owners unbothered with soil regeneration: "Une vaine et fatale théorie sortie des cercles académiques, est venu [sic] fortifier cet élan vers les arbres d'une rapide croissance" (1820, p. 520). A few decades earlier, François Rozier had seen in these intensive farming practices symptoms of a pathology responsible for the decrease in diversity of France's treescape: "La *peuplomanie* fit déraciner les avenues plantées en ormeaux, en tilleuls" (1786, p. 623).[10] Diagnosing these manic tendencies towards poplar planting as chronic cases of dendromania, the naturalist uses sylvan terminology to denounce the detrimental over-commodification of trees in the name of financial interest.

Eugénie Grandet also clinically exposes how capitalism's uncontrollable drive asphyxiates and destabilizes the French countryside's economic landscape. The felling of tree farms alongside the Loire necessitates extensive ground-levelling efforts by a large workforce to prepare the land for the cultivation of wheat fields: "trente ouvriers s'occupaient à déblayer, combler, niveler les emplacements autrefois pris par les peupliers." (*CH*, III, p. 1080) The language of woodwork becomes recuperated by monetary concerns. Techniques of cooperage craftsmanship are stylistically repurposed to capture the way Grandet watchfully stacks and conceals his gold inside barrels: "quand Mme et Mlle Grandet étaient bien endormies, venait le vieux tonnelier choyer, caresser, couver, *cuver*, *cercler* son or." (*CH*, III, p. 1070, my emphasis) As wine semantically turns into gold, the casking and slow maturation of alcohol becomes analogous to the securing and fructification of liquid assets. Over time, the wooden repository used to store coins morphs into a symbolic manifestation of Grandet's speculative success. Once added to his landed property income, the considerable profits derived from his "deux mille arpents de forêt coupés à blanc" and "l'argent de ses peupliers" (*CH*, III, p. 1099) offer

10 See Rozier, 1786, p. 623.

the material condition to initiate substantial investments in *fonds publics*. A revelatory sign of Grandet's mounting misery, intensive sylviculture and land exploitation expose the destructive consequences of reading the world through rational calculations. Unquenchable thirst for money takes the form of a "vegetative" misery — taken in the etymological sense of *vegetare*, as a system that grows slowly but exponentially.

A hopeless *dendromaniac*, Grandet curates his relationships the same way he manages his groves. If the narrator first describes the loyal servant Nanon as a "créature humaine", her subjugation to Grandet's crushing authority reduces her to a tree-shaped organic matter:

> La Grande Nanon, ainsi nommée à cause de sa taille haute de cinq pieds huit pouces, appartenait à Grandet depuis trente-cinq ans. [...] Juge de sa force corporelle en qualité de tonnelier, il devina le parti qu'on pouvait tirer d'une créature femelle taillée en Hercule, plantée sur ses pieds comme un chêne de soixante ans sur ses racines. (*CH*, III, p. 1041–1042)

Sylvan knowledge indexes Nanon's value. The conflation of garden maintenance terminology with plant measurements makes her the arborified object of Grandet's horticultural gaze. Her powerful "bras nerveux" (*CH*, III, p. 1042) equate her muscle tissues with vegetal-like veins and ribs (*nervure*), while the comparison of her stature with that of an oak — an extremely dense, durable and high-end type of timber — evokes her sturdiness, physical strength and maturity. The parallel with Hercules is also reminiscent of the poplar tree's mythological symbolism: Virgil recounts that Hercules, upon his victory against Cacus on the Aventine Hill, was celebrated with crowns and garlands of poplar branches.[11] A lightweight and very soft type of hardwood, poplar timber is prized for its workable texture. Trimmed to Grandet's desire, Nanon reads as a coveted hybrid that combines the solidity of the oak with the malleability of the poplar. Her commodification as a tree growing on Grandet's plots underscores an exploitative worldview that conceptualizes relationships in terms profitability and ownership. A new form of dendrophilia emerges — a botanical attraction stimulated by the financial excitement derived from timber profits.

The same logic of pleasure and gain occurs when Grandet takes a bet on his wife's health to make sure Eugénie does not inherit her mother's

11 See Virgil, 1868 (VIII, v. 276-286).

share of the estate. Warning him against these dangerous calculations, Cruchot tells Grandet: "arrive qui plante, vous êtes majeur, vous savez vous conduire" (*CH*, III, p. 1164). A 19th-century equivalent of *advienne que pourra*, the expression takes the form of a vegetable gambit that ponders whether it is worth it to risk one's morals — and Madame Grandet's life — to ensure financial success. Madame Grandet's transformation reaches full form as her end nears, when her physical decline unfolds as a slow and sublime wilting: "Elle était frêle autant que les feuilles des arbres en automne" (*CH*, III, p. 1170). As the narrator stresses her anguish at the thought of leaving Eugénie alone — "Elle tremblait de laisser cette brebis, blanche comme elle, seule au milieu d'un monde égoïste" (*CH*, III, p. 1171) —, her feverish spasms draw a homonymous *parenté* with the *peuplier tremble*; the only tree, Pliny the Elder explains, "dont les feuilles [font] du bruit entre elles" with their "pétiole tremblant" (1877, p. 582). Haptic sensitivity to the sonorous friction of leaves articulates a new kind of phonological system capable of formulating Madame Grandet's final distress. Parallel to the autumn foliage of decidous trees, the "qualités morales qui venaient fleurir sur sa face" (*CH*, III, p. 1162) blossom in a final sublimatory revelation of her martyrdom that turns physical decay into flowering virtue. As Grandet treats his family relationships with the same rigor with which he manages his groves, the relentless pursuit of profitability reveals his loss of morals.

In 2022, scientists Yousra Hamrouni *et al.* introduced a new metric called the "Poplar Index" in the geoscientific journal *Remote Sensing*. Designed to generate a "national map of poplar plantations", the index proposes an "operational approach for monitoring the [...] resource over large areas for forest managers" (2022, p. 1). While the poplars that grow in the pages of *Eugénie Grandet* similarly register valuable lessons on the methods and history of tree exploitation, Balzac also acknowledges the generative potential of plants for grasping the unquantifiable logics of the modern economy. Poplars exceed a pure ornamental function. An ecologically conscious reading of *Eugénie Grandet* that recounts poplars' rapid growth, attractive yield, and invasive rootstock unavoidably unearths new interpretative skill sets to grasp Balzac's rendering of capitalist modernity. Botanical attunement does not view trees as signs of an immutable rootedness, but as growing indicators of a shifting economic landscape. It invites us to lower ourselves to root level to explore the phyto-sensitive contact zone where the linearity of newly farmed landstrips converges with the straight lines of the text.

Pierre FORFERT
Yale University

ACKNOWLEDGMENTS

I am indebted to my grandfather, André Cluzeau, for sharing his horticultural wisdom and for teaching me to look up and appreciate all that poplars have to offer. I also extend my gratitude to the anonymous reviewers for their valuable insights and suggestions.

WORKS CITED

Arnould Paul, 2004, "Nouvelles forêts, vieilles forêts, forêts de l'entre deux (XIXe et XXe siècles): rationalité économique et fertilité symbolique", in *Les Forêts d'Occident du Moyen Âge à nos jours*, ed. by Andrée Corvol, (Rennes: Presses universitaires de Rennes), p. 253–277.

Arnould Paul, 2003, "Les Peupleraies dans le paysage et l'économie", in *Les Sources de l'histoire de l'environnement*, ed. by Andrée Corvol, 3 vols (Paris: L'Harmattan), III, p. 15–26.

Castex Pierre-Georges, 1965, "Introduction", in Honoré de Balzac, *Eugénie Grandet*, (Paris: Garnier), p. XV–LXVI.

Corvol Andrée, 1987, *L'Homme aux bois. Histoire des relations de l'homme et de la forêt XVIIe-XXe siècle* (Paris: Fayard).

Datty M., 1805, *Des plantations, de leur nécessité en France, de leur utilité dans les départements du midi, pour l'assainissement de l'air; ou, Traité de la culture des arbres forestiers, de leur usage dans l'économie, la médecine et les arts* (Arles: Gaspard Mesnier).

Douette-Richardot Nicolas, 1806, *De la pratique de l'agriculture* (Paris: A-J Marchand).

Duhamel du Monceau Henri-Louis, 1780, *Des Semis et plantations des arbres, et de leur culture; ou méthode pour multiplier et élever les arbres, les planter en massifs et en avenues; former les forêts et les bois; les entretenir, et rétablir ceux qui sont dégradés* (Paris: La Veuve Desaint).

Fougeroux de Bondaroy Auguste-Denis, 1786, "Mémoires sur les différentes espèces de peupliers, et sur les avantages qu'on peut attendre de leur culture", in *Mémoires d'agriculture, d'économie rurale et Domestique* (Paris: Chez Cuchet), p. 75–106.

Hamrouni Yousra, Véronique Chéret *et al.*, 2022, "Sentinel-2 Poplar Index for Operational Mapping of Poplar Plantations over Large Areas", *Remote Sensing*, 14, p. 1–33.

Haraway Donna, 2015, "Anthropocene, Capitalocene, Plantationocene, Chthulucene: Making Kin", *Environmental Humanities*, 6, p. 159–165.

Haraway Donna, Noboru Ishikawa *et al.*, 2016, "Anthropologists Are Talking — About the Anthropocene", *Ethnos*, 83, p. 535–564.

Le Floch Sophie and Daniel Terrasson, 1999, "Entre agriculture et forêt, des enjeux majeurs pour un arbre ordinaire: le peuplier", *Annales de géographie*, 609–610, p. 603–614.

Léorier M, 1830, "Observations" in *Recueil agronomique, publié par les soins de la Société des sciences, agriculture et belles-lettres du département de Tarn-et-Garonne* (Montauban: Lapie-Fontanel), p. 8–18.

Lukács Georg, 1967, *Balzac et le réalisme français*, trans. by Paul Laveau (Paris: Éditions Maspero).

Pacini Giulia, 2018, "'La Tige monarchique [et] l'arbre de la République': Trees and the Body Politic in Revolutionary France", *Journal for Eighteenth-Century Studies*, 41.3, p. 407–425.

Pasco Allan H., 2017, "Balzac, Money and the Pursuit of Power", in *The Cambridge Companion to Balzac*, ed. by Owen Heathcote and Andrew Watts (Cambridge: Cambridge university Press), p. 67–80.

Péraud Alexandre, 2012, "Langue de bois pour siècle de fer: l'inscription problématique de la langue économique dans le roman du XIXe siècle", Congrès international de la Société des Études romantiques et dix-neuviémistes, *Le XIXe siècle et ses langues*, <https://serd.hypotheses.org/files/2017/02/Langues-Peraud.pdf > [accessed 12 July 2024].

Pliny the Elder, 1877, *Histoire naturelle*, ed. by Émile Littré, 2 vols (Paris: Chez Firmin-Didot), I.

Rauch François-Antoine, 1818, *Régénération de la nature végétale, ou recherches sur les moyens de recréer, dans tous les climats, les anciennes températures et l'ordre primitif des saisons, par des plantations raisonnées*, 2 vols (Paris: P. Didot L'Ainé), I, p. 409–417.

Recueil agronomique, publié par les soins de la Société des Sciences, Agriculture et Belles-Lettres du département de Tarn-et-Garonne, 1826, 46 vols (Montauban: Chez Lapie-Fontanel), VII, p. 40–41.

Rougier de la Bergerie Jean-Baptiste, 1820, *Mémoire au Roi et aux Chambres législatives, sur la destruction des bois et sur la grave conséquence qui peuvent en résulter* (Paris: Dentu).

Rozier François, 1786, *Cours complet d'agriculture théorique, pratique, économique, et de médecine rurale et vétérinaire*, 10 vols (Paris: Hôtel Serpentes), V, p. 623–624.

Saint-Maurice Pelée de, 1762, *L'art de cultiver des peupliers d'Italie, avec des observations sur le choix, la disposition des pépinières, leur culture, & sur celle des arbres plantés à demeure* (Paris: Chez la veuve d'Houry).

Spandri Francesco, 2020, "Morphologie de la richesse chez Balzac", *French Forum*, 45, p. 261–274.

Virgil, *L'Énéide*, 1868, trans. by Charles Nisard (Paris: Chez Firmin Didot), VIII, p. 346–361.

PEASANTS V. PASTORAL

Some Uses of Animality in Balzac's *Les Paysans*

THE PARISIAN PASTORAL(IZING) GAZE

Honoré de Balzac's novel *Les Paysans*, published in part in 1844 and posthumously in full in 1855, centers on class struggle and issues of land use in the French countryside. While these themes have been well studied, I wish to highlight an element complementary to — and even mutually dependent on — an analysis of class tensions in the text, particularly as they are articulated in rural space: namely, the view of the non-human natural world (the 'environment') and the role of the human within it. As I will show, *Les Paysans* dramatizes an interplay between a Parisian aesthetic-political approach to the land that functions within the codes of a romantic pastoral. The peasants, who have a more proximate relationship to the land, offer a counter-pastoral discourse, which disrupts, even negates, the logic of wealthy landowners and other consumers from the capital. These ruptures play out through a series of interactions between what we might call the Parisian bloc (which I take to include Blondet and the Montcornet household and staff) and the peasants, wherein representational poetics come head-to-head with on-the-ground reality. We might trace these perspectives in the order they appear in the text, the former first embodied by Émile Blondet, whose stay in Bourgogne acts as a through line for the entire novel.

Blondet, whose voice opens the text through a letter he writes to his friend Nathan back in Paris, is a bourgeois journalist, on holiday in Bourgogne, staying with his friends, the Count and Countess de Montcornet at their estate, les Aigues. Blondet's multiple identity as journalist, relatively recently socially ascended urban bourgeois, and lover (he will end up with the Countess by the end of the novel) coalesce to offer a view of the countryside that is *perceived* (at least by Blondet) to be mimetic, all while embracing artistic metaphor, floral symbolism and a general romantic idealization of the landscape. Remaining primarily within an artistic register — comparing the countryside to romanesque or painterly representations of nature — Blondet's conception of the land falls quite straightforwardly within the pastoral mode. Indeed, at the end of his stroll through the grounds of les Aigues, he concludes: "Quand vous vous promenez dans ce parc, [...] l'Arcadie mythologique devient pour vous plate comme la Beauce. L'Arcadie est en Bourgogne et non en Grèce, l'Arcadie est aux Aigues et non ailleurs" (*CH*, IX, p. 56).

The repetition of Arcadia is striking here. The reference moves from simile, in which the park flattens the myth of Arcadia, narratively and geographically, via the comparison to the Beauce, to metaphor and even replacement, les Aigues *becoming* and thus concretizing Arcadia. Blondet's allusion to the Beauce is particularly interesting; in addition to its being literally quite flat, this is also a primary agricultural region, particularly as wheat became an increasingly important cash crop. The busting of a mythical Arcadia is thus associated with a projection onto agriculturally productive space. In comparison with Blondet's developing pastoral fantasy of Bourgogne — which, we will remember, is the interior of an estate and not 'true' nature or wilderness — this movement points to the formation of a new conception of the countryside in the nineteenth century, which is neither completely wild or *natural*, nor functional in an agro-industrial sense.

This partially happened through the creation of new forms of pseudo-natural entertainment for audiences in Paris. As Nicholas Green shows, urban gardens and carnivals, guidebooks and tours, *maisons de campagne* and pictorial genres including dioramas, picturesque paintings and travel prints constituted a broader attempt to re-insert a kind of nature (man-made but seemingly non-artificial) into bourgeois urban lifestyles. These developing genres and institutions participated in the creation of a discourse about the countryside, where "the codes of landscape art which were fixed at the beginning of the century furnished the grammar and syntax put to work across the whole spectrum of picturesque nature commodifications on offer in the capital" (Green, 1990, p. 94). With this in mind, we might understand Blondet's foray into the countryside — and also the presence of the Montcornets, who have also recently moved to Bourgogne — as a collision of this urban idealization of the land and its material reality.

The peasant interrupts Blondet's epistolary wanderings, if only briefly. The journalist comes upon a "tableau" of a mill and its surroundings, "ses arbres, ses canards, son linge étendu, sa maison couverte en chaume, [...] sans compter un garçon meunier qui déjà m'éxaminait" (*CH*, IX, p. 52). First, Blondet enumerates aspects of the mill scene which contribute to a charming unity. The miller boy, associated with land-based labor, is vital to the functionality of the real-life mill. However, the lexical turn provoked by "sans" suggests that his presence is antagonistic to the rest of the scene; that is, he risks compromising the efficacy of the mill-ideal (which is, through the distance created by the artistic framing of the "tableau", separate from the material landscape). The boy adds a sort of eeriness, as Blondet remarks that "[e]n quelque endroit que vous soyez à la campagne, et quand vous vous y croyez seul, vous êtes le point de mire de deux yeux couverts d'un bonnet de coton" (*CH*, IX, p. 52).

The peasant body — and, even more, the peasant gaze — interrupts Blondet's bourgeois fantasy of romantic solitude in nature; while the journalist attempts to view the scene through the aesthetic constraints of landscape, he becomes himself the object of observation. This disruption is as political as it is aesthetic. In *Le temps du paysage*, Jacques Rancière argues that, in the late eighteenth and early nineteenth centuries, landscape came to be increasingly associated with social and political order. During this time, two visions of land emerged:

> d'un côté, une figure aristocratique élégamment vêtue autour de laquelle se déploie un paysage qui est sa propriété et où seules quelques taches de noir dans les blés ou sur les près suggèrent les hommes du peuple qui y trouvent leur modeste place; de l'autre, un décor de paysage appartenant à tous et à personne, à ceux qui se promènent et à ceux qui travaillent (Rancière, 2020, p. 94).[1]

1 Of course, Blondet is not representative of the artistocracy, but rather the Parisian bourgeoisie. In *Les Paysans*, the lines between the Parisian bourgeois and the aristocracy, represented by the Count and Countess of Montcornet — who themselves are representative of two different kinds of artistocracy in post-Revolutionary France and who both also recently arrived in Bourgogne — are blurred. The more important class distinction is between what we might call the Parisian bloc, the provincial bourgeois, represented by the usurer Rigou and Gaubertin, and the peasants. The town bourgeois also contribute to the animalization of the peasant (Rigou, for example, describes the peasants in this way on more than one occasion). Their relationship to the land is different than that

The very possibility of a shift in perspective from Blondet to the miller boy suggests the threat (at least to Blondet's imaginary) of these competing landscapes. If *Les Paysans* is a story of class warfare, then, it is also — and following Rancière, these things are related — a story of developing views of the countryside, the validity and functionality of such views, and their capacities for social repression or liberation.

"EST-CE LÀ MON SEMBLABLE?" ANIMALIZATION OF THE PEASANT 'OTHER'

In this interaction, the reader perceives a glimpse, albeit brief, of the failure of a sort of bourgeois pastoral fantasy.[2] This will become clearer in the second chapter, ironically titled "Une bucolique oubliée par Virgile". This chapter, in which narrative voice shifts from Blondet to a more typical Balzacian narrator, provides a critical mirror to Blondet's letter, as the text retraces the journalist's walking trajectory, rewriting his initial encounter with Bourgogne. The narration in this retelling is padded with theatrical allusions that simultaneously highlight the cultural, representative relationship between the capital and the countryside, and call into question the reality and affective limits of the latter.[3]

After several minutes of walking, Blondet finds himself at the top of the river Avonne, next to a lush prairie, enjoying the "nature sauvage et solitaire" surrounding les Aigues (*CH*, IX, p. 70), when his enjoyment is interrupted by the sight of a peasant. The introduction of the peasant

of the Parisian bloc, as they do not perpetuate the same romantic fantasies; still, their economic interest in the land is not altogether dissimilar from Montcornet's.

2 My understanding of the pastoral, following Terry Gifford, is as a concept or "cultural function" (2014, p. 26), rather than a genre or mode. I argue that Balzac's ironic interpellation of pastoral language signals that he experiments in *Les Paysans* with the pastoral as a point of view. With this in mind, and with the manipulations of idealized nature laid out by Nicholas Green, I think it reasonable to extend our understanding of the pastoral to the Parisian bourgeois imaginary.

3 "Les beautés de la nature semblent bien mesquines, comparées à leur représentation au théâtre. […] Sans l'intérêt particulier qui vous attache, comme Blondet, *aux lieux honorés par les pas, éclairés par les yeux* d'une certaine personne, on envierait aux oiseaux leurs ailes pour retourner aux perpétuels, aux émouvants spectacles de Paris et à ses déchirantes luttes." (*CH*, IX, p. 66)

in the scene plays into the theatrical tropes evoked earlier, as the narrator assigns this group a dramaturgical position opposite that of the bourgeoisie (ostensibly the main characters), describing the former as "comparses si nécessaires à l'action, qu'on hésitera peut-être entre eux et les premiers rôles" (*CH*, IX, p. 70). Again, as above, the presence of the peasant threatens the spectacle in which Blondet wishes to engage. Here, though, his identity is interrogated further:

> Sa barbe blanche, clairsemée, donnait quelque chose de menaçant à son profil par la raideur des poils coupés court. Ses yeux, trop petits pour son énorme visage, inclinés comme ceux du cochon, exprimaient à la fois la ruse et la paresse; mais en ce moment ils jetaient comme une lueur, tant le regard jaillissait droit sur la rivière. [...] Tout citadin aurait frémi de lui voir aux pieds des sabots cassés, sans même un peu de paille pour en adoucir les crevasses. Assurément, la blouse et le pantalon n'avaient de valeur que pour la cuve d'une papeterie. (*CH*, IX, p. 71)

The peasant is first compared to an animal. This is not altogether surprising, and certainly not unprecedented in *Les Chouans* (1829), a novel that shares many similarities with *Les Paysans*, Balzac introduces the peasant with a similar animalizing gesture.[4] In some ways, this plays into norms of prior literary representation, such as in La Bruyère's *Les Caractères* (1688). In this text, which provides an early example of the peasant figure in modern French literary production, he is mistaken for an "animal farouche" (1926, p. 332) before he is seen as human, in a similar semantic movement as Balzac's in the passage above.

Still, this comparison signals something greater about the place of the peasant in a bourgeois landscape. In the opening to this chapter, the narrator bemoans the ennui induced by the countryside for the Parisian "qui n'est ni chasseur ni agriculteur" (*CH*, IX, p. 66). A landowner required to spend more time on the land would develop "quelque passion pour la géologie, la minéralogie, l'entomologie, ou la flore du département" (*CH*, IX, p. 66).[5] These material relationships with the

4 On animality in *La Comédie humaine*, see Wilds, 2017 and Preuss and Schönbeck, 2015.

5 An interesting discrepancy exists between different versions of the text in this spot: in the Pléiade version, there is no specific mention of specimen collecting; however, in the version published by Folio Classique and prefaced by Louis Chevalier, the same excerpt reads, "quelque passion pour les lépidoptères, les coquilles, les insectes, ou la flore du département" (1975, p. 56). I would argue that the text of the Folio edition further emphasizes the allusion to natural history, particularly through the use of the scientific name

land, figured through the position of the hunter, the farmer or, in the last instance, the natural historian, establish a relatively clear relationship of dominance of the human over the animal. Comparing the peasant to an animal, then, and particularly to an agricultural animal-cum-commodity (the pig, whose relative the boar is also prey to the hunt), not only places him in a subservient position, but indeed conflates him with agricultural production and capitalism, as he becomes little more than a resource — like the land itself.[6]

The theme of animalization continues throughout the novel, arising especially when there is a contest over land. In a scene much later in the novel, the Count de Montcornet and his guard Michaud observe peasants coming to glean:

> il y avait une centaine de créatures [...] des vieilles au cou de dindon, à l'œil chauve et rogue, qui tendaient la tête comme des chiens d'arrêt devant la perdrix, des enfants silencieux comme des soldats sous les armes, des petites filles qui trépignaient comme des animaux attendant leur pâture, les caractères de l'enfance et de la vieillesse étaient opprimés sous une féroce convoitise, celle du bien d'autrui qui devenait le leur par abus. (*CH*, IX, p. 323–324)

The peasant is sequentially likened to a turkey (a hunting fowl), a hunting dog, and a farm animal waiting to be taken out to pasture. Francesco Spandri highlights a "non-sens de la terre" that Balzac attaches to the peasant, in both his journalistic and novelistic writing (including *Les Paysans*), particularly in their thirst for land and their desire to divide large landholdings for their benefit. Acting from this non-sense — literally lack of sense or even *anti*-sense — peasants become "une force sociale qui agit contre la raison, mieux, d'une force sociale qui se sent désormais légitimée à agir contre la raison" (Spandri, 2019, p. 521). What I wish to highlight here is not the inherent non-sense of the peasant as written by Balzac, but the mechanism by which the peasantry is rendered senseless — that is, incapable of sense — by the Blondet/Montcornet

---

for the genus including butterfly and moths (*Lepidoptera*), and the explicit relationship that this creates between the bourgeois collector and the animal specimen. This more explicit presence of the animal, and specifically of an insect, establishes a resonance with the end of the novel, when the peasants impersonate insects to trick the Montcornets and gain access to more wood.

6 This is further highlighted by the idea that the peasant's clothing (essentially rags) might be turned to paper in the "cuve d'une papeterie" (*CH*, IX, p. 71).

bloc. In the passage above, this happens through the animalization of the peasant, which accentuates the difference between the bourgeois/aristocratic figure and the wild 'other' so much as to exclude the latter from the realm of human logic.

Sylvia Wynter argues that "Man", the ideal Western political and economic subject — white, male, land-owning (or, later, capable of amassing capital) — "over represents itself as if it were the human itself", rendering it impossible for certain groups identified as 'other' to achieve full humanity (Wynter, 2003, p. 260). The creation of "Man" requires a Chain of Being with grades of rationality related to degrees of humanness, which in turn allows for the "slandering" of racially- and socially-coded others, who are identified as subhuman in relation to Western Man (*ibid.*).[7] For Wynter, the Mad person, and later the poor person, would come to function within Europe in a parallel way to the Black enslaved person in the colonies, occupying a less-than-human position within the social order (*ibid.*, p. 304). In my reading, I extend this to include also the French peasant, who undergoes, in the passage above, parallel processes of dehumanization, differentiation, and denial of reason. Of course, the stakes for such dehumanization are different within metropolitan France and in its colonies; still, Balzac's representation of the peasant suggests that the colonial-imperial mindset that legitimized violence toward the racialized other also underwrote the Parisian approach to the peasant.[8]

When Blondet asks of the peasant, "Quelles peuvent être les idées, les mœurs d'un pareil être, à quoi pense-t-il? [...] Est-ce là mon semblable?" (*CH*, IX, p. 71), then, this question is not rhetorical. The "thingification"

7 Wynter's Chain of Being is, of course, related to natural historical and natural philosophical hierarchies of beings, creating a link with the novel's several allusions to natural history. In his *Systema Naturae* (1737), the Swedish naturalist Carl Linnaeus codifies and 'scientizes' the *scala natura*, or Great Chain of Being, a hierarchical ordering of existence in Aristotelian thought and which was particularly popular in medieval Christianity. Linnaeus' text provides the basis of modern natural historical collecting. See Arthur O. Lovejoy, *The Great Chain of Being*.

8 Mel Chen describes a form of dehumanization theorized in Marxist discourse that depicts the alienated laborer as animal(ized). The transformation of relations required by capitalism result in the "loss of a laborer's connection to its once-elaborate human nature [...] leaving it in the world of the 'animal function'" (Chen, 2012, p. 46). While Chen recognizes the capacity of this argument to highlight social injustices, they note that Marx still creates/maintains a hierarchy of animacy reminiscent of the Great Chain of Being.

of the peasant represented lexically by a form of "cela" seems to confirm Blondet's understanding of him as an insurmountable other and his impression that "[n]ous n'avons de commun que la forme, et encore!..." (*CH*, IX, p. 71). Observing a "rigidité particulière au tissu des gens qui vivent en plein air", whose skin turns to leather and whose nerves weaken (*CH*, IX, p. 71), he reiterates environmental determinist hypotheses widespread in medical and scientific discourse about European colonies, which point to physiological-biological differences in populations provoked by differing climates.[9] While the French peasant inhabits the same climate as Blondet, his relatively greater physical exposure to that climate, which is another formulation of his proximity to the natural world, is enough to cause noticeable physical difference, even decay into animality.

Blondet seems to answer his own question when he exclaims, "Voilà les Peaux-Rouges de Cooper, [...] il n'y a pas besoin d'aller en Amérique pour observer des Sauvages" (*CH*, IX, p. 71). The translation and spread of James Fenimore Cooper's work in France, along with several theatrical portrayals of Native Americans during this time, likely ensured that its use in comparison here was easily legible to Balzac's readership.[10] The comparison was also widespread in the literary production of the period. *Les Chouans*, for example, was originally meant to be titled *Le Dernier des Chouans*. This obvious allusion to Cooper's novel reinforces a symmetry between the Indigenous American and the French peasant. The comparison is sometimes also extended to city dwellers, as in Balzac's *Le Père Goriot* (1833) and, later, Alexandre Dumas' *Les Mohicans de Paris* (1859).

While cultural representations of the Native American in the nineteenth century were moving away from the social sublime of the eighteenth century, toward the grotesque and caricatural,[11] Balzac's reading of Cooper's Indigenous subject departs from both these tropes. In an article published in the *Revue Parisienne*, Balzac writes of Cooper:

> Cette prose magique non-seulement montre à l'esprit ce fleuve, ses rives, les forêts et leurs arbres, mais elle y parvient en donnant à la fois les moindres

9 On the prevalence of such medical thinking, see Schiebinger, 2017.

10 The novel, published in 1826, was translated to French that very same year by Auguste-Jean-Baptiste Defauconpret.

11 See Meglin, 2000. In addition to providing a helpful review of the tropes of the representation of the New World "*sauvage*", this is one of the only studies of the ballet adaptation of *Le Dernier des Mohicans* (titled *Les Mohicans*), which ran for two nights in 1837.

> circonstances et l'ensemble. [...] Le même génie qui, après vous avoir lancé en pleine mer, passionne l'immense étendue de l'Océan, sait vous faire frissonner en vous laissant apercevoir des Indiens derrière les troncs d'arbres, dans l'eau, sous les rochers. Quand l'esprit des solitudes vous a parlé, quand le calme frais de ces éternels ombrages vous a séduit, quand vous planez sur cette puissante végétation, vous avez le cœur en émoi. (Balzac, 1840, p. 71–72)

For Balzac, then, the genius of Cooper's writing is his ability to subsume the Indigenous subject into a landscape, which itself presents a sort of American(ized) pastoral. As Tom Lynch suggests, colonial spaces in Australia and North America provided Europeans with an opportunity to actualize notions of idyllic pastoralism both materially and ideologically, as "the settler colony was often envisioned as a type of Arcadia" (2022, p. 136).

The pastoral thus moves away from aesthetic mode to become a vehicle for colonial-imperial ideology. Jennifer Yee also notices this, identifying a "sinister pastoral" at play in Balzac's writing. This sinister pastoral is rooted in a "fantasy of self-realization in the form of mini-despotism and non-accountability" and a "desire for an imagined land of aristocratic/autocratic self-fulfillment in the enslavement of others" uniquely possible in the New World (Yee, 2016, p. 76–77). The comparison of the peasant to the Indigenous American is not only an ontological classification, but a way for Blondet to comprehend the former's presence within his own conception of the countryside. While the peasant initially disrupts Blondet's pastoral fantasy, his becoming-*Sauvage*, which echoes the reference to "nature sauvage et solitaire" that precedes this run-in, completes it, as Blondet's pastoral discourse becomes one of domination.[12]

Blondet's and later Montcornet's worldview thus reproduce the sinister pastoral — and, notably, extend it to French rural land and people — by negating the peasant's humanity, such that, via animalization or a rendering "sauvage", the latter becomes part of the non-human natural world. In this way, the former are able to maintain the domineering and proprietary view of landscape that Rancière describes, which itself requires a limiting of lower-class human life, except inasmuch as it

12 This "nature sauvage" also exists in Blondet's letter, where the journalist writes about "une nature luxuriante et parée, [...] quelque chose de sauvage et d'ébouriffé, de secret, de pas commun" (*CH*, IX, p. 51–52).

can be abstracted into the scene. The inhumanity of the peasant functions both as an aesthetic strategy, which, by naturalizing the peasant, maintains the balance of the *tableau*, and as a political strategy, where the domination of the countryside is facilitated by a disregard for the peasant, made ontologically 'other'. The trouble comes, as we will see, when the peasant resists such a categorization.

THE PEASANT'S COUNTER-PASTORAL

Blondet's perspective is only part of the story, and the journalist's projections onto Fourchon are interrupted when the latter starts talking. Fourchon, and the young boy Mouche, who initially blends into the environment enough to escape Blondet's view were it not for his "yeux de chat" (*CH*, IX, p. 72) are lying in wait for an otter. Fourchon explains that the otter, a scientific specimen (he repeats this twice in as many pages), is desired by a local doctor Gourdon, who keeps a natural history cabinet and who will pay the peasant for it (*CH*, IX, p. 73). Blondet, remarking that he has not even seen an otter at the Muséum national d'Histoire naturelle (*CH*, IX, p. 74), happily plays into Fourchon's ploy.

Here, then, Fourchon uses the animal to play into a certain relationship that he understands Blondet and other bourgeois to have with the non-human natural world, mitigated in this instance through natural history collecting. What's more, Fourchon appears here quite conscious of the projected animalization of the peasant by the Parisian. When Blondet questions how they would catch the otter, Fourchon replies, "nous sommes si bêtes, nous aut' *pésans*! que nous finissons par entendre les bêtes" (*CH*, IX, p. 75, emphasis in the original). The old man embraces his supposed stupidity, which, through the repetition of the word "*bête*", brings him into proximity with the animal world; however, this proximity is counter-intuitively the basis of the legitimation of a certain kind of knowledge, which overpowers, at least in this moment, Blondet's. Of course, the reader quickly finds out that this is a scam: Blondet pays Fourchon ten francs, the otter is said to have disappeared (Fourchon blaming Blondet), and later the Count's valet tells Blondet that the Count also fell prey to this prank upon his arrival at les Aigues. While this is only comical (without any real repercussions for Blondet), it signals a generic shift — that is, a shift in the kind of story Blondet is able to tell, if only to himself, about the countryside — which I argue is triggered by the peasants' actions.

In *Discourse/Counter-Discourse*, Richard Terdiman argues that, though dominant discourses situate themselves as "natural", and universal, the heterogeneity intrinsic to language provides for counter-discourses that respond dialectically to any given discourse (1985, p. 16). Drawing on this conception of counter-discourse, and Jean-François Lyotard's notion of the "figure", Lawrence Schehr develops a theory of difference in the realist novel, wherein the introduction of the 'other' into a narrative offers an ironic challenge to the universal(ist) goal of realist mimesis and the hegemonic discourses underwriting bourgeois cultural production. The figure, according to Schehr, "interrupts and differs from the flow of the discursive by introducing what is not comfortably represented in discourse" (2003, p. 30). In the above instance, the peasant acts as a 'figure of alterity' that contests Blondet's idealizing discourse and the associated Parisian environmental imagination. Indeed, by using this discourse *against* Blondet, Fourchon flips the very genre of the interaction, from romantic pastoral to farce.

The primary tension in the novel develops between the peasants, who for generations have foraged for firewood and grain from the grounds of les Aigues, and the Count de Montcornet, who seeks to disallow such practices. Montcornet's reasoning for this, informed by his second-in-command, Michaud, is primarily economic, as the peasants' foraging decreases the property's total yield value by some 30% (*CH*, IX, p. 124). The count, via the proxy of his *garde champêtre*, begins to crack down on these practices, threatening legal proceedings against any peasants caught with fresh wood, and instituting a system of gleaning permits that drastically reduces peasant access to harvests.

While tensions between foraging peasants and landowners existed in France from the fourteenth century, they reached a head in the nineteenth-century, particularly with the passage of the Forest Code of 1827, which severely limited local use-rights.[13] In the 1840s, Karl

13 For a longer history of forest rights in France, see Sahlins, 1998, especially p. 13–18. See also Matteson, 2015.

Marx commented on the increasing illegality of gathering dead wood and the related creation of value in a resource that previously had had none.[14] This feeds into Marx's broader views of alienation from nature, via a dualistic domination of the earth, which meant, as John Bellamy Foster summarizes, "both the domination of the earth *by* those who monopolized land and hence the elemental powers of nature, and also the domination of the earth and of dead matter (representing the power of landlord and capitalist) *over* the vast greater part of humanity (by being alienated in favor of the very few)" (2000, p. 74). While *Les Paysans* is set before the Forest Code, Montcornet's policing of the forest and his clamping down on gleaning are representative of a broader capitalist approach to land. The intermingling of Montcornet's and Blondet's perspectives through the text suggests that this commodification and control of the countryside is not altogether incompatible with a pastoral idealization of landscape; rather, these outlooks represent two sides of the same coin, the fantasy of the land-as-Arcadia masking the political violence of property.

The peasants subvert the Count's rule, via the appropriation of a parasitic animal practice. For two decades, the reader learns, peasant women have been cutting the base of the trees (some five hundred to six hundred of them!), effectively killing them and making their wood available for foraging the following spring (*CH*, IX, p. 319). The marks left on the trees mimic those made by the *ver blanc*, a nuisance well-documented in agricultural literature of the period. This insect, "le désespoir du propriétaire", destroys crops and "échappe sous terre à la circulaire administrative" (*CH*, IX, p. 320). If the worm, part of the natural and not the social world, escapes legal punishment, it also escapes definition by naturalists who, despite their most ardent research, cannot understand the diverse mechanisms of the entire insect world (*CH*, IX, p. 320). The peasants, having themselves learned about this practice through their own observation of the worm, replace naturalist knowledge with a sort of landed knowledge born of their proximity to the non-human natural world. If Blondet's alleged mimetic representation of the countryside in his initial letter is shown by the narrative to be flawed, the peasants perform their own act of mimesis-mimicry. This

14 John Bellamy Foster suggests that it was this topic that encouraged Marx to pursue political economy (2000, p. 67).

latter mimesis differs from Blondet's in its materiality, as it is physically acted out on the landscape, rather than remaining in the realm of aesthetic representation. While in Blondet's pastoral discourse, proximity to Nature works to dehumanize the peasant, here, the peasant strategically co-opts the doubly resistant ecological-ontological position of the animal to subvert Montcornet's capitalist domination of the forest.[15]

One morning, Blondet notices patches of brown among the trees and invites the Countess de Montcornet on a ride through the forest to investigate. At first, the forest is a lovers' idyll, "où la brise apportait les senteurs de serpolet, [...] où la lumière se veloute en s'y perdant [...]" (*CH*, IX, p. 329). The idyll turns eerie, however, when they hear a sound. The Countess initially mistakes it for an animal, to which Blondet responds, "– Ce bruit, chère institutrice d'histoire surnaturelle, n'est pas le bruit fait par un animal; il y a je ne sais quoi d'intelligent qui annonce l'homme" (*CH*, IX, p. 331). This observation, which re-iterates the same failure of natural history to comprehend the peasant-nature assemblage, triggers the degeneration of this scene into deadly chaos. Moments later, the couple hears the sound of "un être égorgé" (*CH*, IX, p. 331), what will turn out to be the killing of the *garde champêtre*'s greyhound, a murder that foreshadows the eventual murder of Michaud and the departure of the Montcornets from les Aigues (the victory of the peasants).

In this episode, peasants blend into the forest like in Balzac's description of Cooper's Native American. However, through their strategic manipulation of this (mis)categorization of their own (in)humanity, they undermine the Parisian pastoral fantasy. Whereas Fourchon turns the idyll into a farce, here the peasants once again change the genre, making it a horror story. The peasants' counter-discourse becomes a more explicit counter-pastoral. This notion of counter-pastoral draws on Leo Marx's "complex pastoral design", wherein a "counterforce" undermines and destabilizes the idealized, "simple" pastoral (Marx, 1964, p. 25). This counterforce appears, in a manner not dissimilar to Schehr's figure, through ironic disruptions in a text (the sound of the

15 Such subversions to forest restrictions by the peasantry were not uncommon in this period. In 1829, the War of the Desmoiselles in Ariège constituted a series of attacks on forest watch stations and charcoal makers' huts, by peasant men disguised as women. During this year, there were also riots and other collective actions. See Sahlins, 1998.

train in Thoreau's *Walden* is a classic example in Marx's analysis). In *Les Paysans*, the instigator of the counter-pastoral is not technology, but the peasantry, who act through a sort of environmental agency, becoming socio-political actors capable of refusing Parisian pastoral discourse. They do so by ironically occupying categorizations such as the animal-human and the wild man as a means of subverting the ideological projections of Parisians onto the landscape and onto the peasant figure.

CONCLUSION

What I mean by the environmental agency of the peasantry is twofold. First, they establish themselves as legitimate actors within the countryside, through their encroachment on the Montcornets' land and the major changes that they bring about on the landscape (which materially destroy Blondet's ability to map Arcadia back onto this space at the end of the novel). Interestingly, though, they do this not by defending their own humanity within the paradigm of elitist thought. By embracing the animality imposed on them and *becoming* animals (if only in disguise), they prove possession of a kind of reasoning exterior to Blondet's or Montcornet's classifications. This is to say, rather than attempting to refute claims of "non-sense" within bourgeois/artistocratic logic, they display a different kind of sense that operates outside of this paradigm, troubling it by its very existence.

To be clear, this sense does not underwrite an environmentalist ethic. Quite the contrary: in the peasants' primary subversion of the Montcornets, they are parasites — to the Montcornets, certainly, but also, ecologically, to the forest. And though they technically win out in forcing the Montcornets to leave, the end result is ambivalent, as they have cleared the entire forest and park and replaced it with agricultural production. We should take Blondet's ironic exclamation — "Voilà le progrès!" (*CH*, IX, p. 347) — with a grain of salt, given his own culturally-informed environmental imagination. Still, what is clear in this scene is that the peasants have transitioned not from one form of domination of the landscape to a natural restoration or symbiosis, but to another form of domination.

In *Mythes balzaciens*, Pierre Barbéris describes *Les Paysans* as a "roman dans lequel on voit le siècle basculer" (1972, p. 63). While he makes this claim with regard to the moral and political affiliations of wealth, I think it can extend to other cultural evolutions, including shifting perspectives on landscape and land use. This novel, perhaps more explicitly than any other preceding it, dramatizes competing views of the countryside. The peasants' victory is indicative of a general shift in French society, which increasingly recognizes them as a social force and results in universal male suffrage in 1848, making the peasant officially a political actor. The transition of the parks of les Aigues (already manufactured and not natural, but also not productive) to arable land also signals a process that takes shape over the entirety of the nineteenth century, namely the rise of agricultural capitalism. It is ultimately unclear in this context if the peasants have escaped the larger horror story to which their own actions have also contributed. While Blondet and the Countess de Montcornet ride off into the sunset, blissfully ignorant of the future, the peasants remain attached to the land. The narrative ends as it began, giving the final word to Blondet, who raises the question of the "social machine" (*CH*, IX, p. 347). In this way, then, the humanity of every character in the story is troubled in the end, as the peasant, like the bourgeois, figure as mere cogs in the machinery of capital.

Abigail FIELDS
University of Kansas

WORKS CITED

Balzac Honoré de, 15 juillet 1840, "Lettres sur la littérature, le théâtre et les arts, Ire. À Madame la Comtesse E.", *La Revue Parisienne*, p. 47–98.

Chevalier Louis (préface de), 1975, Honoré de Balzac, *Les Paysans* (Paris: Gallimard, "Folio Classique").

Barbéris Pierre, 1972, *Mythes balzaciens* (Paris: Armand Colin).

Bellamy Foster John, 2000, *Marx's Ecology: Materialism and Nature* (NYU Press).

Chen Mel, 2012, *Animacies: Biopolitics, Racial Mattering and Queer Affect.* (Duke University Press).

Gifford Terry, 2014, "Pastoral, Anti-Pastoral, and Post-Pastoral", in *The Cambridge Companion to Literature and the Environment*, ed. by Louise Westling (Cambridge University Press).

Green Nicholas, 1990, *The Spectacle of Nature: Landscape and Bourgeois Culture in Nineteenth-Century France* (Manchester University Press).

La Bruyère Jean de, 1926, *Les Caractères* (Paris: Hachette).

Lynch Tom, 2022, *Outback and Out West: The Settler-Colonial Environmental Imaginary* (University of Nebraska Press).

Marx Leo, 1964, *The Machine in the Garden: Technology and the Pastoral Ideal in America* (Oxford University Press).

Matteson Kieko, 2015, *Forests in Revolutionary France: Conservation, Community and Conflict, 1669–1848* (Cambridge University Press).

Meglin Joellen, 2000, "*Sauvages*, Sex Roles, and Semiotics: Representations of Native Americans in the French Ballet 1736–1837, Part Two: The Nineteenth Century", *Dance Chronicle*, 23, no. 3, p. 275–320.

Preuss Matthias and Sebastian Schönbeck, 2015, "Bêtes Studies: Flaubert's and Balzac's Lessons in Natural History", *Journal of Literary Theory*, 9, no. 2, p. 250–270.

Rancière Jacques, 2020, *Le Temps du paysage. Aux origines de la révolution esthétique* (Paris: La Fabrique).

Sahlins Peter, 1998, *Forest Rites: The War of the Demoiselles in Nineteenth-Century France* (Harvard University Press).

Schehr Lawrence, 2003, *Figures of Alterity: French Realism and its Others* (Stanford University Press).

Schiebinger Londa, 2017, *Secret Cures of Slaves: People, Plants, and Medicine in the Eighteenth-Century Atlantic World* (Stanford University Press).

Spandri Francesco, 2019, "Balzac et le non-sens de la terre", *French Studies*, 73.4, p. 513–524.

Terdiman Richard, 1985, *Discourse/Counter-Discourse: The Theory and Practice of Symbolic Resistance in Nineteenth-Century France* (Cornell University Press).

Wilds Travis, 2017, "Animality and Contagion in Balzac's *Père Goriot*", *SubStance*, 46, no. 3, p. 173–182.

Wynter Sylvia, 2003, "Unsettling the Coloniality of Being/Power/Truth/Freedom: Towards the Human, After Man, Its Overrepresentation — An Argument", *CR: The New Centennial Review* 3, no. 3, p. 257–337.

Yee Jennifer, 2016, *The Colonial Comedy: Imperialism in the Realist French Novel* (Oxford University Press).

PANTHERS AND PANTHEISM

Animal Sympathy and Balzac's Mystical Biology

Upon first glance, Honoré de Balzac's *Une passion dans le désert* (1830) and *Séraphîta* (1834) tell two rather different stories; when placed together, however, the two texts cohere in significant ways, exploring largely analogous interspecies relationships between creatures who occupy different rungs along a hierarchical *échelle des êtres*. In *Une passion*, Balzac depicts the relationship between a panther and a soldier who works to cultivate the human qualities of his feline companion; in *Séraphîta*, meanwhile, Balzac explores the romantic triangle between two humans and an androgynous angel who likewise works to cultivate the *angelic* qualities of her/his human companions. Drawing from a wide range of scientific and philosophical influences, most notably Étienne Geoffroy Saint-Hilaire's transformist *unité de composition* and Emmanuel Swedenborg's metaphysics, Balzac constructs a mystical-biological framework in which all organic matter is in perpetual upward motion towards the divine, with individual organisms transforming into increasingly complex lifeforms as they adapt to their respective milieux.

Despite their timbral differences, *Une passion* and *Séraphîta* thus ultimately share the same narrative backbone (to speak in comparative anatomical terms): they both explore the conditions under which kinship can take place across zoological boundaries in Balzac, dramatizing the rituals and modes of communication, linguistic or otherwise, that emerge when negotiating the alterity of an unknowable other with whom one would make kin. In this regard, Balzac's oeuvre proves remarkably sensitive to considerations around alterity and continuism that continue to inform contemporary animal studies scholarship. Following an exploration of Balzac's biological reference points, we will compare the relational dynamics of *Une passion* and *Séraphîta* in an effort to concretize what interspecies kinship looks like in Balzac's framework — that is, one in which nonhuman creatures bear analogous cognitive and physical attributes to human beings, are (sometimes harshly) evaluated along a single, hierarchical scale, but are also capable of the same environmentally induced transformations as humans. A closer look at Balzac's mystical biology reveals an animal sympathy that is much less anthropocentric, and much more mindful of nonhuman modes of being, than would *prima facie* appear to be the case.

WHAT'S GOOD FOR THE GOOSE IS GOOD FOR REALIST CHARACTER STUDIES

Balzac's investment in animality is a point of contention in the scholarship; while Allen Thiher suggests that "What is innovative in Balzac is that he is writing a discourse in which human beings are squarely recognized as part of the animal kingdom" (Thiher, 2001, p. 69), Richard Somerset detects a cynical marketing tool meant to create "an air of scientificity" (Somerset, 2002, p. 104). Famously, in his 1842 "Avant-Propos" to *La Comédie humaine*, Balzac suggests that the very conceit of his literary enterprise is tied to the study of nonhuman animals, declaring: "Cette idée vint d'une comparaison entre l'Humanité et l'Animalité" (*CH*, I, p. 7). Just as zoologists can study an animal's milieu to understand its nature, argues Balzac, novelists can study the physical surroundings of the human animal to understand how different environments shape this organism into different social types: the laws surrounding species and character formation become interchangeable.

Balzac anchors his "Avant-Propos" in the 1830 anatomical debates between Geoffroy Saint-Hilaire and Georges Cuvier. Where Cuvier maintained that all of life is organized along four distinct *embranchements* of *animaux vertébrés*, *mollusques*, *articulés*, and *rayonnés* (Cuvier, 1817, p. 57–60), Geoffroy Saint-Hilaire detected a structural analogousness between cephalopods (decidedly mollusks) and vertebrates; this cross-*embranchement* analogousness pushed him to then extrapolate upon his more radical theory of "*l'unité de composition*" (Geoffroy Saint-Hilaire, 1830, p. 48):

> Il n'est qu'un même mode de formation pour engendrer les faits organiques, soit que son action, s'arrêtant de bonne heure, donne les animaux les plus simples, soit que cette action, persévérant jusqu'au terme de toute sa capacité possible, amène la plus grande complication des organes. [...] Pour cet ordre de considérations, il n'est plus d'animaux divers. Un seul fait les domine, c'est comme un seul être qui apparaît. Il est, il réside dans l'Animalité; être abstrait, qui est tangible par nos sens sous des figures diverses. (*Ibid.*, p. 22)

Geoffroy Saint-Hilaire thus proposes a transformist vision in which one singular anatomical design morphs into increasingly complex life-forms via direct environmental influence. As Toby A. Appel notes, while the fixist Cuvier may have been deemed the unofficial victor due to his professional stature, he came to be seen in literary circles as a leader of a "retrograde movement of science" (Appel, 1987, p. 199), while writers like Balzac and Sand were "drawn toward Geoffroy's philosophy by its romantic, pantheistic, and unified vision of the world" (*ibid.*, p. 190).

Indeed, in his "Avant-Propos", Balzac celebrates Geoffroy Saint-Hilaire as "le vainqueur de Cuvier" (*CH*, I, p. 8), identifying *l'unité de composition* as a pillar of his own realist process of studying human characters as organisms shaped by their environment: "L'animal est un principe qui prend sa forme extérieure, ou, pour parler plus exactement, les différences de sa forme, dans les milieux où il est appelé à se développer. [...] La Société ne fait-elle pas de l'homme, suivant les milieux où son action se déploie, autant d'hommes différents qu'il y a de variétés en zoologie?" (*CH*, I, p. 8). Balzac's suggestion that the tools for studying nonhuman animal life are just as applicable to human life does much to compromise any sort of sharp ontological divide between human beings and the rest of the animal kingdom.

Nevertheless, *La Comédie humaine* is also marked by a certain anthropocentrism that echoes Geoffroy Saint-Hilaire's hierarchical vision of *l'échelle des êtres*. Indeed, unlike later Darwinian evolutionary models for which the ability to survive (regardless of anatomical complexity) becomes the primary criterion through which to evaluate an organism, the idea of a universal anatomical structure that transforms along a singular spectrum of complexity winds up privileging a view in which human beings are demonstrably, *objectively* superior beings to other animals. *L'unité de composition* thus poses the paradox of simultaneously promoting a radical continuism that would bridge ontological gaps across the animal kingdom, while also maintaining a rigidly hierarchical *échelle des êtres* reminiscent of classical natural history. With this framing in mind, Balzac can be rather categorical when he declares that, as sophisticated as nonhuman animal life might be, human beings are vastly more interesting: "les habitudes de chaque animal sont, à nos yeux du moins, constamment semblables en tout temps; tandis que les habitudes [...] d'un prince, d'un banquier, d'un artiste, d'un bourgeois, d'un prêtre et d'un pauvre sont entièrement dissemblables et changent au gré des civilisations" (*CH*, I, p. 8). Upon first glance, this position appears quite dismissive of the potential richness of nonhuman modes of being. It is with such statements in mind that we can make sense of the otherwise perplexing scarcity of nonhuman animals in *La Comédie humaine.* As Christèle Couleau rightly points out, despite the privileged status afforded to animality in the "Avant-propos", "si l'on sonde *La Comédie humaine*, on constate évidemment un passage au second plan, à la fois quantitatif et qualitatif, du personnel animal" (Couleau, 2009, p. 1).

We ought to return, however, to Balzac's assertion that it is perhaps merely "à nos yeux" (*CH*, I, p. 8) that nonhuman animals seem to lead monotonous lives, a qualifier that signals a self-awareness around the limits of his human lens. In this sense, Balzac anticipates a type of ontological caution characteristic of contemporary animal studies scholarship. In *Thinking Animals: Why Animals Studies Now?* (2012), Kari Weil highlights this sensitivity to perspective and nonhuman alterity upon which much of contemporary animal studies stands, seeing therein "an attempt to recognize and extend care to others while acknowledging that we may not know what the best form of care is for another whom we cannot presume to know. It is a concern with and for alterity" (Weil, 2012, p. 17).

In bearing in mind Balzac's "à nos yeux", we can appreciate the extent to which his interspecies interactions are tied to the question of perspective and this "concern with and for alterity" to which Weil refers. When read in the light of Saint-Hilairian transformism, *Une passion* and *Séraphîta* are both narratives about extending care to an other while negotiating a certain tension between continuism and alterity, experimenting with the possibilities of analogousness and ontological hierarchy underpinning *l'unité de composition.* In both texts, Balzac explores a series of projections, analogies, and communicational compromises that allow for a nuanced vision of interspecies kinship — in Balzac's fluid but hierarchized system, a human-to-panther dynamic is altogether analogous to a human-to-angel one, with both dynamics revealing a sophisticated relational mode of being.

MAKING KIN BY DESERT

Une passion follows a soldier who loses his battalion during the French invasion of Egypt, only to awaken in a cave in which he finds a surprisingly docile panther. While he first contemplates killing the animal, he then hears "dans son cœur une sorte de remords qui lui criait de respecter une créature inoffensive. Il lui semblait avoir trouvé une amie dans ce désert sans bornes" (*CH*, VIII, p. 1228). This physical space of the desert "sans bornes" mirrors the story's interspecies dynamic that blurs the *bornes* between the two creatures. Indeed, the soldier gradually humanizes the panther as the bond between the two strengthens: the panther receives a name (Mignonne); she is repeatedly described as being "comme une femme" (*CH*, VIII, p. 1231); and she even develops a meaningful form of communication with the soldier. The story ends abruptly when the protagonist stabs Mignonne in an act of self-defense, having potentially misread a display of affection as an attack (therefore suggesting that their communications are not entirely in sync after all). The final sequence's ambiguity has pushed scholars like Couleau to call into question Mignonne's status as a character: "rien n'explicite au bout du compte sa réaction finale […]. L'animal est donc *in extremis* rendu à son opacité, renvoyé à son altérité. Alors que le texte tendait à l'humaniser de plus en plus, il n'est décidément pas un personnage comme les autres" (Couleau, 2009, p. 9). Couleau argues that Mignonne is instead an indecipherable entity that receives a series of anthropocentric projections from the reader and soldier, whose "vision désirante et déformante" (*ibid.*, 8) fails to do justice to this animal other's identity.

A closer look at this human/panther dynamic suggests, however, that the idea of animal characterhood is more complex than this character/not-a-character binary, and that the projecting at play is part of a more sophisticated series of two-way negotiations inherent in any interspecies interaction. The question is not whether Mignonne deserves to be called "un personnage comme les autres", but rather what type of sympathy can exist in this Saint-Hilairian backdrop between two species who are simultaneously united by an anatomical analogousness, but divided by a firmly hierarchical system.

From their earliest interactions, the soldier and Mignonne are entangled in a web of communication. The question of language is of course vital in the discussion of animal sympathy in French letters from René Descartes onwards. Critics like Régine Borderie, Kathleen R. Hart, and Élisabeth Plas have all made nods to the Cartesianism hovering over *Une passion*, drawing attention to the climactic moment in which the soldier declares of Mignonne, "Elle a une âme" (*CH*, VIII, p. 1231).[1] This idea of an animal soul runs directly counter to Descartes's famous theory of the animal-machine; while the scholarship has acknowledged this intertextual dialogue, it is important to turn to the substance of Descartes's argument (which is based on the question of language) in order to fully appreciate its placement in the story.

Indeed, Plas argues that the soldier's affirmation is insufficiently earned and "presque insatisfaisante", writing that "La découverte de l'âme de la panthère ne s'inscrit pas dans le prolongement d'une réflexion sur l'intelligence des animaux [...] Elle interrompt au contraire une contemplation des 'attraits' de la panthère" (Plas, 2021, p. 257). For Plas, this marks but one of many moments in which the soldier clumsily projects an ontological status onto the panther; and yet, this reading ignores the paragraph immediately beforehand, which develops at length the quasi-linguistic exchanges between the two beings. In *Discours de la méthode* (1637), Descartes argues that the absence of a linguistic capacity in animals "ne témoigne pas seulement que les bêtes ont moins de raison que les hommes, mais qu'elles n'en ont point du tout" (Descartes, [1637] 1953, p. 165). In the paragraph preceding the announcement of Mignonne's soul, the text insists upon the communicative fluidity between the two species: the soldier "avait fini par connaître les différentes inflexions de sa voix", suggesting that there is a trackable logic behind Mignonne's signifiers; likewise, the panther is able to recognize and respond to the name the soldier has given her: "Quelque rapide que

1 See: Borderie, 2009, p. 5; Hart, 2012, p. 404; Plas, 2021, p. 255–257.

fût son élan, [...] elle s'y arrêtait tout court, au mot de 'Mignonne'" (*CH*, VIII, p. 1230–1231). In granting the panther a soul, the soldier does not make a facile statement on his admiration, but rather acknowledges that the two species have established the conditions for a communicative responsiveness. Balzac's intertextual dialogue thus takes up Descartes's own conditions, granting Mignonne an "âme" only once her ability to take part in a pseudo-linguistic exchange has been advanced.

Accordingly, for all the projecting upon Mignonne that critics like Couleau and Plas justifiably accuse the soldier of committing, there is also what Haraway would call a "mutually responsive" (Haraway, 2008, p. 23) element to their relationship. In her *When Species Meet* (2008), Haraway considers another famous human/feline encounter in French letters, that of Derrida in *L'Animal que donc je suis* (2006), in which the philosopher describes a moment of epistemological crisis that occurs when he notices his cat looking at him naked, causing him to feel shame, and then shame *for* his shame before this cat that is itself naked but visibly unperturbed (Derrida, 2006, p. 18). Haraway takes Derrida to task here for letting prudish hangups before his cat interfere with a courteous greeting that would more fully take into consideration the animal other before him. If Derrida's text can reflect on the nature of thought and the ontological status of nonhuman animals, there is little mind given, Haraway suggests, to the ability of human beings to themselves *respond*, that is, to allow for the type of bidirectional communication needed for interspecies kinship:

> Actually to respond to the cat's response to his presence would have required his [...] asking what this cat on this morning cared about, what these bodily postures and visual entanglements might mean and might invite [...] Instead, he concentrated on his shame in being naked before this cat. Shame trumped curiosity, and that does not bode well for an autremondialisation. (*Ibid.*, p. 23)

Just as Haraway argues that Derrida's sexual embarrassment ends up interfering with the possibility of an interspecies mutual responsiveness, the dominant critical interpretation of *Une passion* as a thinly veiled erotic tale has ended up selling short the mutually responsive nature of this human/panther encounter.[2] Bearing in mind the sheer physicality

2 See Plas, 2021, p. 210–213 for more on the history of sexual interpretations of the story. This interpretation continues to be a dominant one; see, most recently, Schuerewegen, 2024.

of their exchanges, as well as the soldier's recurrent feminization of the panther ("C'est comme une petite maîtresse!" [*CH*, VIII, p. 1225]), it is of course impossible to miss the sexual undertones of their rapport. If, however, as Haraway wishes that Derrida had been able to do with his cat, we put aside the sometimes comical, sometimes vexing sexual overtones of this feline/human encounter (whose erotic nature is never overtly articulated, after all[3]), we retain a story that revolves around two species adapting to their readings of the other. In all facets of their interactions, we detect that the soldier adjusts his mannerisms to make them more legible to this panther other; in other words, the soldier does not stop, as does Derrida, at the idea that Mignonne has her own, inaccessible perspective on him, but rather pushes things further by demonstrating an attempt to be responsive to his reading of Mignonne's perspective. The scholarship's emphasis on the soldier's potentially *déformant* point of view is a useful reminder of the ontological haziness of the text, but this haziness does not preclude kinship. Rather, this gesture offers a reflection on interspecies entanglement and modes of relating; as Haraway argues, this is the space in which meaningful interspecies encounters can occur, it "is communication about relationship, the relationship itself, and the means of reshaping relationship and so its enacters" (Haraway, 2008, p. 26).

In this respect, the Saint-Hilairian idea of a complexity-based, hierarchical divide between the human and the panther does not compromise the possibility of kinship. Following the logic of *l'unité de composition*, there is in the panther (lower on the *échelle* as she may be) a capacity that is analogous to that of human language. It then becomes the responsibility of the human to understand what this analogous function is (that is, her various growls, purrs, and gazes), as well as to find the mechanisms through which to make his own linguistic function comprehensible to her. Signficantly, the soldier takes into consideration the sounds that most track with this nonhuman other, gradually adapting his voice to a falsetto call that is responsive to the panther's aural perspective: "Enfin sa compagne avait fini par prendre l'habitude de le regarder quand il criait en voix de fausset: '*Mignonne*'" (*CH*, VIII, p. 1228). From this moment onwards, the story tracks the development of a series of rituals that

3 Göran Blix has even pointed to the logical, narrative inconsistencies behind readings that would insist upon a sexual relationship here (Blix, forthcoming).

allow for increasingly precise exchanges: "Mignonne arriva les babines sanglantes, elle reçut les caresses nécessaires que lui fit son compagnon, en témoignant même par plusieurs *rourou* graves combien elle en était heureuse. Ses yeux pleins de mollesse se tournèrent avec encore plus de douceur que la veille sur le Provençal, qui lui parlait comme à un animal domestique" (*CH*, VIII, p. 1229). With this emphasis on social expectations ("les caresses *nécessaires*"), joyful exchange, a bidirectional communication of purrs and speech, and an attention to gaze, Balzac highlights precisely the sorts of elements that Haraway finds missing in Derrida's feline encounter:

> Can I, the philosopher, respond to an invitation or recognize one when it is offered? What if work and play, and not just pity, open up when the possibility of mutual response, without names, is taken seriously as an everyday practice available to philosophy and to science? […] And what if the question of how animals engage one another's gaze responsively takes center stage for people? (Haraway, 2008, p. 22)

This reformulation of *la question animale* in a manner that takes seriously mutual response is crucial to appreciating Balzac's nonhuman others. Even the tragic ending of the story, far from being the moment of human/animal disconnect that the scholarship has sometimes suggested, is rather presented in the text as analogous to numerous human-human encounters, with the story's frame narrator declaring that the two characters "ont fini comme finissent toutes les grandes passions, par un mal-entendu"; the moment is not framed as one of incomprehensible animal opacity, but rather as a recognizable dynamic between two agents, human or otherwise — thus can the narrator's interlocutor respond in instant recognition: "Et quelquefois dans les plus beaux moments, […] un regard, une exclamation suffisent" (*CH*, VIII, p. 1231–1232).

In its attention to whether Mignonne can be considered a character, or whether the soldier's gaze relies on too anthropocentric of a lens, the scholarship has posed a series of vital questions on animality that nevertheless allow the idea of animal identity to undercut the sophisticated interspecies kinship to be found in Balzac. Lorraine Daston has warned against the facile conflation of anthropomorphism and anthropocentrism in animal studies, writing: "Perhaps if we could formulate questions about understanding other minds in some other mode than 'What is it like to a be an X?' we might partly redeem [...] the pleasures of anthropomorphism" (Daston, 2005, p. 54). And, indeed, *Une passion* cannot answer the question of what it is like to be a panther, but its exploration of animal kinship (by way of feline anthropomorphism) is extraordinarily valuable. In Balzac's Saint-Hilairian transformism, species identity is not fixed, but is rather defined by one's evolving rapports to one's dynamic milieu. In the *désert sans bornes*, the principles of *l'unité de composition* allow for a form of kinship that enables these two species to meaningfully, adaptively respond to one another.

MAKING KIN BY FJORD

In analyzing the panther of *Une passion*, Plas suggests that "Plus que tout autre personnage balzacien et sans doute en raison de sa nature animale, Mignonne défie la connaissance et la représentation à tous les niveaux de la narration" (Plas, 2021, p. 264). However, the titular, androgynous angel of *Séraphîta*, whose gender identity and temperament radically shift depending on who is observing him/her, surely offers Mignonne some serious competition. Throughout the novel, Balzac reflects on the idea of communication across the *échelle des êtres*. As the human beings and angelic figure in the text are both linguistic entities, their exchanges are, on the hand, more easily trackable than those that take place between the soldier and panther. On the other hand, there are significant differences in what human language and the Swedenborgian conception of angelic language can express; as such, the moments of disconnect and projection between them, as well as the vital moments of communicational negotiation, become all the more urgent. In what follows, we will consider the balancing act between continuism and alterity that defines the relationships within Balzac's mystical hybrid of Saint-Hilairian and Swedenborgian thought.

In his "Avant-propos", Balzac signals the intimate connection he detects between Swedenborg and Saint-Hilaire, seeing in Swedenborg "les rudiments de la belle loi du *soi pour soi* sur laquelle repose l'*unité de composition*" (*CH*, I, p. 8). He pushes this connection still further in *Séraphîta*: the titular character, when elaborating her/his Swedenborgian philosophy, turns to transformism as a pillar of her/his vision of universal harmony, anachronistically advancing Saint-Hilairian theory in a novel set in 1800 by suggesting that God works "par l'unité de composition" (*CH*, XI, p. 826–827). In his analysis of Balzac's (mis) readings of Swedenborg, K.-E. Sjöden suggests that the author sought "chez Swedenborg que l'appui de [ses] propres théories" (Sjöden, 1963, p. 299), noting that Balzac's actual engagement with the Swedish philosopher appears to be relegated to the anonymously published *Abrégé des ouvrages d'Ém. Swédenborg* (1788). Indeed, in *Séraphîta*, much of the dramatic sense of the novel ultimately comes from Balzac's own (sometimes disjointed) grafting of *l'unité de composition* onto the Swedenborgian bestiary of humans and angels — while certain classical visions of the *scala naturae* such as Charles Bonnet's *Palingénésie philosophique* (1769) could include angels in their taxonomies, Balzac works to include them here with a more precise evolutionary mechanism.

Séraphîta offers a time-lapsed vision of species transformation, tracking Séraphitüs/Séraphîta's attempts to bring out the angelic traits of his/her human admirers Minna and Wilfrid in a collective effort to transcend/evolve to the next rung of the *échelle des êtres*. Just as the interactions between the soldier and Mignonne are occasionally marred by moments lost in interspecies translation, human and angel alike consistently run into the wall of alterity here. Virtually every scene in the novel is cut short by a moment in which either the human or angel side realizes that an intended message is not properly going through. In the opening sequence of the novel, during a romantic ski expedition with Séraphitüs above the fjord Stromfjord, Minna catches in the angelic gaze a "regard qui la pénétra comme un rayon de soleil traverse le prisme [...]. Elle sentit, sans le comprendre, un abîme entre eux" (*CH*, XI, p. 742). As the novel continues, this *abîme* is increasingly framed as a gulf between *species*. True to the Saint-Hilairian framework, the human and angel experiences contain enough analogous dimensions for a type of sympathy to emerge, but there is everywhere a hierarchical distinction that complicates the possible interactions — thus does Séraphitüs accusingly bemoan Minna's humanness for being overly attached to the material world: "Restes-y, jouis par les sens, obéis à ta nature" (*CH*, XI, p. 746).

As in *Une passion*, the possibilities of interspecies kinship are explored most saliently through the question of language, here once again with an attention to the bidirectional nature of communication. Minna and Wilfrid repeatedly fail to grasp the complexity of angelic, Swedenborgian philosophy, with Séraphitüs/Séraphîta exasperatedly demanding: "Cessez, cessez de m'interroger, nos langages sont différents" (*CH*, XI, p. 827). Importantly, these moments of misunderstanding go in both directions; Séraphitüs/Séraphîta is attuned to the fact that his/her perspective makes it impossible to fully understand these human others. Recalling the "à nos yeux" of the "Avant-propos", Séraphitüs/Séraphîta reflects on his/her gaze in declaring: "Ceux qui sont tout esprit ne pleurent pas [...]. Comment pleurerais-je? Je ne vois plus les misères humaines" (*CH*, XI, p. 745). This inability to see what human eyes see makes it so that he/she is indeed incapable of fully grasping human modes of thinking: "De là vient la solitude où vivent les Esprits Angéliques et leur dédain de ce qui fait les joies humaines. [...] s'ils en entendent les langages, ils n'en comprennent plus les idées" (*CH*, XI, p. 848–849).

The text thus stages a series of negotiations in which the involved species work to bypass these communicative blocks to adapt responsively to one another. Séraphîta later chastises Wilfrid for dealing with her in a jealous, overly *human* way that feels unresponsive to her nature, guiding him in a different, angelic direction: "Si vous aviez l'intelligence de ma nature, vous m'auriez fait de la musique, vous auriez endormi mes ennuis; mais vous m'aimez pour vous et non pour moi" (*CH*, XI, p. 751). This accusation of egocentrism is in effect an accusation of anthropocentrism: in engaging with her from his human perspective, Wilfrid fails to extend care that would be responsive to this angel other.

For all the scholarly attention paid to the soldier's anthropocentric projections onto Mignonne, the sense of projection in *Seraphîta* is much more pervasive. The ever-shifting gender identity of the double-named titular character is described accordingly:

> L'imagination de Minna était complice de cette constante hallucination sous l'empire de laquelle chacun serait tombé, et qui prêtait à Séraphîtüs l'apparence des figures rêvées dans un heureux sommeil. Nul type connu ne pourrait donner une image de cette figure majestueusement mâle pour Minna, mais qui, aux yeux d'un homme, eût éclipsé par sa grâce féminine les plus belles têtes dues à Raphaël. (*CH*, XI, p. 741–742)

Elisabeth Gerwin reads these gender projections in a manner that emphasizes how identity never exists in isolation, but rather in dynamic co-production, arguing that "in this context gender identity emerges in a very modern guise: as a mutable function of the individual's relation to others" (Gerwin, 2020, p. 17). We see here a manner of conceptualizing identity that can be productively applied to the discussion of interspecies kinship in Balzac, recalling the sympoiesis, or *making-with*, underlying Haraway's theory of the Chthulucene (Haraway, 2016, p. 33). Fittingly, when Minna tells Séraphitüs, "Je voudrais être tout toi!", the angelic figure responds by directing her towards a pantheistic merging of the *Tout-Puissant* with all life, thus endorsing a type of ecological sympoiesis on the grandest scale: "si tu veux être pure, mêle toujours l'idée du Tout-Puissant aux affections d'ici-bas, tu aimeras alors toutes les créatures, et ton cœur ira bien haut!" (*CH*, XI, p. 743)

In a novel in which language is consistently an obstacle to interspecies understanding, Séraphitüs/Séraphîta's transformation scene is forthright about its abandoning of linguistic convention. The angel's final interactions with Wilfrid and Minna transcend linguistic expression altogether: "Ces derniers chants ne furent exprimés ni par la parole, ni par le regard, ni par le geste, ni par aucun des signes qui servent aux hommes pour se communiquer leurs pensées, mais comme l'âme se parle à elle-même; car à l'instant où Séraphîta se dévoilait dans sa vraie nature, ses idées n'étaient plus esclaves des mots humains" (*CH*, XI, p. 851). In this brief passage, speech, gaze, gesture, and sign are all given the same status in opposition to angelic communication; the mechanisms through which nonhuman animals like Mignonne communicate are placed on a level playing field with human language in their shared juxtaposition to this ultimate, divine form of communication. The gaze of the nonhuman animal is thus analogous to human language, and both are simply phenomena to be negotiated en route to this ideal of angelic communication, a model of responsiveness "aux pieds de laquelle rampent les Formes et les Espèces de l'Animalité pour reconnaître leur chemin" (*CH*, XI, p. 849).

Interspecies kinship is a sophisticated dance in Balzac. Within his fantastical vision of *l'unité de composition*, there is an ontological continuism that is nevertheless compromised by the rigid hierarchizing of all life along a linear spectrum of progressive development. In both *Une passion* and *Séraphîta*, Balzac does not shy away from this overarching tension within *l'unité de composition*; rather, these texts deftly experiment with this continuism/alterity dichotomy at all stages of their interspecies encounters, asking the vital questions of what constitutes responsiveness and kinship across *l'échelle des êtres*. Indeed, both texts consider the analogous communicative capacities of their nonhuman others, gradually pointing towards novel ways of learning to be responsive to nonhuman responses across the *échelle*; hierarchized as this vision may be, there is a genuine sensitivity to alterity that still embraces the possibility for kinship in Balzac's world.

Christopher Robison
Swarthmore College

WORKS CITED

Appel Toby A., 1987, *The Cuvier-Geoffroy Debate: French Biology in the Decades Before Darwin* (New York: Oxford University Press).

Blix Göran, "Balzac zoographe: l'histoire naturelle de l'amitié dans *Une passion dans le désert*" (forthcoming, unpublished manuscript).

Borderie Régine, 2009, "Le Propre de l'homme: ses figurations animalières dans les portraits de *La Comédie humaine*", *La Comédie animale: le bestiaire balzacien*, ed. by Aude Déruelle, <http://balzac.cerilac.univ-paris-diderot.fr/collectionenligne.html> [accessed 13 January 2025].

Couleau Christèle, 2009, "Les Animaux sont-ils des personnages comme les autres?", *La Comédie animale: le bestiaire balzacien*, *La Comédie animale: le bestiaire balzacien*, sous la ed. by Aude Déruelle, <http://balzac.cerilac.univ-paris-diderot.fr/collectionenligne.html> [accessed 13 January 2025].

Cuvier Georges, 1817, *Le Règne animal distribué d'après son organisation, pour servir de base à l'histoire naturelle des animaux et d'introduction à l'anatomie comparée* (Paris: Deterville).

Daston Lorraine, 2005, "Intelligences: Angelic, Animal, Human", in *Thinking with Animals: New Perspectives on Anthropomorphism*, ed. by Lorraine Daston and Gregg Mitman (New York: Columbia University Press), p. 37–58.

Derrida Jacques, 2006, *L'Animal que donc je suis* (Paris: Galilée).

Descartes René, [1637] 1953, *Discours de la méthode*, in *Œuvres et Lettres* (Paris: Gallimard, « Bibliothèque de la Pléiade »), p. 123–179.

Geoffroy Saint-Hilaire Étienne, 1830, *Principes de philosophie zoologique, discutés en mars 1830, au sein de l'Académie royale des sciences* (Paris: Pichon et Didier).

Gerwin Elisabeth, 2020, "Beyond Pleasure: Androgyny in Balzac's *Séraphîta*", *French Studies*, 74:1, p. 17–34.

Haraway Donna, 2008, *When Species Meet* (Minneapolis: University of Minnesota Press).

Haraway Donna, 2016, *Staying with the Trouble: Making Kin in the Chthulucene* (Durham: Duke University Press).

Hart Kathleen R., 2012, "Strangers to Ourselves: Animality and Theory of Mind in Honoré de Balzac's *A Passion in the Desert*", *Style*, 46:3–4, p. 399–419.

Plas Élisabeth, 2021, *Le Sens des bêtes: rhétoriques de l'anthropomorphisme au XIXe siècle* (Paris: Classiques Garnier).

Schuerewegen Franc, 2024, "La Queue de la panthère: remarques sur l'analyse", *Poétique*, 195, p. 111–119.

Sjöden Karl-Erik, 1963, "Balzac et Swedenborg", *Cahiers de l'Association internationale des études françaises*, 15, p. 295–307.
Somerset Richard, 2002, "The Naturalist in Balzac: The Relative Influence of Cuvier and Geoffroy Saint-Hilaire", *French Forum*, 27:1, p. 81–111.
Thiher Allen, 2001, *Fiction Rivals Science: The French Novel from Balzac to Proust* (Columbia: University of Missouri).
Weil Kari, 2012, *Thinking Animals: Why Animal Studies Now?* (New York: Columbia University Press).

THE ECOLOGY OF EMOTIONS

Exploitation of Nature in Balzac's *Le Lys dans la vallée*

> Si vous voulez voir la nature belle et vierge comme une fiancée, allez là par un jour de printemps; si vous voulez calmer les plaies saignantes de votre cœur, revenez-y par les derniers jours de l'automne; au printemps, l'amour y bat des ailes à plein ciel, en automne on y songe à ceux qui ne sont plus.
> *CH*, IX, p. 987–988.

In his prefatory "Historique du procès" leading to the 1836 publication of *Le Lys dans la vallée*, Honoré de Balzac writes that in the novel he aspired to "étudier la langue française aussi bien que les fibres les plus déliées du cœur, et aborder la grande question du paysage en littérature" (*CH*, IX, p. 922). Set in the natural "paysage" of the Touraine deep within the Indre Valley, Balzac's work does, in fact, explore human love through metaphorical and symbolic language, recounting the forbidden yet unconsummated affair between the coming-of-age Félix de Vandenesse and the older, married mother of two, Comtesse Henriette de Mortsauf, during the Bourbon Restoration. Penned as a confessional letter to his new lover, Comtesse Natalie de Manerville, Félix narrates his past love, the "fantôme" that haunts him through "d'imposants souvenirs ensevelis au fond de [son] âme" (*CH*, IX, p. 970). Beginning with his childhood, he recalls the affair in the Touraine, his short time with Lady Arabelle Dudley in Paris, and his return to the countryside to be at the deathbed of Henriette. Jean-Hervé Donnard points out the autobiographical inspiration for *Le Lys* as well as the stylized depiction of the Touraine: "Si la localisation géographique est précise, la topographie et la toponymie subissent des remaniements" (1978, p. 894). The writer's literary Touraine "est synonyme de beauté, de bonheur et de profusion. [...] En archéologue de la vie sociale, Balzac souhaite certes conserver la mémoire des paysages mais invite également le lecteur à saisir la poésie des lieux".[1] What, though, is the relationship between landscape as object of realist description ("mémoire") and its status as "poésie"? Balzac's work demonstrates the intersection of human feeling, expressed through language, and the portrayal of the nonhuman/natural landscape. In-between the two, the human and the natural, lies representation — but for what end goal? On one hand, Balzac's depiction of the Touraine, seen as "synonyme de beauté" and as an artifact that preserves geographic memory, could be taken as a typically Romantic or pastoral exaltation and idealization of nature itself. On the other, an ecocritical reading might suggest that a stark separation between human and nature is always impossible, even within the realm of representation.

REPRESENTATION

James C. McKusick's *Green Writing: Romanticism and Ecology* presents a persuasive debunking of such an opposition that remains salient some twenty years after its publication. McKusick points to the way in which Romantic writers expressed the "adaption of species to their habitats, [and] the interrelatedness all life forms" (2000, p. 28). He highlights the human/cultural role in literary representation, arguing that writing about nature is inevitably filtered: "it remains excruciatingly difficult to discover or describe the process by which consciousness emerges from the raw sensory data of experience, since human beings always do that kind of meta-analysis through an invisible cultural/political filter" (*ibid.*, p. 16). Furthermore, he argues, "our perception and conception of 'nature' is always filtered, categorized, and constructed by our perceptual/cognitive apparatus" (*ibid.*, p. 17). Therefore, as contemporary

1 "L'Œuvre de Balzac en Touraine", http://www.lysdanslavallee.fr/fr/contenu/loeuvre-de-balzac-en-touraine-0 [accessed 18 December 2024]. This citation comes from a digital collaborative between the Conseil général de l'Indre-et-Loire and organizations including the Société des Amis d'Honoré de Balzac et de la Maison de Balzac.

ecocritical readers concerned with notions of place/space, one could ask: To what extent and with what accuracy does *Le Lys* imagine and preserve "la mémoire des paysages?" Can the sentimental education of Félix (and Henriette) also be read as a memorialization and exaltation of landscape, even if fictionalized, and even if, as will be argued here, exploited for sentimental representation? This analysis explores these questions and the larger issue of literary representation — the human writing nature — by situating *Le Lys* within an ecocritical framework and investigating Balzac's portrayal of the Touraine through his narrator's rhetorically exploitative lens.

While nineteenth-century critics have explored the city/nature divide that the Industrial Revolution forced into the open, this dichotomy has been critiqued as too deterministic and simplistic.[2] However, it would be equally reductive to presume that those experiencing the early Industrial Revolution's transitions in quotidian life would not have been acutely aware of the differences, both material and phenomenalistic, between the natural world/countryside and the developing cities. Balzac is hardly considered a founder of ecological consciousness or a nature writer. And yet, *Le Lys* offers a way to explore not simply what the author thought about nature, but how the natural world was imbricated with human emotions through his realist Romanticism or Romantic realism. Is Balzac's countryside constructed as it is in pastoral novels such as George Sand's *François le champi* (1848), as an idyllic refuge from the economic and social problems of the industrialized city? Does Balzac reveal the dynamics between humans and nonhumans/natural space or does he in fact map the social *through* natural symbols, reinforcing human-to-human and human-to-nature hierarchies prevalent at the time? Balzac's writing of the natural landscape in (and of) the *Le Lys dans la vallée*, whose title itself points to both floral nature ("le lys") and nature-as-symbol (*le lys* standing in for Henriette in the title), reveals the inseparability of human analysis in representation, as consistent with McKusick's claim: there is no writing about nature without or beyond a cultural, social perception. In Balzac's novel, though, it is not only a filtered, cultured/socialized worldview that is presented and mapped onto nature, but also an exploitation of natural representation intended for human purposes. While critical attention has been given to Félix's

2 For more on the city/nature divide, see Green, 1990.

metonymic floral arrangements, this article goes a step beyond to argue that most, if not all, of the floral, *champêtre*, "wilderness" depictions are explicitly used for human consumption and representation.[3] *Le Lys* creates an ecology of emotions that reinforces an anthropocentric view only "natural" at the time.

PAYSAGE

Sent to the countryside, "cet éternel remède des affections" (*CH*, IX, p. 985), the young Félix de Vandenesse falls in obsessive love with Comtesse Henriette de Mortsauf, who, eternally dutiful to the despotic Comte de Mortsauf and their two feeble children, transforms under Félix's gaze into a lily, an incarnated flower that blooms and withers conforming to sentiment. In this text, nature seems to exist solely to express the human and for human use alone. The verdant landscape, the pure air of the valley, the Indre River, the walnut trees, and the ecology of Félix's beloved's space are enveloped within human perception, exploited for emotional representation at both the diegetic (i.e. floral language) and extradiegetic (i.e. epistolary confession) levels.

At first, the natural environment in *Le Lys* can be read as idealized and romanticized, a space where protagonists and readers become "comme les peintres", who come to the valley to create their paintings (*CH*, IX, p. 989). Describing this land to Natalie, Félix writes that "l'œil se perd sous un ciel chaud et vaporeux", offering "un des milles points de vue de ce beau pays" (*CH*, IX, p. 989). This novel, one of Balzac's *Études de Mœurs*: *Scènes de la vie de campagne*, is saturated with depictions of the land, landscape, and flora of the region, prompting the ecocritical reader, to anticipate a narrative lens comparing the natural milieu of rural life to the cityscape as can be found in other stories of the *Comédie humaine*. However, depictions of the Parisian salons and political controversies are sparse and limited to Félix's account of his affair with Lady Dudley. Unlike *Les Paysans* (1855), which offers a deep commentary on industrialized agriculture and the exploitation of the poor, the focus of *Le Lys*

3 See, for example, Comfort, 1998, p. 31–38.

is not on the opposition between the countryside and the city. It is not a story that elaborates upon the city-country dichotomy typical of the époque. The reader beholds Balzac's study of the *paysage*, the aesthetic beauty of a Touraine yet to be adulterated by "too" much progress. The countryside, where numerous real and fictionalized sick were sent to be healed, physically or mentally, appears as a hopeful space for an apathetic young man on the precipice of his sentimental education, and the right place to encourage the health of an anemic daughter and suffering mother.

And yet, Félix and Henriette are never quite fully cured in and by the space: they are enclosed by their own gaze on the imaginary horizon, always on the threshold, pacing the terrace, slipping between inside and outside, and within, a constructed natural domain that reflects the social construction of the human world. As Karen Quandt explains: "The spectacle of nature […] is not merely an intellectual or aesthetic experience […] Nature provokes a physical response, and an 1830s romanticism veering towards a more immediate and visceral experience of nature (Sand) and society (Balzac) did not shy away from this new sense of penetration" (2017, p. 365). This "natural" place in *Le Lys*, whose hyperbolized representation promises infinite love — "L'amour n'est-il pas dans les espaces infinis de l'âme, comme est dans une belle vallée le grand fleuve où se rendent les pluies, les ruisseaux et les torrents, où tombent les arbres et les fleurs" (*CH*, IX, p. 1129–1130) — paradoxically limits (and is limited by) the natural to the social domain.

EMOTION

The representation of the environment in *Le Lys* is in fact a representation of the ecology of emotions and the limits this entails. Even before the looming reality of the increasingly insalubrious cities began their sprawl into rural space and before the corresponding rural exodus to the city, Balzac's vision of the countryside, as imagined in this love story, implies a problematic fate of natural space: already dominated by the human gaze, agricultural use, and the social constructions of lineage and estates, the landscape falls victim to an anthropocentric, unidirectional view placing human emotion above all else. As Francesco Spandri writes, "ce retour du sol à la vie 'sous toutes ses formes, végétale, économique, spirituelle' n'échappe pas aux tensions d'un équilibre toujours précaire entre pessimisme et utopie" (2019, p. 523). There is a clear ecological tension in this text, hidden beneath a flowery rhetoric, but indicative of Balzac's modern ideology wherein human economy (human use of land for profit and for emotional expression) spreads beyond the city.

By 1835, natural space as depicted by Romantic writers was already imbricated within an emotional context equating human affect with the natural world and evoking feelings of "melancholia and nostalgia toward the past times" (Moruno, 2011–2012, p. 248). The Romantic period, as Dolores Martín Moruno suggests, "provided a fertile ground for the development of ecological concerns" (*ibid.*) as it connected human sentiment intimately to the natural nonhuman world. Nature as an object of study for creative reflection and as a proxy for human emotions helped set the stage for a conception of ecology historicized and contextualized within emotional experience rather than solely as "a scientific discipline to describe the mutual relations of plants, animals, geography and the climate to each other and to their environment" (*ibid.*, p. 247–248). By the mid to late century, poets and writers explored the relationship between artistic production and the projection of emotions onto environment. John Ruskin's description of this relationship as "pathetic fallacy" would eventually be a basis for affect theory. The Romantic "invention of nature" (*ibid.*, p. 248) thus included a conception of nature and ecology rooted in human-nature relationships and expressed through art in rhetorical devices such as personification and anthropomorphism. With the progressive industrialization of the nineteenth century, humans sought refuge, escape, and reconnection in the earlier romanticized and idealized versions of the land.

Le Lys could be read in this vein. Touraine is depicted as an escape from the potentially dangerous political scene in Paris. Félix is sent to the countryside to be healed from his "apathie": "La campagne, cet éternel remède des affections auxquelles la médecine ne connaît rien, fut regardée comme le meilleur moyen de me sortir de mon apathie" (*CH*, IX, p. 985–986). In fact, the natural space is not only seen as a remedy, but as a medium to reinvigorate and inspire feelings. As Christophe

Morhange points out, "Pour Balzac, ces lieux communiquent à l'âme leur sérénité. Ils semblent avoir, dans un premier temps, un pouvoir quasi magique de guérison [...] La perception du paysage de la vallée correspondait donc à la construction d'un espace idéalisé" (1991, p. 48). Furthermore, just as for Romantic writers, nature serves as a site that renders expressiveness possible by the abundant signs readily available to the protagonists' gaze within the symbolic register. Félix's first descriptions of the Touraine reveal a freedom unknown to him in Paris: "Pour la première fois de ma vie, je pouvais m'arrêter sous un arbre, marcher lentement ou vite à mon gré sans être questionné par personne" (*CH*, IX, p. 986). He describes a freedom to wander, to idle, to explore the physical sites of "les beautés de la nature champêtre" (*CH*, IX, p. 986), without being "écrasé par les différents despotismes qui, peu ou prou, pèsent sur toutes les jeunesses" (*CH*, IX, p. 986).

Even during his childhood, Félix had been drawn to the external world, feeling neglected by his family. His unencumbered, joyful moments were in the garden where he could enjoy the kinesthetic closeness of the natural world: "Je bénissais mon abandon, et me trouvais heureux de pouvoir rester dans le jardin à jouer avec des cailloux, à observer des insectes, à regarder le bleu du firmament" (*CH*, IX, p. 971). Despite the refuge this space provides, it does not offer him full independence. In the garden after dark, Félix's mother catches him staring at a star. She mocks him after his governess inquires as to where he is: "Que faisiez-vous donc là? me dit-elle. – Je regardais une étoile. – Vous ne regardiez pas une étoile, dit ma mère qui nous écoutait du haut de son balcon, connaît-on l'astronomie à votre âge?" (*CH*, IX, p. 972) Accused of not turning off a spigot in the garden, Félix is punished: "Mais, châtiment horrible! je fus persiflé sur mon amour pour les étoiles, et ma mère me défendit de rester au jardin le soir [...]. J'eus donc souvent le fouet pour mon étoile" (*CH*, IX, p. 972). The star, unlike his family became not only the object of his attention but his confidant: "je lui disais mes chagrins" (*CH*, IX, p. 972). Early on, nature provides Félix with the emotional space to feel and express his sentiments. Similarly, Madame de Mortsauf is off limits to Félix, out of physical reach, but within sight and confidante status. She becomes the physical incarnation of his star after their first encounter: "ma chère étoile s'était donc faite femme en conservant sa clarté, ses scintillements et sa fraîcheur" (*CH*, IX, p. 985).

This childhood scene not only foreshadows Félix and Henriette's relationship, but also sets up Félix's positioning to the countryside. It is simultaneously a site of escape and dreaming, a recipient for Félix's inner thoughts and feelings, and a source of possible punishment and confinement. In the Touraine there are man-made gardens and named domains, governed by the human. In other words, the natural cannot and does not escape the social, despite the possible freedom the countryside seems to offer. There is no attainable, inhabitable nature-space outside the social realm or outside the symbolic register. Félix, after all, could only speak to the star from within an enclosed space; "his" nature would always be infected by the mocking and punishments of his superior, reinforcing familial and social hierarchies.

This despite the fact that when Félix first arrives in the countryside, the Touraine appears to promise a literal freedom, a continuous space to explore by foot and by sight. As Owen Heathcote explains, "At first sight, Touraine seems to represent unadulterated joy. Félix de Vandenesse's walk into the valley of the Indre is, in this respect, justly famous as a moment of newfound freedom" (2003, p. 17). But his exploration is recounted through a confessional lens: the narrative voice inevitably frames and dictates the spatial limits through representation itself. "Le sentiment du beau" is juxtaposed with "la poésie des sites" (*CH*, IX, p. 986). Félix loves the Touraine "comme un artiste aime l'art" (*CH*, IX, p. 988). Félix's depiction of the Touraine cannot be separated from his telling of it, as Heathcote justly notes:

> Touraine, that seemingly quintessential evocation of spontaneous, unmediated, unadulterated nature, is also, at least in part, artificial, created, as Félix admits [...] Touraine is enveloped not just by its 'tapisseries' but by memory which is, as we have seen, also associated with the 'productions marines' of the Loire. Touraine is, therefore, doubly encased and encasing – in 'nature' and in 'art'. (2003, p. 17)

Through its literary purpose of artistic expression and as an emotional exploit, the natural landscape can only be seen from within human perception and representation. Again, Heathcote's analysis is useful: "This linking of language, feeling and landscape is particularly evident in the Touraine letter-novels, *Sténie* and *Le Lys*, where the emotions of the narrator colour the events, characters and environments described" (*ibid.*, p. 24). Heathcote's analysis reinforces the objective Balzac set out in his preface, to study language, feeling, and *paysage*, demonstrating the interconnected of the three through literary representation.

EXPLOITATION

Félix almost immediately turns Henriette vegetal, into an object amongst the landscape, using the natural to describe the human and as a way to represent his feelings: he catches sight of a "point blanc" that "brillait dans ce vaste jardin comme au milieu des buissons verts éclatait la clochette d'un convolvulus, flétrie si l'on y touche" (*CH*, IX, p. 988). Comparisons between Henriette and her surroundings continue throughout the text. She is "le lys de cette vallée" (*CH*, IX, p. 987), her voice the "chant d'hirondelle joyeuse" (*CH*, IX, p. 995), her eyes are "verdâtres", and her complexion is "comparable au tissu des camélias blancs" (*CH*, IX, p. 996). Even her mood is represented by a seasonal vocabulary; Félix explicitly describes her emotions as "natural" and cyclical: "La renaissance de Mme de Mortsauf fut naturelle, comme les effets du mois de mai sur les prairies, comme ceux du soleil et de l'onde sur les fleurs abattues. Comme notre vallée d'amour, Henriette avait eu son hiver, elle renaissait comme elle au printemps" (*CH*, IX, p. 1101). Here, the valley is appropriated linguistically and possessively by Félix; it is no longer *the* valley, but "*notre*" valley of love, employed for their use. As Anne-Marie Perrin-Naffakh has aptly pointed out, nature is interpreted time and again in *Le Lys* from within the narrator's subjectivity.[4] Even with Henriette's eventual death, she is linked to the space from where she seemed to grow in Félix's eyes: "il y eut un gémissement unanime mêlé de pleurs qui semblait faire croire que cette vallée pleurait son âme" (*CH*, IX, p. 1212). Here, is it not only Félix who sees her and mourns her, as part of the land, but also the *campagnards* and the valley itself; the emotions of the people and the valley are indistinguishable, "unanime",

4 See Perrin-Naffakh, 1994, p. 77: "Pour les deux protagonistes au moins, paysages et sentiments sont d'emblée consubstantiels [...] les paysages ont pour trait commun d'être indissociables de la subjectivité des personnages". See also Kadish: "Félix, as describer of nature, to believe that landscape exists as some static aesthetic phenomenon in the eternal present of his own subjective vision" (1983, p. 13).

"mêlé". Henriette's burial amongst the "cailloux et le gravier de la terre" weakens Félix ("mon courage m'abandonna" [*CH*, IX, p. 1212]), again highlighting the continuity of nature and human emotion.

Rarely is nature depicted as solitary and autonomous, examined in its own state, set apart from Félix's perspective. As an epistolary narrator, Félix uses nature to convey the symbolic meaning of his first love to Natalie. Even before recounting his recent past, he describes his earliest memories using nature similes, linking sentiment to nature from his first paragraph: "J'ai d'imposants souvenirs ensevelis au fond de mon âme comme ces productions marines qui s'aperçoivent par les temps calmes, et que les flots de la tempête jettent par fragments sur la grève" (*CH*, IX, p. 970). Projecting his feelings onto the space, Félix fills the landscape with rhetoric, so that the possible infiniteness of the countryside collapses in on itself and reflects back to him, enclosing the human within the natural, claiming its purpose, its use, and its poetic inspiration for human consumption and circulation. Throughout his letter, Félix equates human emotion with nature, drawing on comparisons and metaphors to explain his experience to Natalie: "Si pour beaucoup d'êtres les passions ont été des torrents de lave écoulés entre des rives desséchées, n'est-il pas des âmes où la passion contenue par d'insurmontables difficultés a rempli d'une eau pure le cratère du volcan?" (*CH*, IX, p. 1061) Here, Félix does not describe and exalt nature's power in and of itself, but uses it to symbolize his passion. Nature becomes a sort of echo chamber for the characters: "c'est presque toujours à travers l'émotion qu'un paysage est perçu, interprété, construit [...] La nature se fait langage, écho ou interprète de l'humain sinon personnage de l'histoire" (Perrin-Naffakh, 1994, p. 74). According to Michel Collot, this type of relationship reveals a narcissism inherent to the "valorisation romantique du paysage", valuing nature solely in relation to the human: "La correspondance entre le paysage et l'état de l'âme est un mirage, le pur produit d'une conscience narcissique qui projette son image dans un monde réduit au rôle du miroir" (2005, p. 79).

Nature is used by Félix and Henriette to express their feelings through nonverbal means, which are equally described through a self-referencing and aggrandizing rhetoric. Félix creates bouquets to offer Henriette as an expression and representation of his love. He explores the land, throwing himself into it, for the purpose of extracting flowers to be contained in vases and to represent his feelings: "Je m'élançai dans les champs, dans les vignes, et j'y cherchai des fleurs pour lui composer deux bouquets" (*CH*, IX, p. 1053). While Félix considers the aesthetic harmony of the flowers' colors and leaves "tout en cueillant une à une, les coupant au pied, les admirant, je pensai que les couleurs et les feuillages avaient une harmonie", he immediately connects this harmony to human language, sensorial experience, and sentiment: "une poésie qui se faisait jour dans l'entendement en charmant le regard, comme les phrases musicales réveillent mille souvenirs au fond des cœurs aimants et aimés" (*CH*, IX, p. 1053). This "language of flowers", as Kathleen Ann Comfort explains, "was prevalent in nineteenth-century France, which by all accounts was in rapture over things floral" (1998, p. 32). Balzac situates the literary, symbolic use of flowers within a social trend of the time, recognizing the impact of customs on his readership and within the natural world he creates within *Le Lys*. Doris Kadish's reading that the lily motif is both an explicit "symbol of purity and equated with the novel's pristine, virtuous heroine, Mme de Mortsauf" and more implicitly, the "*fleur-de-lis*, symbol of monarchy" (1983, p. 8) offers further support to the argument that nature is exploited for even more than sentiment: it represents the political sphere and social fabric of human interactions, as is indicative of Balzac's emphasis on social-economic-political mapping. Félix and Henriette will never be together within the social domain; for them the natural one represents the only space of possibility, but this too, is dominated by an inescapable social hierarchy.

HUMAN

The estates of the Touraine are owned and named; humans possess the land. The Comte de Mortsauf, "le représentant d'une famille historique en Touraine, dont la fortune date de Louis XI" (*CH*, IX, p. 989–990) is proud to display his land and farm to Félix, with possessive adjectives dominating the tour of the grounds: "mes seigles", "sa haie", "ses cours et ses bâtiments" (*CH*, IX, p. 1014). The literal exploitation of the land for agricultural and economic purposes, passed back to the aristocracy by the Restoration, is explicit in the text, with the land linked to human ownership and wealth: "La Comtesse de Mortsauf devenait ainsi l'une des plus riches héritières du Maine [...], le comte pouvait acheter deux domaines voisins qui valaient environ neuf mille livres de rente" (*CH*, IX, p. 1039). The land secures the Mortsaufs' social status, providing wealth and lineage, while also bringing different social groups together. During the harvest, "les vendangeurs sont nourris au logis. Ces repas étant les seuls où ces pauvres gens aient, chaque année, des aliments substantiels et bien préparés, ils y tiennent comme dans les familles patriarcales les enfants tiennent aux galas des anniversaires. [...] La maison est donc pleine de monde et de provisions [...], les rangs sont confondus: femmes, enfants, maîtres et gens" (*CH*, IX, p. 1059–1060). The careful management of the estate produces an abundance of ripe grapes wherein the "ciel y sourit toujours en Touraine", producing not only crops but "plaisir" for the different classes (*CH*, IX, p. 1059). This countryside, this Touraine, is not an unadulterated, *sauvage* space, and Balzac would perhaps never have claimed it was. Balzac's nature is one that is created in a narrative space, across diegetic levels, and with an awareness of social construction and a construction of memory istelf: "la mémoire des créateurs est imprégnée de divers modèles plus ou moins canoniques, modèles qui risquent de se surimposer à la représentation spontanée de la nature" (Vanoncini, 2004, p. 356). Or, to employ Roland Chollet's words, Balzac created the Touraine, rather than reproducing it,

> L'enjeu est ici une autre Touraine, *qui naîtra du roman* – et non l'inverse –, Touraine inventée d'après la 'vraie', rechargée de désir, d'affectivité insatisfaite, plénitude qui a l'intensité du vide dont elle procède. Cet espace maternel, essentiellement mélancolique, celui de la maternité sans la mère, caractérise la Touraine balzacienne mais aussi d'autres paysages de *La Comédie humaine* et peut-être, d'une manière plus générale, l'image de la nature chez Balzac (2003, p. 174).

This is not to say that there is no place for Balzac's representation of natural space in contemporary ecocritical studies or in an attempt to "reach the utopian reconciliation of man and nature" based on "hope, a revolutionary emotion, which projected our memories of a past unity with nature in a future (re)union" (Moruno, 2011–2012, p. 256). The use of nature to express sentiment can be a driving force in its continued representation, preservation of "la mémoire", and protection: "The prevailing vision of humanity-in-nature in the world-system is one in which humans terraform and extract for profit — an instrumentalization of nature that inevitably rebounds on humanity" (Rose, 2024, p. 9). Current concerns surrounding environmental protection suggest that human sentiment is necessary for ecological preservation, as Kay Milton proposes in *Loving Nature: Towards an Ecology of Emotion*: "But to be effective, they have to be affective. The motivating force of an argument (and of anything else) lies in its emotional impact" (2002, p. 95). The question must be asked: Could Balzac have let nature stand alone and outside of emotional and literary exploitation, where nature is shown to have its own agency and autonomy through a symbiosis that envelopes humans within the natural? As Michel Juffré argues in *À la recherche d'une humanité durable*, there are avenues for an ideology shift, for humans to value nonhuman life and lifeforms differently, more equally, and reject teleological and hierarchical positioning of the human as the highest life form. Balzac's narrative style in *Le Lys* is essentially anthropocentric. Despite the interludes of aestheticized, idealized romantic depictions of flowers and rivers and hills, the voice is confessional, an epistolary form that narrates and thus dominates. The form does not cede to the content but rather works to emphasize the narrator's exploitation of the natural environment to express his feelings, his ultimate perspective, cemented within the socio-political-anthropocentric Balzacian map. As was his objective, Balzac did not only endeavor to "aborder la grande question du paysage en littérature" in this work, but also to study language and human emotion — "je voulais surtout étudier la langue française aussi bien que les fibres les plus déliées du cœur" (*CH*, IX, p. 922) – binding language, sentiment, and landscape representation inextricably together at *Le Lys*'s literary inception.

Abbey Carrico
Virginia Military Institute

WORKS CITED

Chollet Roland, 2003, "*Sténie*, la Touraine inventée", *AB*, p. 163–178.

Collot Michel, 2005, *Paysage et poésie du romantisme à nos jours* (Paris: Librairie José Corti).

Comfort Kathleen Ann, 1998, "Floral Emblems of Health in Balzac's *Le lys dans la vallée*", *Dalhousie French Studies*, 44, p. 31–38.

Donnard Jean-Hervé, 1978, "Introduction" to *Le Lys dans la vallée*, *CH*, IX, p. 875–913.

Green Nicholas, 1990, *The Spectacle of Nature: Landscape and Bourgeois Culture in Nineteenth-century France* (Manchester University Press).

Heathcote Owen, 2003, "The Work of Memory: Sexuality, Violence and Writing in Balzac's Touraine", *Journal of Romance Studies*, 3.2, p. 15–29.

Juffré Michel, 2018, *À la recherche d'une humanité durable* (Paris: L'Harmattan).

Kadish Doris Y., 1983, "The Ambiguous Lily Motif in Balzac's *Le Lys dans la vallée*", *The International Fiction Review*, 10.1, p. 8–14.

McKusick James C., 2000, *Green Writing: Romanticism and Ecology* (New York: St. Martin's Press).

Milton Kay, 2002, *Loving Nature: Towards an Ecology of Emotion* (New York: Routledge).

Morhange Christophe, 1991, "*Le Lys dans la vallée*: Modèle d'organisation et de signification de l'espace", *Mappemonde*, 1.3, p. 46–48.

Moruno Dolores Martín, 2011–2012, "Feeling Nature: Emotions and Ecology", *Bollettino Filosofico*, 27, p. 247–261.

Perrin-Naffakh Anne-Marie, 1994, "*Le Lys dans la vallée*: Variations sur le thème végétal", *Champs du signe*, 4.1, p. 71–84.

Quandt Karen F., 2017, "Embodying Ecopoetry: Victor Hugo, Love, and Landscape", *Nineteenth-Century Contexts*, 29. 5, p. 365–381.

Rose Kristin, 2024, "Post-extraction Possibility: Genre and Landscape in George Eliot's The Mill on the Floss", *Novel: A Forum on Fiction*, 57 (1), p. 1–21.

Spandri Francesco, 2019, "Balzac et le non-sens de la terre", *French Studies*, 73.4, p. 513-524.

Vanoncini André, 2004, "Balzac et les couleurs", *AB*, p. 355–366.

NIGHT AIR

Miasma Theory and *La Cousine Bette*

Throughout his work, Balzac presents the French capital as a site of natural and climatic significance, repeatedly pointing to an inextricable association between ecological particularities and night time. Nocturnal scenes set in the city streets abound in the Paris cycle and present an urban topography characterised by cold, humidity and mud; the opening moments of *Ferragus* as Auguste de Maulincour stalks Clémence Desmarets in the shadows of rue Soly and *Splendeurs et misères des courtisane*'s sinister rue de Langlade chapter offer two memorable examples. Night time and nocturnal space provide fruitful tools for Balzac to think about a myriad of questions in his writing, including social class, the environment, public health, gender and modernity, while his depiction of a deleterious night constitutes one of the structural motifs that underpin *La Comédie humaine* overall. Yet there has been no in-depth examination of the significance of the nocturnal experience in this author's work to date, still less of the environmental perspective which permeates his nocturnal poetics.

The present essay focuses on the culmination of Balzac's ecological interpretations of the Parisian night in one of his final major works, *La Cousine Bette* (1846). Through the metaphor of nocturnal miasma, the novel represents the spread of contagion and vice in the July Monarchy cityscape, where no part of the ecosystem is left unscathed. This historical period is characterised by a marked surge in nocturnal entertainments and curiosity regarding nightlife more generally, as well as by the rise of the public health movement. *La Cousine Bette*'s miasma metaphor thus reproduces anxieties regarding the blurring of social boundaries in contemporary Parisian nightlife and questions state-advanced claims that physical and moral disease can be geographically and socially circumscribed. By bringing nocturnal superstitions and hackneyed tropes into dialogue with contemporary debates in medical humanities and urban planning, *La Cousine Bette*'s miasma metaphor presents a productive site for Balzac to investigate spatial segregation and change in July Monarchy society, and a compelling locus for the manifestation of middle-class fears regarding a morally corrupt night. Ultimately, by drawing attention to the social alienation of the popular classes and proponents of nocturnal counter-culture, *La Cousine Bette*'s miasmic imagery demonstrates the impossibility of the July Monarchy regime propped up by a bourgeoisie whose capitalist interests impose an increasingly outdated diurnal bias on contemporary life.

Written in the summer of 1846 and serialised in *Le Constitutionnel* from October of the same year, *La Cousine Bette* tells the story of the vengeful Lisbeth Fischer who enlists the seductive skills of her friend and accomplice Valérie Marneffe to bring about the downfall of her Hulot relatives. Beginning in July 1838 and ending in early 1846, it spans a significant portion of the July Monarchy and thus offers contemporary readers a panorama of the regime just as it enters the period of crisis which will ultimately lead to its collapse in 1848.[1] In tracing the miasma metaphor woven through *La Cousine Bette*, this article recontextualises the novel, allowing a new interpretation where Balzac's resurrection of outmoded superstitions regarding miasmic "night air" (Baldwin, 2003, p. 413) brings together two subjects of significant contemporary discourse, urban public health and nightlife, at a critical historical moment. The enmeshed nature of July Monarchy society is evoked at the novel's outset by means of the *quartier du Doyenné*'s fetid night air, setting up a thread of contagion that contaminates all that follows and culminates in Valérie Marneffe's deathbed "miasmes délétères" (*CH*, VII, p. 433), a concluding torrent of tears, and the baron Hulot's escape from the city's miasmic clutches. Building on the notion of an olfactory revolution in the early nineteenth century (Corbin, 1982), the article considers the 1832 cholera epidemic and concomitant rise of the hygiene movement and consequent preoccupation with air quality and contagion. Night air became imbued with socio-cultural significance under the July Monarchy given the changing nocturnal experience and concerns that "la nuit parisienne sert d'en-dessous, de souterrain quotidien, comme si elle couvait une explosion à venir" (Delattre, 2003, p. 38). I argue

1 A poor harvest and consequent rise in food prices in the summer of 1846 marked the beginning of the end for the July Monarchy regime.

that the language of miasma theory is manipulated in *La Cousine Bette* in a bid to interrogate socio-political change and prejudices regarding the nocturnal city in July Monarchy France, before closing with some remarks on how this contextualisation of *La Cousine Bette* alongside miasma theory and nocturnal culture finds fruitful parallels in today's post-Covid-19 society and provides important historical context for current environmental trends in Night Studies scholarship.

Scholars such as Corbin (1982), Barnes (2006), and Vigarello (2014) have previously investigated dirt, odour and air in nineteenth-century Paris, revealing a significant ecological dimension to analysis of the capital city. Studies of mud (Lascar, 2009) and smells (Dupuis, 2009) in Balzac's Parisian fiction have similarly highlighted these characteristics of the nineteenth-century city; however, their comments pertain mostly to the daytime. The Parisian night scenes in Balzac's novels demonstrate a uniquely nocturnal microclimate, a fact which shows the significance of the connection between Parisian ecology and the nocturnal experience in these works, as well as suggesting a wider connection between night time and public health in nineteenth-century Paris. The singular night-time ecology established in the early *rue du Doyenné* episode of *La Cousine Bette* operates as a vector for July Monarchy moral judgment and socio-political criticism, and the metaphor of spreading miasma initiated in these moments replicates the authoritie's warnings of moral contamination in the face of growing curiosity about the nocturnal experience. More broadly, the motif of a harmful, insalubrious night that recurs across *La Comédie humaine* and reaches its pinnacle in *La Cousine Bette* attests to a developing awareness of the inextricable relationship between humans and the environment in the face of nineteenth-century industrialisation and urbanisation.

THE "DRAME BIOLOGIQUE"[2] OF THE *QUARTIER DU DOYENNÉ*

In contrast to the business of the daytime city, the tranquillity that descends after dark allows space for the natural world to return to the fore. The early night scene of *La Cousine Bette* set in the deprived *quartier du Doyenné* — home to the novel's eponymous character and her eventual co-conspirator Valérie Marneffe — illustrates this nocturnal deceleration and concomitant ecological resurgence. Chevalier has highlighted "les fondements biologiques" (2002, p. xix) of social discord during this period and this is borne out in the environmental and medical emphasis that characterises this nocturnal street scene and which recurs throughout the novel.[3] Societal division is embedded from the outset through the striking contrast which the *quartier du Doyenné* provides with the comparative affluence of Bette's Hulot relatives. The novel's opening details the bright daylight, fresh air and spaciousness of the Hulot residence, thus highlighting the severity of the family's subsequent *chute* to the *quartier du Doyenné*. The gas lighting and wide avenues of the more prosperous parts of July Monarchy Paris have not yet reached the *quartier du Doyenné*.[4] By foregrounding the shadowy gloom, Balzac draws a connection between the late hour, the narrow "ruelles", "petits jardins" and "baraques" (*CH*, VII, p. 80), and the diseased atmosphere of this neighbourhood:

> Enterrées déjà par l'exhaussement de la place, ces maisons sont enveloppées de l'ombre éternelle que projettent les hautes galeries du Louvre, noircies de ce côté par le souffle du Nord. Les ténèbres, le silence, l'air glacial, la

2 Chevalier, 2002, p. xvii.

3 During the 1832 epidemic, the nocturnal hours were a moment of further social segregation with a clear divide between those circulating in the elite neighbourhoods where nocturnal entertainments carried on as normal and the socially-disadvantaged who inhabited the cholera-stricken parts of the city.

4 In these decades before Haussmannisation, the work of urban reconstruction had already begun. The narrow streets of pre-modern Paris began to be supplanted with spacious boulevards and improvements were made in street lighting. These changes served at first as a social indicator: gas lighting was first introduced to areas frequented by the elite, while the less effective *réverbère à l'huile* remained in the more deprived neighbourhoods for some years longer.

> profondeur caverneuse du sol concourent à faire de ces maisons des espèces de cryptes, des tombeaux vivants. Lorsqu'on passe en cabriolet le long de ce demi-quartier mort, [...] l'âme a froid, l'on se demande qui peut demeurer là, ce qui doit s'y passer le soir, à l'heure où cette ruelle se change en coupe-gorge, et où les vices de Paris, enveloppés du manteau de la nuit, se donnent pleine carrière. (*CH*, VII, p. 100)

This passage and the surrounding paragraphs develop an idea first mentioned in *Splendeurs et misères des courtisanes*, underlining the link between the nocturnal hours and the unique "conditions atmosphériques" and "nature étrange" of the *rue de Langlade* (*CH*, VI, p. 447). Balzac presents a microclimate that is specifically nocturnal: repetition of "froid" and reference to "le souffle du Nord" convey the drop in temperature, while a semantic field of moisture — "l'air glacial", "un marais", "un océan de pavés moutonnants" (*CH*, VII, p. 100) — is woven throughout the description. These details are compounded by repeated references to this group of dwellings as a "pâté de maisons" (*CH*, VII, p. 99); a term that denotes a block of houses, "pâté" also signifies a defensive fortification surrounded by water, further underlining the geographical and social alienation of this area and its inhabitants. These dank and poorly ventilated streets present a landscape intimately associated with disease in the July Monarchy consciousness. The 1832 cholera epidemic and resulting deaths of more than twenty thousand Parisians had brought attention to the topography of the disease.[5] Particularly prevalent among the poorer population, cholera became intertwined in the public mind with the more deprived parts of the city: "toute une répartition sociale se lit en cette répartition de la mortalité [...] tout un paysage urbain aussi" (Chevalier, 2002, p. xviii). The epidemic also brought miasma theory to the forefront of July Monarchy discourse as a potential airborne explanation for disease transmission. Night air therefore proves significant in this representation of the Doyenné area, as it establishes the humid conditions essential to miasma. If, as Jean-Luc Steinmetz asserts, "rarement l'eau nous apparaît comme une simple présence" in the novels of *La Comédie humaine*, night air also proves "porteuse de sens" (1969, p. 24) in *La Cousine Bette* and Balzac is exploiting recent subjects of public concern in July Monarchy society in order to manipulate his readers' sensibilities.

---

5 For more on this topic, see Leca, 1982; Kudlick, 1996; Chevalier, 1958.

Together with the cholera epidemic, the early decades of the nineteenth century also witnessed the development of the public hygiene movement in France and the consequent appearance of a number of publications on public health, including Alexandre Parent-Duchâtelet's treatise on the city's sewerage system: *Essai sur les cloaques ou égouts de la ville de Paris* (1824) and Louis-René Villermé's work on the correlation between health and social class: *Tableau de l'état physique et moral des ouvriers employés dans les manufactures de coton, de laine et de soie* (1840). Imagery related to human waste gradually became associated with the urban imaginary in the years following and further established the July Monarchy myth of a miasmic city swirling with pestilent vapours such that writers such as Jules Janin were led to declare that "Paris est bâti sur un vaste cloaque" (1839, p. 6). Balzac's interpretation of the *quartier du Doyenné* lends further credence to this contemporary connection between the city streets, damp pestilence and human filth, echoing night scenes in *Splendeurs et misères des courtisanes* (1838–1847) — where the *rue de Langlade* chapter focuses on description of refuse and foul matter and spells out links to prostitution by means of fantastic imagery — and *Gambara* (1837) — where "égout" (*CH*, X, p. 460) imagery is coupled with description of a morally corrupt working class and a disgusted elite. Given the close relationship between disease and air quality for his bourgeois readership, Balzac's representation of the dark and dank streets of popular Paris likely evoked revulsion. "Souligner la fétidité des classes laborieuses, et donc mettre l'accent sur le risque d'infection que leur seule présence comporte, contribue à entretenir cette terreur justificatrice dans laquelle la bourgeoisie se complaît et qui endigue l'expression de son remords" (Corbin, 1982, p. 168). The watery miasmic metaphor is unique to *La Cousine Bette*, however, and represents the culmination of Balzac's thinking on the insalubrious and hostile night. Used to emphasise the spread of moral corruption throughout French society, the "parfum choisi" (*CH*, VII, p. 101) exuded by Valérie in the Doyenné episode is inextricably associated with the area's pestilential night air and her refusal to play the *honnête femme* given as the reason of this intoxicating scent. The moral lesson of Valérie's behaviour becomes clear later when her scent re-emerges in a distorted form as the "miasmes délétères" (*CH*, VII, p. 433) of her deathbed. The danger associated with the surrounding atmosphere is further underlined through the character of Crevel and his olfactive profession of perfumer. As a result of his association with the contaminated Valérie Marneffe, he too will perish.

The relationship between a watery atmosphere and death in Balzac's novels is exemplified in the Doyenné episode through the intertwining of vocabulary relating to both themes (Besson, 2003, p. 307–329). Alongside the aforementioned lexical field of moisture, the protracted demise of this "demi-quartier mort" is suggested through references to "cryptes" and oxymoronic "tombeaux vivants" (*CH*, VII, p. 100). Compounded by the late hour, this death imagery recalls the eighteenth-century "poésie de la nuit et des tombeaux" (Van Tieghem, 1921, p. 7) and, coupled with the solitary nature of this landscape, bears traces of macabre romanticism. Despite this scene's situation early in the novel, there is a clear sense of an ending. "Le résidu d'un ancien quartier en démolition depuis le jour où Napoléon résolut de terminer le Louvre" (*CH*, VII, p. 99), the Doyenné scene fulfils Balzac's "mission d'historien" (Guichardet, 1999, p. 166) as he records the signs of destruction and disrepair marking these "maisons condamnées à disparaître" (*CH*, VII, p. 100), a detail that also hints at the eventual fate of those who inhabit this neighbourhood.[6] This destruction is echoed in Valérie's physical decay and death later in the novel. Valérie's ending is already written, not only in the fatal night air, but in the very ruins which surround her home: "ces prétendues maisons", "un océan de pavés moutonnants", "des steppes de pierre de taille et de démolitions" (*CH*, VII, p. 100).[7] Reduced on her deathbed to an "amas de pourriture" (*CH*, VII, p. 431), "tas de boue" and "chair décomposée" (*CH*, VII, p. 432), her husband "pestiféré" (*CH*, VII, p. 433), Valérie suffers a physical decomposition that replicates the debris and putrefaction of the Doyenné landscape and illustrates the logical conclusion of the blurring of physical and moral hygiene prevalent in public discourse of the period.[8]

The author's "mission d'historien" (Guichardet, 1999, p. 166) notwithstanding, Balzac adapted reality to suit his literary purpose.

---

6 Before the Second Empire era of Haussmannisation, the comte de Rambuteau undertook the refurbishment of the urban landscape and carried out some reconstruction projects, as in this case.

7 On nineteenth-century Parisian ruins, see Tranca, 2016.

8 The hygienist movement blurred the lines between the physical and moral in discussions of public health reform. For example, Parent-Duchâtelet published works on both sewerage and prostitution.

"L'exactitude du tableau paraît incertaine, et l'ensemble visiblement noirci" (*ibid.*, p. 168). Balzac's bleak interpretation is also at odds with other contemporary records of the area, most notably those joyful evocations of "la bohème du Doyenné" (Houssaye, 1896, p. 26) offered by the "Jeune-France" writers: "C'était dans notre logement commun de la rue du Doyenné, que nous nous étions reconnus frères. [...] Nous étions jeunes, toujours gais, souvent riches..." (Nerval, 1853, p. 7).[9] This "Jeune-France" association of the *quartier du Doyenné* with the socially marginalised does chime with *La Cousine Bette*. But, in contrast to Nerval's bohemian brotherhood, the inclusive "on" used by Balzac's narrator accentuates the otherness of those who occupy this silent and solitary neighbourhood. Night ("l'heure où cette ruelle se change") facilitates a shift towards the supernatural and the streets of the *quartier du Doyenné* become an exotic space of "fantômes" and "tombeaux vivants" (*CH*, VII, p. 100), reminiscent of gothic and fantastic nights. Once again, we find here an echo of the *rue de Langlade* scene in *Splendeurs* which explains to the reader that "en y passant pendant la journée, on ne peut se figurer ce que toutes ces rues deviennent la nuit" and "ces rues [...] prennent à la nuit une physionomie mystérieuse et pleine de contrastes" (*CH*, VI, p. 446–447). Playing on contemporary curiosity regarding the nocturnal city, Balzac exploits night's lack of visibility to render the familiar strange and impenetrable, since, as Delattre has noted, "le sentiment de l'étrangeté nocturne de la grande ville prouve enfin que Paris n'est pas seulement inconnu aux provinciaux, mais aussi à ses propres habitants" (2003, p. 63). The Doyenné neighbourhood is physically separate as well: its situation "beaucoup plus bas" and its houses "enterrées" due to "la profondeur caverneuse du sol" (*CH*, VII, p. 100). Vocabulary related to burial ("cryptes", "tombeaux") further emphasises this theme of an underground existence.[10] These hidden depths suggest not only Lisbeth's "sauvagerie de la passion" (Conrad, 2018, p. 194), but go further, reproducing the contemporary trope of night as a frontier as well as the nineteenth-century night's function as a "révélateur souterrain" (Csergo, 1997, p. 107). Balzac's narrator therefore

9 Théophile Gautier, Camille Rogier, Arsène Houssaye, and Gérard Nerval, lived in the rue du Doyenné as young writers and artists of modest means. For more on this topic, see Wagneur, 2010, p. 85–102.

10 On the topic of what lies beneath nineteenth-century Paris, see Goulet, 2021.

fulfils the role of explorer, unearthing the hidden depths of the city that darkness reveals. From a more sinister perspective, these references to underground Parisian existences tap into the "anxiety-laden sense of subterranean forces threatening the health, both physical and moral, of the overground city" (Prendergast, 1992, p. 75) which preoccupied the July Monarchy middle classes. Night is shown to exacerbate this threat, hence: "l'obligation que l'état du quartier lui faisait [à Bette] de se retirer avant la nuit close" (*CH*, VII, p. 101). *Splendeurs* also refers to this idea: "tout homme à qui le Paris du soir reste inconnu serait saisi d'une terreur triste en tombant dans le lacis de petites rues qui cercle cette lueur reflétée jusque sur le ciel." (*CH*, VI, p. 446) As Csergo explains: "ville de l'ombre et des ténèbres, le Paris nocturne et souterrain devient celui des 'plus basses classes du peuple', des classes dangereuses enfouies au plus profond de la société et que la modernisation ne peut extirper" (1997, p. 108).

To the July Monarchy's diurnal capitalist culture, night time and its associated population represents danger; participation in urban nightlife threatens the bourgeois way of life. Night's potential as a new landscape for exploration is tempered by concerns regarding the destruction of middle-class convention and domesticity. The contagion comprised in the night air of the *quartier du Doyenné* thus appears not only physically threatening, but morally so, at a time when "[des] théories selon lesquelles l'environnement est responsable de l'état physique et moral des populations s'affirment […] sous la forme de topographies médicales assimilant l'obscur et le malsain, voyant dans la nuit un immense égout à ciel ouvert, traquant l'ombre jusque dans le jour douteux des ruelles médiévales" (Delattre, 2003, p. 38). Intersecting the trope of the mysterious and macabre romantic night with the social reality of the period, Balzac describes a perilous "coupe-gorge" (*CH*, VII, p. 100), playing on contemporary fears regarding nocturnal safety in the city (Kalifa, 1997, p. 121) and the novel's miasma metaphor further feeds night's reputation as the natural habitat of the "classes dangereuses", emphasising the ease with which its moral contagion can spread. In so doing, this *quartier du Doyenné* scene hammers home the inextricable link between this nocturnal landscape and the lower classes who inhabit it.

THE "MANTEAU DE LA NUIT" METAPHOR

"Le pavé, beaucoup plus bas que celui de la chaussée de la rue du Musée, se trouve au niveau de celle de la rue Froidmanteau." (*CH*, VII, p. 100) The reference to the "rue Froid-manteau" in this Doyenné scene is of particular significance in establishing the notion of a nocturnal microclimate. By accentuating the "manteau de la nuit" (*CH*, VII, p. 100) metaphor, Balzac is returning to imagery which appears elsewhere in *La Comédie humaine*.[11] The rue Froidmanteau also appears in a night scene in *Gambara* (1837) where it is described as "une sorte d'égout que la police tolère auprès du Palais-Royal assaini" (*CH*, X, p. 460) and thus presents an earlier iteration of the blurred lines between physical filth and moral disease in the Parisian nightscape.[12] As for the "manteau de la nuit", *Splendeurs et misères des courtisanes* evokes a "froid malsain [qui] pose sur vos épaules un manteau moite" (*CH*, VI, p. 446). The explicit immorality of the rue de Langlade in this scene offers a further example of the unique and unhealthy microclimate which characterises Balzac's night scenes. Beyond Balzac, the relationship between the "manteau de la nuit" and urban contagion occurs in the wider July Monarchy literary imagination, as in George Sand's Parisian novel *Horace* where all the elements of Balzac's "manteau de la nuit" metaphor are present but without the fantastic connotations of Balzac's versions: "J'étais à l'ambulance, roulé dans mon manteau, par une de ces froides nuits du printemps qui semblaient donner plus d'intensité au fléau [...] lorsque je sentis une main se poser sur mon épaule" (1840, p. 236).

The "manteau de la nuit" image recurs throughout literature. In Shakespeare, "night's cloak" (2008, p. 380) shields the lover Romeo, while Edward Young's "Night Thoughts" praised the curtain of darkness as the source of poetic imagination. During the Renaissance, the metaphor was frequently used in a religious sense to represent the Virgin's protective cloak of stars.[13] But these positive connotations of a gentle,

11 For more on this metaphor, see Oster, 2013.

12 The street name is hyphenated in *La Cousine Bette*, further emphasising its meaning.

13 For a cosmological interpretation of the "manteau de la nuit" during the renaissance, see Ménager, 2005, p. 75–78.

mysterious and protective night are missing from Balzac. Instead, the "manteau de la nuit" of *La Cousine Bette* manipulates contemporary anxiety regarding miasmic night air and the deviant nocturnal activities of the popular classes. Balzac's "manteau" is more in keeping with the night of terror in Racine's *Andromaque*: "Mais quelle épaisse nuit tout à coup m'environne? / De quel côté sortir? D'où vient que je frissonne? / Quelle horreur me saisit? Grâce au ciel, j'entrevoi… / Dieux! Quels ruisseaux de sang coulent autour de moi!" (2022, p. 82) The "manteau de la nuit" in *La Cousine Bette* fits with this tragic conception of the night. It allows bourgeois readers to project their horrified imaginings on to the enveloping darkness and to anticipate the dreadful fate which awaits those who immerse themselves in it.

The "manteau de la nuit" reemerges later in the novel as Crevel breaks the news of Valérie Marneffe's rejection to the waiting Hulot. The second scene set in the night-time street, it invites comparison with the earlier Doyenné episode. Here, gas lighting signifies a more affluent setting, but the trope of miasmic moisture remains:

> "Que diable faites-vous là?… vous vous promenez par une jolie petite pluie fine. À nos âges, c'est mauvais. Voulez-vous que je vous donne un bon conseil? Revenons chacun chez nous; car, entre nous, vous ne verrez pas de lumière à la croisée…"
>
> En entendant cette dernière phrase, le baron sentit qu'il avait soixante-trois ans, et que son manteau était mouillé. (*CH*, VII, p. 229)

Miasma has crept beyond the boundaries of the *quartier du Doyenné* and penetrated the upper echelons of society. The night air and Marneffe's "parfum choisi" of the earlier Doyenné scene have wrought visible changes in Hulot. Brought low, both physically and emotionally, he is susceptible to the nocturnal damp — and renewed references to the unstable urban landscape (an echo of the ruins in the *quartier du Doyenné*) hint at this vulnerability: "[Crevel] apercevait, dans les ténèbres de la rue de Babylone, le grand Hulot, un peu voûté, se glissant le long des planches d'une maison en construction" (*CH*, VII, p. 229). A watery theme is again apparent — "glissant", "phoque", "dauphin", "se brouiller" (*CH*, VII, p. 228–231) —, reflecting the baron's melancholy, which reaches such a pitch that he later contemplates death by water, by throwing Crevel and himself into the river (*CH*, VII,

p. 231).[14] While Crevel's instruction "Ne faites pas de tapage nocturne" (*CH*, VII, p. 230) references a common complaint of the July Monarchy middle classes, beneath its humorous surface, there lies a potential warning: if Hulot had followed bourgeois convention and retreated to the safety of his home as night fell, his health would not be at risk. Participation in July Monarchy nightlife appears to bring only misfortune.

FROM DEATH TO RESURRECTION

The consequences of the *quartier du Doyenné*'s deadly nocturnal ecology finally become evident at Valérie's deathbed: "j'ai vu la vengeance partout dans la nature" (*CH*, VII, p. 432). The corrupt Parisian night air has morphed her "parfum choisi" (*CH*, VII, p. 101) into "miasmes délétères" and "fétidité" (*CH*, VII, p. 433). The revival of outdated miasma theory is echoed in the multiple references to the medieval origins of the "maladie perdue" which finally afflicts Valérie Marneffe and Crevel. This connection with night air is amplified by the link between disease and environment in Bianchon's explanation that there is no cure "dans les climats tempérés" but that "elle est guérissable aux Indes" (*CH*, VII, p. 428). In contrast to the mysterious "wasting away" of the nineteenth-century romantic heroine (Rogers, 1983, p. 246), Valérie's non-adherence to the behaviour of a "femme comme il faut" allow for detailed references to contagion — "viciation", "corrompait", "infecte", "infection"—, disease and death — "maladie", "moribonde" — and air— "les fenêtres ouvertes et les plus puissants parfums", "miasmes délétères" (*CH*, VII, p. 431–433). The vocabulary that related to night air at the novel's outset now refers to Valérie's person. This corrupt air does not spare Lisbeth either and she finally succumbs to "l'affreuse agonie d'une phtisie pulmonaire" (*CH*, VII, p. 448).

But night air is not universally fatal in *La Cousine Bette.* Steinbock's suicide attempt also unites the tropes of night time, poisonous air and death but in the end, "la porte ouverte, l'air afflua, l'exilé fut sauvé"

14 See Petitier (2002, p. 51) on water and melancholy in *Ferragus*.

(*CH*, VII, p. 110). Conversely, because Valérie herself is the source of the pestilential air, she cannot be saved. This ties in with Crevel's comparison of Valérie with physical harm: "quelle femme! Elle me remue autant qu'une colique, quand elle me regarde froidement…" (*CH*, VII, p. 229), and his subsequent declaration: "me voilà guéri des femmes comme il faut" (*CH*, VII, p. 235). Finally, the escape of baron Hulot is of particular interest, since he manages to cast off the nocturnal "manteau moite" even as Valérie and Crevel perish.

After his social descent, Hulot is discovered living in the *quartier du Petit-Pologne*, in a new place of residence whose description replicates tropes of the *quartier du Doyenné* in its references to nature — "Pépinière", "végètent", "florissent", "fangeux" — and to urban reconstruction: "la truelle est, à Paris, plus civilisatrice qu'on ne le pense!" (*CH*, VII, p. 437) Like the *quartier du Doyenné*, the natural world is again associated with the lower classes. But the baron finds a new life for himself thanks to his willingness to integrate with the lower social orders. Unlike Crevel, whose desire for a "femme comme il faut" proves his downfall, Hulot's social adaptability where one finds "l'aristocratie coudoyée là par une infime Bohême" (*CH*, VII, p. 437) is what saves him. Much of the contemporary concern regarding urban nightlife was predicated on apprehension about social mixing since the nocturnal street had traditionally been viewed as the natural habitat of the lower classes, as well as anxiety regarding the erosion of the capitalist foundations of July Monarchy society. Thus, Hulot's survival despite his earlier immersion in the Doyenné night air interrogates the alarmist public discourse on the Parisian night and the "classes dangereuses". Hulot's survival is clear from the outset: "un conseiller d'État qui fait la pluie et le beau temps au Ministère" (*CH*, VII, p. 102). His climatological mastery allows him to shake off the contagious miasmic night air, and his later residence in "le passage du Soleil, dont le nom est une de ces antithèses familières aux Parisiens, car ce passage est doublement obscur" (*CH*, VII, p. 437) demonstrates his enduring capacity to turn a situation to his advantage.

The novel's theme of watery miasma and its stealthy penetration of French society reaches its climax in the final paragraphs, through the motif of tears. Lisbeth weeps at Valérie's bedside (*CH*, VII, p. 433) but later it is the Hulots who succumb one after another: Adeline "fondit en larmes", "le baron [...] avait les yeux humides", even Atala "fond en larmes" (*CH*, VII, p. 446). At Lisbeth's deathbed, the family unites "tous en larmes autour de son lit" and her funeral procession "fut mené par toute une famille en larmes" (*CH*, VII, p. 448). Following Hulot's final betrayal, "la baronne, administrée la veille, était à l'agonie et se voyait entourée de sa famille en larmes" and even in death, Adeline is crying: "Et l'on vit, ce qui doit être rare, des larmes sortir des yeux d'une morte." (*CH*, VII, p. 451) This concluding torrent of tears verges on the ridiculous, but the accumulation effect is purposeful. The final message is one regarding contagion. In the end, no-one is spared the consequences of the *quartier du Doyenné*'s miasmic night air.

The theme of a deleterious Parisian night underpins Balzac's writing on French society in *La Comédie humaine.* But what is made explicit in earlier novels has become more nuanced in his later writing. Rather than the world of solicitation and prostitution as evoked in *Splendeurs et misères des courtisanes*, the metaphor of nocturnal miasma in *La Cousine Bette* emerges as the inevitable conclusion of the author's musings on vice. Playing on outmoded miasma theory, the novel interrogates July Monarchy assignation of moral meaning to nightlife by demonstrating how moral corruption has penetrated all parts of society, as well as the ultimate failure of state efforts to enforce spatial segregation. Rather than night air, ultimately it is Valérie, as the incarnation of vice, who is revealed as the source of this watery metaphor: "c'est une anguille qui vous coule entre les mains" (*CH*, VII, p. 236).

The concept of night air offers a valuable framework through which to examine Balzac's Paris in light of recent scholarship on the relationship between humans and their environment. Looking to the post-Covid-19 era, sociologist Des Fitzgerald has advocated for a move "against green cities" (2023) in order to shift perspectives on the relationship between people, health and cities, echoing the problematic re-emergence of the natural world at night time in Balzac's pessimistic portrait of the miasmic city. Current avenues of inquiry in the nascent field of Night Studies also replicate Balzac's thinking in *La Cousine Bette*, from Nick Dunn's observation of the nocturnal transformation of urban space "when dynamics of human movement and occupation are profoundly altered" (2021, p. 193), to a recent call for the study of "nighttime ecology" (Gaston, 2019, p. 481). In this essay, I contend that the socio-cultural shifts and new understanding of the night-time city which the recent pandemic has engendered were in fact anticipated almost two hundred years earlier in Balzac's writing on the insalubrious, hostile and harmful night.

Charlotte BERKERY
University College Cork

WORKS CITED

Baldwin Peter C., 2003, "How Night Air Became Good Air, 1776–1930", *Environmental History*, 8, p. 412–429.

Barnes David, 2018, *The Great Stink of Paris and the Nineteenth-Century Struggle against Filth and Germs* (Baltimore: John Hopkins University Press).

Beaumont Matthew, 2016, *Nightwalking: A Nocturnal History of London, Chaucer to Dickens* (London: Verso).

Besson Lucette, 2003, "L'eau de mort ou le thème de la noyade chez Balzac", *AB*, p. 307–329.

Chevalier Louis (ed. by), 1958, *Le Choléra: la première épidémie du* XIX*e siècle* (La Roche-sur-Yon: Imprimerie Centrale de l'Ouest).

Chevalier Louis, 2002, *Classes laborieuses classes dangereuses à Paris pendant la première moitié du* XIX*e siècle* (Paris: Perrin).

Conrad Thomas, 2018, "Du bon usage des passions", *AB*, p. 193–212.

Corbin Alain, 1982, *Le Miasme et la jonquille. L'odorat et l'imaginaire social (*XVIII*e–*XIX*e siècles)* (Paris: Aubier).

Csergo Julia, 1997, "Dualité de la nuit, duplicité de la ville", *Sociétés et Représentations*, 4, p. 105–120.

Delattre Simone, 2003, *Les Douze Heures noires. La Nuit à Paris au* XIX*e siècle* (Paris: Albin Michel).

Dunn Nick, 2021, "Nocturnal Urban Natures: Multispecies encounters in the pandemic city after dark" in *Proceedings: II International Conference on Night Studies* (Lisbon: ISCTE, Instituto Universitario de Lisboa), p. 192–206.

Fitzgerald Des, 2023, *The Living City: Why Cities Don't Need to be Green to be Great* (Basic Book).

Gaston Kevin J., 2019, «Nighttime Ecology: The 'Nocturnal Problem' Revisited», *The American Naturalist*, 198, p. 481–502.

Goulet Andrea, 2021, "Anthropocene Under Paris? Rethinking the Quarries and Catacombs", *Dix-Neuf*, 25, p. 225–241.

Guichardet Jeannine, 1999, *Balzac "archéologue de Paris"* (Geneva: Slatkine Reprints).

Houssaye Arsène, 1896, *Souvenirs de jeunesse: 1830–1850* (Paris: E. Flammarion).

Janin Jules, 1839, *Les catacombes: romans, contes, nouvelles et mélanges littéraires* (Paris: Werdet), III.

Kalifa Dominique, 1997, "L'Attaque nocturne", *Sociétés et Représentations*, 1, p. 121–138.

Kudlick Catherine J., 1996, *Cholera in Post-Revolutionary Paris: A Cultural History* (Berkeley and Los Angeles: University of California Press).
Leca Ange-Pierre, 1982, *Et le choléra s'abattit sur Paris: 1832* (Paris: Albin Michel).
Mathias Manon, 2024, *Gut, Brain, and Environment in Nineteenth-Century French Literature and Medicine* (London: Routledge).
Ménager Daniel, 2005, *La Renaissance et la nuit* (Geneva: Droz).
Nerval Gérard de, 1853, *Petits Châteaux de Bohème* (Paris: Eugène Didier).
Oster Patricia, 2013, "Voile de la nuit (Le)", in *Dictionnaire littéraire de la nuit*, ed. by Alain Montandon (Paris: Honoré Champion), II, p. 1533–1547.
Parent-Duchâtelet Alexandre, 1824, *Essai sur les cloaques ou égouts de la ville de Paris* (Paris: Crevot).
Petitier Paule, 2002, "La Mélancolie de *Ferragus*", *Romantisme*, 117, p. 45–58.
Prendergast Christopher, 1992, *Paris and the Nineteenth Century* (Oxford: Blackwell).
Racine Jean, 2022, *Andromaque* (Paris: Éditions Ligaran).
Rogers Nancy, 1983, "The Wasting Away of Romantic Heroines", *Nineteenth-Century French Studies*, 11 (Spring-Summer), p. 246–256.
Sand George, 1840, *Horace* (Paris: Michel Lévy).
Shakespeare William, 2000, *The Oxford Shakespeare: Romeo and Juliet* (Oxford: Oxford University Press).
Steinmetz Jean-Luc, 1969, "L'eau dans *La Comédie humaine*", *AB*, p. 3–30.
Tranca Alexandra, 2016, "From Pompeii to Paris: ghostly cityscapes and the ruins of modernity in Théophile Gautier and Eugène Atget", *Word and Image*, 32, p. 251–263.
Van Tieghem Paul, 1921, *La Poésie de la nuit et des tombeaux en Europe au XVIIIe siècle* (Paris: F. Rieder).
Vigarello Georges, 2014, *Le Propre et le sale: l'hygiène du corps depuis le Moyen Âge* (Paris: Points).
Villermé, Louis-René, 1840, *Tableau de l'état physique et moral des ouvriers employés dans les manufactures de coton, de laine et de soie* (Paris: Jules Renouard et Cie).
Wagneur Jean-Didier, 2010, "L'invention de la bohème: entre bohème et bohême", in *Bohème sans frontière*, ed. by Pascal Brisette and Anthony Glinoer (Rennes: Presses universitaires de Rennes), p. 85–102.

LE CHEF-D'ŒUVRE INCONNU, OU LA DISPARITION DE L'HERBE VERTE

À lire *Le Chef-d'œuvre inconnu* du point de vue de l'écocritique, c'est-à-dire en se focalisant sur la nature et sa présence dans le conte de Balzac, on remarque non seulement un huis clos dans la ville de Paris, représentée comme sous cloche, tel un aquarium, mais aussi une absence de paysage – et donc une absence d'une certaine forme de nature. Cependant, même réprimée, la nature ne finirait-elle pas par ressurgir ? L'on en viendrait alors à considérer l'incendie final comme la victoire de la nature sur ce que l'art peut avoir d'artificiel : l'autodafé, réel ou suggéré, donnerait à lire une forme de morale écologique, un retour salutaire au naturel et à la nature[1]. En comparant toutefois les différentes versions du texte, on remarque une curieuse disparition, celle de l'« herbe verte », ainsi qu'un effacement de la bucolique Grenadière. C'est à partir de cette mise à distance de la nature au sein des variations, entre la version de 1831 et celle de 1845, qu'il convient de repenser le conte[2].

---

1 Il n'en demeure pas moins que, en notre temps "post-Balzac", art et écologie paraissent aller de plus en plus de pair. Certes, les réactions-happenings dans les musées ces dernières années sont pensées comme éminemment médiatisables : l'Art est ce qui permettra d'être vu sinon entendu, et c'est cet effet de visibilité exacerbée qui est recherché par ceux qui abîment, se collent la main, projettent de la soupe ou de la peinture voire essaient de casser les vitrines de toutes ces toiles célèbres autant que célébrées que sont nos chefs-d'œuvres bien connus. Tout ceci a donc lieu dans un cadre qui est celui d'une volonté de prise de conscience d'une catastrophe écologique en devenir, mais il reste notable que ce soit dans le monde de l'art que cette crise ait été rendue la plus visible. Ajoutons que les incendies picturaux les plus contemporains sont souvent affaire politique : Edward Ruscha avait fait brûler le Los Angeles County Museum en 1965, dans le droit fil des émeutes de Watts, et, plus récemment, au lendemain de *Occupy Wall Street*, vers 2009, Alex Schaefer s'est mis à représenter des banques américaines prises par le feu, comme si de tels enflammements pouvaient suffire à mettre à mal le capitalisme.

2 Balzac a souvent repris son texte, d'abord en 1832, puis plus longuement en 1837, et c'est la version de 1845, avec sa conclusion en incendie, qui semble avoir eu sa préférence ; étant donné que cette date de 1845 accompagne l'épigraphe « A un Lord » et les célèbres pointillées initiaux. Ce passage entre différentes versions est au cœur de l'ouvrage de

Du caractère exceptionnel du *Chef-d'œuvre inconnu*, il a beaucoup été question ailleurs : texte court, il fait paradoxalement partie des écrits balzaciens les plus glosés, de ceux qui intéressent tout autant les spécialistes de littérature que les critiques d'art et les amateurs d'esthétique. Et s'il s'agit d'un texte sur l'origine du beau, sur ce que le génie peut avoir de dangereusement « fou », c'est également un texte sans « origine » : l'on en connaît les versions publiées, mais il n'y a pas trace de manuscrit. Tant et si bien que certains ont supposé que Théophile Gautier et non Balzac en avait été le réel auteur – proposition qu'infirme l'étude biographique, étant donné que la première version du texte parut bien avant la rencontre entre les deux hommes, en 1835[3]. Au mieux pourrait-on accepter que Gautier aurait, dès 1837, quelque peu repris l'ultime version, dont la trame demeurerait balzacienne. L'origine du texte constituerait alors un écho ironique à la diégèse, lorsque Frenhofer reprend la toile de Porbus et propose ironiquement d'apposer sa signature au bas de la toile[4].

D'une version l'autre, le conte a toujours lieu en huis clos dans Paris[5] : l'histoire se passe dans un quartier limité et bien connu de la ville, sur la rive gauche. Néanmoins, tandis que deux jours séparent les deux parties du texte en 1831, il faudra trois mois en 1845 à celui qui n'est pas encore connu comme le Poussin pour convaincre Gillette et retrouver Porbus chez Frenhofer. Ce ralentissement du récit lui confère davantage de « réalisme » : la vivacité de la version de 1831 participait du fantastique qui caractérisait alors le genre de ce conte balzacien ; ainsi le jeune homme avait-il encore un « costume » (Balzac, 1831, I, p. 319). Implicitement, passer de deux jours à trois mois permet surtout d'inscrire les saisons au cœur du texte. Les deux versions présentent un personnage qui vient d'arriver à Paris, souffrant du froid, à la toute fin de l'année 1612. Dans la version de 1845, puisque trois mois se sont écoulés, c'est au printemps que se passera l'échange entre les artistes, sur fond de nus et de modèles. Bien entendu, le texte ne le dit jamais

---

Pierre Laubriet (1961) qui révèle combien les éléments ajoutés par Balzac transforment un conte fantastique en nouvelle d'art.

3 Voir Charles de Spoelberch de Lovenjoul, « H. de Balzac et Th. Gautier. À propos du *Chef-d'œuvre inconnu* », *Autour d'Honoré de Balzac*, Paris, Calmann Lévy éditeur, 1899, p. 5.

4 Cet événement n'a lieu que dans la version reprise par Gautier.

5 Dans la première version, le lecteur déduisait que l'histoire se passait dans la ville de Paris, alors que la maison y est clairement située dans la version de 1845.

explicitement, et c'est au lecteur de le déduire. Or, si le printemps est empli de promesses, le fait qu'il ne soit suivi ni d'un été ni d'un automne laisse entendre que ces artistes sont confrontés à la stérilité : il n'y aura ni foins, ni vendanges, et le conte est placé sous le signe, éphémère et léger, des fleurs plutôt que sous celui des fruits.

La potentielle froide stérilité de la ville de Paris est accentuée par le fait que la Grenadière a disparu dans la version de 1845. En 1831, on la trouvait à la fin d'une longue digression ayant trait aux aventures de la toile de Marie l'Égyptienne, offerte à Marie de Médicis avant que cette dernière n'ait à s'en séparer. Et le narrateur expliquait alors que c'était la Grenadière qui était la dernière demeure de ce chef-d'œuvre – c'est-à-dire son cadre[6]. Or cette Grenadière sacrifiée entre 1831 et 1845 est devenue le site et le titre même d'un étrange texte, publié en 1832. Contrairement à ce qu'on lit dans *Le Chef-d'œuvre inconnu*, la nature y est féconde, et la beauté sur laquelle s'arrête l'instance narrative est bien celle d'un paysage et de la nature dans son entièreté, et non le cadre d'un quelconque portrait :

> En aucun lieu du monde vous ne rencontreriez une demeure tout à la fois si modeste et si grande, si riche en fructifications, en parfums, en points de vue. Elle est, au cœur de la Touraine, une petite Touraine où toutes les fleurs, tous les fruits, toutes les beautés de ce pays sont complètement représentés. (*CH*, II, p. 423-424)

Cette demeure, renvoyant à la Touraine tout entière, constitue le parfait opposé du Paris froid et stérile de la version de 1845 du *Chef-d'œuvre inconnu* comme si Balzac avait eu besoin que ces deux espaces de vie existent textuellement, en parallèle, sans pour autant qu'ils n'en viennent à se mêler. D'une version l'autre a ainsi été effacé ce souffle que constituait certainement pour Balzac la mention de la Grenadière, double lieu d'origine. Rappelons la nourrice de Saint-Cyr, et ce qui fut peut-être le lieu de nuits passées avec la femme-mère aimée ; et il y aurait en somme, à la Grenadière le lait d'*infans* autant que la présence de celle qui fut là pour soutenir et rendre possible l'écriture adulte, dès ses débuts[7]. Ajoutons que comme l'a judicieusement analysé Corine

---

6 « Aujourd'hui cette magnifique toile est au château de la Grenadière, près de Saint-Cyr, en Touraine » (Balzac, 1831, I, p. 320).

7 Balzac évoque l'importance de cette nourrice dans *Sténie*. Et l'on sait qu'il passa quelque temps à la Grenadière avec Madame de Berny, à qui il aurait avoué son amour dès 1822

Ménage (1982), Balzac s'est fait paysagiste de la Touraine au cœur d'un texte où le panorama, quoi qu'imaginaire, a la part belle. De sorte que lorsque disparait la Grenadière, le Paris qui reste est un cadre des plus tristes et des plus sombres pour le conte, un cadre qui permet à l'histoire de ne pas être dénaturée par le contexte. Ou, pour le dire autrement, il y a effacement d'indices biographiques balzaciens, pour que le conte s'inscrive davantage dans l'histoire du Poussin en devenir[8].

Et si ce Paris peu lumineux est placé sous le signe des fleurs, c'est parce que, dans la première partie du *Chef-d'œuvre inconnu*, il est par trois fois question de ces dernières : « fleur primitive », « fleur de vie » et « fleur de nature », les métaphores florales tissent le bouquet de cette absente que serait la femme que l'on ne saurait voir – ou plutôt que l'on ne sera ultimement pas capable de contempler.

Or ces fleurs, toutes métaphoriques, sont doublement artificielles : dans une des anecdotes du conte, le « damas à fleur » (qui est déjà une manière de donner à voir ces dernières par le biais d'un tissage), Mabuse le transforme en un papier sur lequel il peint des fleurs, et dont il s'habille pour célébrer l'entrée de Charles Quint dans la ville. Imitant un tissu qu'il a perdu au jeu ou en buvant, le peintre se rattrape ainsi par le biais d'une sorte de trompe-l'œil. Les fleurs ne sont donc plus qu'imitation d'une image de fleurs, et cette double médiation, qui passe par le tissage puis par le dessin et la peinture, suppose une mise à mal de la nature.

Tout ceci demande néanmoins à être précisé. Car ce tissu damassé dont se revêtent les dignitaires accueillant Charles Quint était souvent, à l'époque baroque, nommé « brocart ». La ville de Damas, au cœur du nom, marque l'origine byzantine de cette riche toile qui fut, dès le haut Moyen Âge, tissée en France. L'Atilf rappelle que c'est une « Étoffe monochrome, à double face, généralement en soie, ornée de dessins satinés, en relief sur fond mat, formés par le tissage ». Initialement monochrome, le damas suppose des fils de la même couleur que l'étoffe, tant et si bien que, pour voir le motif dessiné en ton sur ton, il faut un

et qui, selon ses confidences à Madame Hanska, « a fait l'écrivain, [...] a consolé le jeune homme » (cité par Bouteron, 1921, p. 582). Balzac et sa *Dilecta* auraient ensuite ensemble séjourné à la Grenadière « pendant quelques mois de l'été et de l'automne 1830 » (Serval, 1928, p. 434).

8 Le Poussin se rend en effet à Paris en 1612, information que Balzac trouva sans doute dans la *Biographie universelle ancienne et moderne* de Michaud.

éclairage oblique. Cette étoffe est sans doute utilisée par Balzac parce qu'il reprend directement la source culturelle, historique et documentaire qu'est pour lui la *Biographie universelle ancienne et moderne* de Michaud. Au sujet de Mabuse, l'on y lit en effet ce passage :

> Le marquis de Aeren se l'était attaché en qualité de peintre. Charles-Quint vint quelque temps après chez ce seigneur, qui n'épargna rien pour recevoir dignement le monarque : il fit habiller les principaux officiers de sa maison en damas blanc. Quand le tailleur vint prendre mesure, Mabuse lui demanda l'étoffe sous prétexte de faire un habillement singulier : il la vendit pour boire, et lorsqu'il fallut paraître, il ne trouva d'autre moyen que de s'affubler d'une robe de papier blanc qu'il peignit en beau damas. L'empereur fut frappé de l'éclat de cette étoffe ; mais le marquis ayant été instruit de la ruse du peintre, le dit à l'empereur, qui ne put s'empêcher de rire d'avoir été ainsi trompé. (Michaud, 1843, p. 589)

Le damas est ici blanc, et c'est avant tout l'éclat de ce blanc, sans doute en ses chatoyants reflets et motifs en blanc sur blanc, qui frappa l'empereur. Toutefois, dans le conte, lorsque Porbus raconte à Poussin l'influence que Mabuse eut sur Frenhofer, l'anecdote est reprise avec une variation intéressante pour qui étudie la présence de la nature dans le texte :

> Mabuse lui a légué le secret du relief, le pouvoir de donner aux figures cette vie extraordinaire, cette fleur de nature, notre désespoir éternel, mais dont il possédait si bien le faire qu'un jour, ayant vendu et bu le damas à fleurs avec lequel il devait s'habiller à l'entrée de Charles-Quint, il accompagna son maître avec un vêtement de papier peint en damas. L'éclat particulier de l'étoffe portée par Mabuse surprit l'empereur, qui, voulant en faire compliment au protecteur du vieil ivrogne, découvrit la supercherie. (*CH*, X, p. 426–427)

La toute métaphorique « fleur de nature », seule et unique fleur du texte qui ne soit pas nommée par Frenhofer, et qui est une manière pour Porbus d'évoquer le talent exceptionnel de ce dernier, sa capacité à donner de la vie aux figures qu'il peint, semble avoir contaminé le damas, qui est désormais « à fleurs ». Étant donné que tout damas, quelle que soit sa couleur, suppose un motif, il n'est pas impossible que le damas blanc initial ait été lui aussi à fleurs. Cependant, Balzac a rendu sa description plus précise, et cette précision importe parce que ces fleurs ne sont plus des fleurs en image du texte, mais constituent des ornements concrets. Ce sont des fleurs dessinées par le tissage du fil sur l'étoffe confiée à Mabuse, puis des fleurs qu'il dessine lui-même sur le papier de son costume en trompe l'œil, à la venue de Charles Quint. Et la blague de Mabuse est une sorte de mise en abyme de la nouvelle tout entière : le peintre imite picturalement la texture du tissu tout comme l'homme de lettre s'essaie, en palinodies, à faire de la peinture. Mais tout comme Mabuse n'avait en réalité pas de costume, sinon un trompe-l'œil, le nu final du texte est une absence, une aporie.

Ces fleurs sur tissu ou sur papier possèdent sans doute cette caractéristique propre au damas de n'être vraiment visibles que dans une certaine lumière. Quelle que soit leur teinte, elles ne se révèlent vraiment que dans la texture. Certes, le texte ne le dit pas directement, mais serait-il alors possible que la Catherine Lescaut de Frenhofer n'ait tout simplement pas été vue par Poussin et Porbus dans le bon angle, sous la lumière adéquate la rendant vraiment visible[9] ? Ce décalage vers l'oblique que demanderait le tissu damassé pour être vraiment vu inscrit un nouvel élément potentiellement fantastique dans le récit, puisque le diable est du côté d'un tel oblique[10]… Ici, la recherche de la présence de la nature amène à une question de représentation et de picturalité : le biais écocritique ne saurait exister sans réflexion esthétique.

De fait, si le terme de *nature* revient souvent dans le conte, le naturel y constitue l'idéal de la *mimesis*, c'est-à-dire ce qu'il faut parvenir à représenter. En d'autres termes, il n'est pas ici question de cette nature que les hommes devraient protéger pour éviter quelque catastrophe écologique, mais de la facette « humaine » sinon « philosophique » de cette dernière. Lorsque Frenhofer déclare que « la mission de l'art n'est pas de copier la nature, mais de l'exprimer » (*CH*, X, p. 418), il propose une esthétique où le vivant n'importe que parce qu'il peut être artificiellement transcrit et dépassé. Et cet étrange paradigme mimétique inventant une artificialité qui le dépasse nous permet d'imaginer un Balzac précurseur de la décadence et du symbolisme, annonçant cette

9 Pour le moment, nous n'avons encore jamais lu une semblable analyse de l'invisibilité de la Belle Noiseuse reposant sur un problème d'angle et de point de vue. Il n'est pas impossible que la réflexion écocritique puisse ouvrir des portes nouvelles à qui s'intéresse à l'esthétique. Précisons néanmoins que cette trouvaille accompagnerait parfaitement la manière dont Georges Didi-Huberman (1985) comprend la nouvelle balzacienne : lorsqu'il explique que la couleur n'est pas une surface et que la toile demande plis et replis, il esquisse sans le dire directement la possibilité d'un regard oblique.

10 Pour Ae-Young (2008), la lutte avec la nature au cœur du texte s'explique par le fait que « le Diable déguisé en Frenhofer jou[e] à être la mère terrible et rivalis[e] avec le père Dieu » (p. 25).

fleur nécessairement absente du bouquet mallarméen, sinon les créations florales gémellaires d'*À Rebours*[11]. Aussi Frenhofer en vient-il presque à s'égarer dans ces fascinants miroitements mimétiques lorsqu'il s'exclame plus loin : « N'est-ce pas ainsi que procède le soleil, ce divin peintre de l'univers. Oh ! nature, nature ! qui jamais t'a surprise dans tes fuites ! » (*CH*, X, p. 425) Si c'est le soleil qui peint, la nature elle-même est œuvre picturale – de sorte que le peintre imite ce qui est déjà une imitation. Cette curieuse présence du soleil, au cœur d'un conte en huis clos, est sujette à caution. Il ne s'agit pas tant de l'astre qui se lève et se couche sur notre quotidien que d'une figure métaphorique divinisée qui, en éclairant, donne à voir et éblouit, tout en se refusant à être saisie. Et sans doute ce glissement vers un monde exclusivement mimétique ne déplairait-il pas à un Timothy Morton qui a su montrer combien la nature, toute thématique soit-elle, est un être de fuite des plus littéraires.

Et si le soleil est personnifié par Frenhofer, l'« œuvre picturale » que serait la nature n'est étonnamment jamais paysage. Lorsque l'on revient sur les différentes versions du texte, si l'on y trouve quelques descriptions d'atelier, si l'on y déchiffre des comparaisons avec la sculpture, toutes les toiles présentent des figures humaines. Dès les toutes premières pages, Balzac joue lui-même les peintres portraitistes : la figure 'rembrandtienne' du vieillard dans l'escalier est ainsi bien connue (*CH*, X, p. 415). Mais dès l'incipit, pour que le lecteur puisse s'imaginer celui que l'on n'a pas encore identifié comme étant le peintre Poussin, l'instance narrative a recours à des comparaisons ainsi qu'à des propositions au conditionnel. Le parallélisme avec la peinture est alors évident : peindre un portrait demande de donner à voir des points de ressemblance, que les comparaisons rendent visibles. Et le conditionnel ajoute à la fiction ce potentiel d'imaginaire qui fait les œuvres d'art.

C'est d'ailleurs pour mieux décrire et portraiturer le personnage de Frenhofer que le narrateur de 1831 évoquait quelque herbe verte :

> Pour toutes ces singularités, l'idiome moderne n'a qu'un mot : c'était indéfinissable !... Admirable expression ! En effet, elle résume la littérature fantastique ; elle formule tout ce qui échappe aux perceptions bornées de notre esprit ; et, quand vous l'avez placée sous les yeux d'un lecteur, il est lancé

11 Je tiens à remercier Göran Blix qui s'est attaché à relire une des versions initiales de cet article et a su me poser les bonnes questions, afin que je puisse tenter de préciser d'avantage cette question de nature.

> dans l'espace imaginaire ; alors le fantastique se trouve tout germé ; il pointe, comme une herbe verte, au sein de l'incompréhensible et de l'impuissance… (Balzac, 1831, I, p. 321–322)

Cette seule et unique « herbe verte » du texte, qui a disparu dans les reprises de 1837, est tout autant métaphorique que l'étaient les fleurs. Sa disparition a sans doute partie liée avec un certain choix d'évolution générique du conte : Balzac est passé d'un conte « fantastique » à un conte « philosophique », et il a de ce fait gommé un passage où la narration insistait sans doute un peu trop lourdement sur le caractère « indéfinissable » et par là-même fantastique de Frenhofer.

Dans la version de 1845, avant les tous derniers mots du conte qui évoquent la destruction du potentiel chef-d'œuvre et la mort de Frenhofer, on retrouve la couleur verte de cette herbe disparue. Le peintre recouvre sa Catherine Lescaut de serge verte, de celle qui était alors utilisée, si l'on en croit la narration, par les bijoutiers pour recouvrir leurs joyaux. Le vert serait ainsi ce qui demeure de la toile, avant sa destruction par le feu – mais ce vert qui cache et recouvre n'est plus celui de l'herbe. Et son artificialité est d'autant plus tangible qu'il rappelle la verroterie que quelque joaillier souhaiterait dissimuler du regard[12].

Soulignons que cette « serge verte » de la toute fin du roman n'est plus affaire de docte discours sur la question du fantastique : elle inscrit, implicitement, une inquiétante étrangeté qui donne à l'ensemble une teneur fantastique. C'est alors au cœur du texte et non plus dans la distante narration s'y rapportant que s'inscrit désormais cette sensation de fantastique que le conte conserve, même dans sa version de 1845. Car si Balzac voulait davantage tendre vers le philosophique, il a conservé des traces de luminosités rousses et vertes qui, en leur contraste, continuent de faire de l'atelier un espace potentiellement diabolique.

Que cette « herbe verte » ait été présente dans un passage ayant trait avec la notion d'indéfinissable demande à être souligné. Balzac n'a en effet de cesse de jouer avec la question de la non-représentation ou plutôt de l'irreprésentabilité. Le pied final et le chef-d'œuvre de Frenhofer ne constituent que le point ultime d'une aventure où la narration est

12 La question de révélation potentiellement « spectaculaire » sinon « éblouissante » est ici essentielle. Le deuxième chapitre du livre de Michel Serres intitulé *Genèse* (1982) met ainsi en scène Poussin et Porbus soulevant le voile de serge verte comme s'il s'était agi d'un rideau théâtral qui donnerait à voir un fragment du corps de quelque danseuse.

possible, mais où l'image ne l'est guère. L'image me paraît ici affaire d'occultation, et le fait qu'une mystérieuse icône de la vierge soudain rendue visible ait été au cœur de la sanctification de la Marie l'Égyptienne n'est peut-être pas un hasard.

Si l'on réfléchit au genre pictural, il n'y a pas trace de paysages ni de natures mortes dans ce récit, et les ateliers eux-mêmes, surtout dans l'ultime version, ne sont en rien aussi colorés, en leur bric-à-brac bohème, que le seront ceux décrits par Gautier, voire par les Goncourt ou par Zola, quelques années plus tard. Outre le Paris représenté comme un huis clos, le conte présente surtout des pièces peu éclairées, des ateliers, certes avec verrière, mais dans lesquels la lumière, tamisée, joue d'artificialité. Sans doute est-ce ainsi qu'est rendue possible l'atmosphère fantastique. Le conte tout entier éclipse les paysages, comme si seul le nu féminin avait importé à ces artistes. Avec la Marie l'Égyptienne, alors que la scène choisie pourrait permettre d'imaginer les bords du fleuve, le désert dans l'arrière-plan etc., il n'est guère fait mention de paysage, et seuls corps et regards sont vraiment décrits. Ceci est d'autant plus étonnant que la toile de la traversée du fleuve par Marie l'Égyptienne est de celles qui demandent un arrière-plan panoramique, une sorte de contexte naturel. Toutefois, refusant *l'ekphrasis*, le narrateur passe sous silence le décor de la scène, qui n'est plus qu'une scène d'échange et de mouvement, une scène décrite avec pudeur et distance.

Balzac s'est soigneusement documenté sur Mabuse, Porbus et Le Poussin, et il sait parfaitement que ces artistes ne se sont pas limités aux nus et aux portraits. Il existe même de nombreuses scènes historiques ou bibliques de « bord de fleuve » signées Poussin qui auraient pu parfaitement correspondre à la mise en scène de Marie l'Égyptienne sur le point d'embarquer. Et nous pouvons en conclure que c'est volontairement que le romancier a choisi de laisser de côté cette question de paysage.

L'absence de nature non-humaine dans les toiles du texte permet alors de s'interroger sur la question même de paysage, mêlant potentiellement esthétique et écocritique. Est-ce que le portrait nie le paysage ? Est-ce que l'absence de paysages dans le récit explique qu'il n'y ait pas de paysages non plus dans les scènes représentées dans les peintures du texte ? L'on en viendrait presque à deviner quelque paysage effacé au cœur des célèbres pointillés qui ouvrent le conte.

À la manière de Frenhofer, Balzac est ainsi revenu sur son texte pour en gommer certaines images, mais tandis que la toile du peintre laisse encore deviner la trace d'un petit pied de femme, le romancier a quant à lui soigneusement effacé tout ce que son texte pouvait transcrire de souffle de vie, de respiration et de présence trop tangible de la nature. Ainsi, l'herbe verte n'est plus déchiffrable nulle part. Et s'il faut bien de l'air pour que puisse poindre la toute première flamme de ce qui sera l'ultime incendie, il n'en demeure pas moins que cette nouvelle fonctionne en huis clos d'artificialité, tout comme une de ces boules de Noël où les faux flocons de neige auraient été remplacés par de vraies cendres.

Virginie A. Duzer
Pomona College, CA

OUVRAGES ET ÉTUDES CITÉS

Ae-Young Choe, 2008, « Une lecture textanalytique du *Chef-d'œuvre inconnu* de Balzac », *Gradiva*, 11, 1, p. 15-27.

Balzac Honoré de, 1831, « Le Chef-d'œuvre inconnu », in *L'Artiste : Journal de la Littérature et des Beaux-Arts*, I, p. 319-323 et II, p. 7-10.

Bouteron Marcel, 1921, « Balzac et Madame de Berny : une correspondance inédite », *Revue Des Deux Mondes (1829-1971)*, vol. 6, n° 3, p. 580-590.

Didi-Huberman Georges, 1985, *La Peinture incarnée*, Paris Éditions de Minuit.

Laubriet Pierre, 1961, *Un Catéchisme esthétique.* Le Chef-d'œuvre inconnu *de Balzac*, Paris Didier.

Lovenjoul Charles de Spoelberch de, 1899, « H. de Balzac et Th. Gautier. À propos du *Chef-d'œuvre inconnu* », *Autour d'Honoré de Balzac*, Paris Calmann Lévy, p. 3-17.

Ménage Corinne, 1982, « Balzac paysagiste : *La Grenadière* », *L'Année balzacienne*, p. 257-271.

Michaud Joseph, 1854, *Biographie universelle ancienne et moderne*, tome 34, Paris Madame C. Desplaces.

Michaud Joseph, 1843, *Biographie universelle ancienne et moderne*, tome 25, Paris A. Thoisnier Desplaces.

Morton Timothy, 2007, *Ecology Without Nature*, Harvard University Press.

Serres Michel, 1982, *Genèse*, Paris Grasset.

Serval Maurice, 1928, « Sites Balzaciens. Au Pays de La Grenadière », *Revue d'Histoire littéraire de La France*, vol. 35, n°. 3, p. 432-438.

BIBLIOGRAPHIE SÉLECTIVE / *SELECTIVE BIBLIOGRAPHY*

Aït-Touati Frédérique, and Coccia Emanuele (eds.), 2021, *Le cri de Gaïa. Penser la terre avec Bruno Latour* (Paris : Éditions La Découverte).

Audier Serge, 2019, *L'Âge productiviste : hégémonie prométhéenne, brèches et alternatives écologiques* (Paris : Éditions La Découverte).

Berque Augustin, 1987, *Écoumène. Introduction à l'étude des milieux humains* (Paris : Éditions Belin).

Besse Jean-Marc, 2000, *Voir la terre : six essais sur le paysage et la géographie* (Le Méjan : Actes Sud).

Blix Göran, 2009, *From Paris to Pompeii. French Romanticism and Cultural Politics of Archaeology* (Philadelphia : University of Pennsylvania Press).

Blix Göran, « Balzac zoographe : l'histoire naturelle de l'amitié dans *Une passion dans le désert* », *Actes du colloque de Cerisy, Balzac et les disciplines du savoir*, Bordas Éric, Del Lungo Andrea, and Glaudes Pierre (eds.) (forthcoming).

Bonneuil Christophe, and Fressoz Jean-Baptiste, 2016, *The Shock of the Anthropocene* (London and New York : Verso).

Chakrabarty Dipesh, 2021, *The Climate of History in a Planetary Age* (Chicago and London : University of Chicago Press).

Charbonnier Pierre, 2020, *Abondance et liberté : une histoire environnementale des idées politiques* (Paris : Éditions La Découverte).

Clark Timothy, 2019, *The Value of Ecocriticism* (Cambridge, UK : Cambridge University Press).

Cohen Jeffrey Jerome, 2015, *Stone : An Ecology of the Inhuman* (Minneapolis : University of Minnesota Press).

Collot Michel, 2022, "Romantisme et écopoétique", *Relief*, vol. 16, no. 1, p. 9–19.

Collot Michel, 2005, *Paysage et poésie du romantisme à nos jours* (Paris : Librairie José Corti).

Coupe Laurence (ed.), 2000, *The Green Studies Reader : From Romanticism to Ecocriticism* (New York : Routledge).

Daston Lorraine, and Mitman Gregg (eds.), 2005, *Thinking with Animals : New Perspectives on Anthropomorphism* (New York : Columbia University Press).

DeLoughrey Elizabeth, and Handley George B. (eds.), 2011, *Postcolonial Ecologies : Literatures of the Environment* (Oxford and New York : Oxford University Press).

Derrida Jacques, 2006, *L'Animal que donc je suis* (Paris : Galilée).

Desblache Lucile, 2006, "Introduction : profil d'une éco-littérature", *L'Esprit Créateur*, 46.2, p. 1–4.

Descola Philippe, 2005, *Par-delà culture et nature* (Paris : Gallimard).

Dufour Philippe, and Mozet Nicole (eds.), 2004, *Balzac géographe : territoires* (Saint-Cyr-sur-Loire : Christian Pirot).

Finch-Race Daniel A., and Posthumus Stephanie (eds.), 2017, *French Ecocriticism : From the Early Modern Period to the Twenty-First Century* (Frankfurt am Main : Peter Lang).

Finch-Race Daniel A., and Weber Julien (eds.), 2017, "French Ecocriticism/ L'Écocritique française", *L'Esprit Créateur*, 57.1, p. 1–8.

Finch-Race Daniel A., and Gosetti Valentina, 2019, "Editorial : Discovering Industrial-Era Francophone Ecoregions", *Dix-Neuf : Journal of the Society of Dix-Neuviémistes*, 23.3–4, p. 151–162.

Foster John Bellamy, 2000, *Marx's Ecology : Materialism and Nature* (New York : Monthly Review Press).

Foster John Bellamy, Clark Brett, and York Richard, 2010, *The Ecological Rift : Capitalism's War on the Earth* (New York : Monthly Review Press).

Foster John Bellamy, 2022, *Capitalism in the Anthropocene : Ecological Ruin or Ecological Revolution* (New York : Monthly Review Press).

Fressoz Jean-Baptiste, 2012, *Une histoire du risque technologique* (Paris : Seuil).

Fressoz Jean-Baptiste, and Locher Fabien, 2020, *Les Révoltes du ciel. Une histoire du changement climatique, XVe-XXe siècle* (Paris : Seuil).

Gaston Kevin J., 2019, "Nighttime Ecology : The 'Nocturnal Problem' Revisited", *The American Naturalist*, 193, p. 481–502.

Gemenne François, and Rankovic Aleksandar, 2019, *Atlas de l'Anthropocène* (Paris : SciencesPo).

Ghosh Amitav, 2021, *The Nutmeg's Curse : Parables for a Planet in Crisis* (Chicago : University of Chicago Press).

Goul Pauline, and Usher Phillip John (eds.), 2020, *Early Modern Écologies : Beyond English Ecocriticism* (Amsterdam : Amsterdam University Press).

Goulet Andrea, 2021, "Anthropocene Under Paris ? Rethinking the Quarries and Catacombs", *Dix-Neuf : Journal of the Society of Dix-Neuviémistes*, 25.3–4, p. 225–241.

Goulet Andrea, "Balzac géologue, ou Horace de Saint-Aubin à l'aube de l'anthropocène", *Actes du colloque de Cerisy, Balzac et les disciplines du savoir*, Bordas Éric, Del Lungo Andrea, and Glaudes Pierre (eds.) (forthcoming).

Green Nicholas, 1990, *The Spectacle of Nature : Landscape and Bourgeois Culture in Nineteenth-Century France* (Manchester and New York : Manchester University Press).

Griffiths Devin, and Kreisel Deanna K., 2020, "Introduction : Open Ecologies", *Victorian Literature and Culture*, 48.1, p. 1–28.

Guattari Félix, 1989, *The Three Ecologies* (New York : Bloomsbury Revelations).

Guest Bertrand, 2017, *Révolutions dans le cosmos. Essais de libération géographique : Humboldt, Thoreau, Reclus* (Paris : Classiques Garnier).

Guichardet Jeannine, 1986, *Balzac archéologue de Paris* (Paris : Sedes).

Hadot Pierre, 2004, *Le Voile d'Isis : essai sur l'histoire de l'idée de nature* (Paris : Gallimard).

Haraway Donna, 2016, *Staying with the Trouble : Making Kin in the Chthulucene* (Durham : Duke University Press).

Haraway Donna, 2008, *When Species Meet* (Minneapolis : University of Minnesota Press).

Hensley Nathan K., and Steer Philip (eds.), 2019, *Ecological Form : System and Aesthetics in the Age of Empire* (New York : Fordham University Press).

Heringman Noah, 2015, "Deep Time at the Dawn of the Anthropocene", *Representations*, 129.1, p. 56–85.

Hunt Stephen E., 2011, *Green Romanticism : the Natural World and Human Well-Being, 1775-1900* (Saarbrücken : VDM Verlag Dr. Müller).

Iovino Serenella, and Oppermann Serpil (eds.), 2014, *Material Ecocriticism* (Bloomington : Indiana University Press).

Jarrige François, 2014, *Technocritiques. Du refus des machines à la contestation des technosciences* (Paris : Éditions La Découverte).

Jarrige Francois, and Le Roux Thomas, 2017, *La Contamination du monde : une histoire des pollutions à l'âge industriel* (Paris : Seuil).

Jeannerod Aude, Schoentjes Pierre, and Sécardin Olivier, 2022, "Littératures francophones & écologie : regards croisés", *Relief*, vol. 16.1, <https://revue-relief.org/issue/view/587> [accessed 7 March 2025].

Kohn Eduardo, 2013, *How Forests Think : Toward an Anthropology beyond the Human* (Oakland : University of California Press).

Kolbert Elizabeth, 2014, *The Sixth Extinction : An Unnatural History* (New York : Henry Holt).

Latour Bruno, 2017, *Facing Gaia : Eight Lectures on the New Climactic Regime* (Cambridge, UK : Polity).

Lloyd Declan, and Mortimer Warren (eds.), 2024, *Digressions in Deep Time : Ecocritical Approaches to Literature and the Arts* (Lanham : MD Rowman and Littlefield).

Malcom Ferdinand, 2019, *Une écologie décoloniale : penser l'écologie depuis le monde caribéen* (Paris : Seuil).

Marsh George Perkins, 2003, *Man and Nature* (Seattle : University of Washington Press).

McKusick James C., 2000, *Green Writing : Romanticism and Ecology* (New York : St. Martin's Press).

Menely Tobias, and Taylor Jesse Oak (eds.), 2017, *Anthropocene Reading. Literary History in Geological Times* (University Park : Penn State University Press).

Merchant Carolyn, 1980, *The Death of Nature : Women, Ecology and the Scientific Revolution* (New York : HarperCollins).

Morgan Benjamin, 2017, "Scale as Form : Thomas Hardy's Rocks and Stars", *Anthropocene Reading : Literary History in Geological Times*, Tobias Menely and Jesse Oak Taylor (eds.) (University Park : Penn State University Press).

Morton Timothy, 2007, *Ecology Without Nature* (Cambridge, MA : Harvard University Press).

Nordhaus William, 2013, *The Climate Casino : Risk, Uncertainty, and Economics for a Warming World* (New Haven : Yale UP).

O'Neal-Henry Anne, and Hollinshead-Strick Cary (eds.), "Fueling the Nineteenth Century : Energy and Nineteenth-Century French Studies", *Nineteenth-Century French Studies*, 53.3–4 (forthcoming).

Ottum Lisa, and Reno Seth T. (eds.), 2016, *Wordsworth and the Green Romantics : Affect and Ecology in the Nineteenth Century* (Lebanon, NH : University of New Hampshire Press).

Pacini Giulia, 2016, "Arboreal Attachments : Interacting with Trees in Early Nineteenth-Century France", *Configurations*, 24.2, p. 173–195.

Posthumus Stephanie, 2017, *French 'Écocritique' : Reading Contemporary French Theory and Fiction Ecologically* (Toronto : University of Toronto Press).

Reno Seth T. (ed.), 2022, *The Anthropocene. Approaches and Contexts for Literature and the Humanities* (Milton Park : Routledge).

Richards Robert J., 2002, *The Romantic Conception of Life : Science and Philosophy in the Age of Goethe* (Chicago : University of Chicago Press).

Romestaing Alain, Schoentjes Pierre, and Simon Anne (eds.), 2015, "Écopoétiques", *Revue Critique de Fixxion Française Contemporaine*, 11, <https://www.fabula.org/actualites/71767/revue-critique-de-fixxion-francaise-contemporaine.html> [accessed 7 March 2025].

Ryan John Charles, 2019, "Foreword : Ecocriticism in the Age of Dislocation ?", *Dix-Neuf : Journal of the Society of Dix-Neuvièmistes*, 23.3-4, p. 163–170.

Sahlins Peter, 1994, *Forest Rites : The War of the Demoiselles in Nineteenth-Century France* (Cambridge, MA : Harvard University Press).

Saito Kohei, 2017, *Karl Marx's Ecosocialism : Capitalism, Nature, and the Unfinished Critique of Political Economy* (New York : Monthly Review Press).

Schoentjes Pierre, 2015, *Ce qui a lieu : essai d'écopoétique* (Marseille : Wildproject).

Schoentjes Pierre, 2020, *Littérature et écologie : le mur des abeilles* (Paris : Éditions Corti).

Séginger Gisèle (ed.), *Urbanature. Savoirs et culture de la biodiversité urbaine*, [https://urbanature.hypotheses.org] [accessed 7 March 2025].

Serres Michel, 1990, *Le Contrat naturel* (Paris : François Bourin).

Simon Anne, 2021, *Une bête entre les lignes. Essai de zoopoétique* (Marseille : Wildproject).

Usher Phillip John, 2019, *Exterranean : Extraction in the Humanist Anthropocene* (New York : Fordham University Press).

Valantin Jean-Michel, 2017, *Géopolitique d'une planète déréglé* (Paris : Seuil).

Weber Andreas, 2019, *Enlivenment : Towards a Poetics for the Anthropocene* (Cambridge, MA : The MIT Press).

Westphal Bertrand, 2007, *La Géocritique : réel, fiction, espace* (Paris : Éditions de Minuit).

Yusoff Kathryn, 2013, "Geologic Life : Prehistory, Climate, Futures in the Anthropocene", *Environment and Planning D : Society and Space*, 31.5, p. 779–795.

Zask Joëlle, 2016, *La Démocratie aux champs : du jardin d'Eden aux jardins partagés* (Paris : La Découverte).

VARIA/*VARIA*

LE MERVEILLEUX NAPOLÉONIEN DANS LES ROMANS DE JEUNESSE DE BALZAC

La transformation de Bonaparte en Napoléon commence bien avant 1804. Dans le *Courrier de l'armée d'Italie*, les exploits du général font de Napoléon « un demi-dieu » (Petiteau, 2004, p. 31), un « être surnaturel » (*ibid.*, p. 40) que l'on retrouve dans l'épopée et au théâtre (Himmelsbach, 1988, p. 80, 218), dans les tableaux de David et de Gros ainsi que, après 1815, dans les chansons de Debraux et de Béranger (Tulard, 1971, p. 31-44). La propagande napoléonienne d'abord et la culture populaire ensuite échafaudent la légende dorée de Napoléon, dont la figure se superpose aux grands conquérants de l'Histoire, au dieu Mars ou à la volonté de la Providence.

De même, la propagande anglaise et les anciens opposants intérieurs produisent, entre 1815 et 1821, plus de cinq cents pamphlets constituant les fondements de la légende noire de l'Empereur (Tulard, 2013). Loin d'adopter la sobriété des libelles de Constant ou de Mme de Staël, Goldsmith et Doris, Rougemaître et De Pradt font de « Buonaparte » un brigand ou un ogre ; ils l'assimilent à l'ange exterminateur Apollyon ou à l'Anti-Christ.

Qu'il soit l'homme du Destin ou le diable, Napoléon dépasse les limites humaines, et son portrait exige le surnaturel. Carrefour « où se superposent les images les plus contradictoires de l'Empereur » (Tulard, 1971, p. 77), *La Comédie humaine* ne fait pas exception dans un siècle littéraire hanté par Napoléon (voir Pagé, 2013 ; Gengembre, 1988) : l'Empereur y apparaît comme le « simulacre de la puissance divine » (*CH*, II, p. 1046) lors de sa dernière revue dans *La Femme de trente ans*, ou figure l'une des « images terribles que le principe du Mal, existant chez l'homme, éternise » (*CH*, XI, p. 487) dans *L'Élixir de longue vie*.

Dans les deux cas, sous la plume de Balzac l'Empereur finit par se transformer « en référence du discours, en élément de langage » (Déruelle,

2021, p. 892-893) ; il devient l'emblème de la Volonté animant les *Études philosophiques* : au-delà du bien et du mal, il est « un homme qui pouvait tout faire », comme le définit Canalis dans *Autre étude de femme*, « parce qu'il voulait tout » (*CH*, III, p. 701).

Si le merveilleux chez Balzac est mis au service du but philosophique consistant à concilier l'Idée et l'image (Amblard, 1972, p. 233), Napoléon constitue la pierre de touche du procédé. Sa figure garantit « une intelligibilité absolue » (Méra, 2004, p. 325) aux forces métaphysiques parcourant *La Comédie humaine* : dans *La Peau de chagrin*, Raphaël éprouve une émotion « semblable à celle que nous avons tous éprouvée devant Napoléon » (*CH*, X, p. 79), alors que la bataille d'Austerlitz évoque, en Louis Lambert, une vision effrayante « comme une page de l'Apocalypse » (*CH*, XI, p. 594).

L'emploi « philosophique » du merveilleux napoléonien n'implique pas l'approbation politique de l'Empereur de la part de Balzac. Son prétendu bonapartisme a souvent été qualifié de supercherie ou de provocation face à la mollesse de la classe politique sous Louis-Philippe (Guyon, 1967, p. 133-135) ; par ailleurs, son admiration pour Napoléon est parfois biaisée par la rentabilité d'opérations commerciales telles que les *Maximes et pensées de Napoléon* (1838, Donnard, 1963). En revanche, les « teintes presque fabuleuses » (*CH*, II, p. 1041) du culte de l'Empereur sont évoquées comme « figure de reproche et de contraste » par rapport au réel (Barbéris, 1972, p. 229).

Le mythe napoléonien dans *Le Médecin de campagne* met en scène la dialectique « besoin-réalité » de Goguelat, sa nécessité d'« élysées compensateurs » (Barbéris, 1970b, p. 1042) face à un monde « qui de plus en plus impitoyablement est celui du désenchantement » (*ibid.*). De même, dans *Une ténébreuse affaire* les *realia* du militaire recouvert de boue jurent avec le mythe de Napoléon, « qui allait avec la rapidité de la foudre » (*CH*, VIII, p. 678), formule figée dans le *Courrier de l'armée d'Italie*.

Balzac démontre maîtriser les codes esthétiques de la légende napoléonienne, qu'elle soit noire ou dorée (Guyon, 1967, p. 134), tirés de l'ensemble hétérogène des documents littéraires, artistiques ou journalistiques sur l'Empereur. Cela nous encourage à revenir sur le rôle de Napoléon en tant qu'emblème philosophique dans *La Comédie humaine*, en nous demandant à quel point la légende napoléonienne a pu contribuer à l'élaboration de l'esthétique romanesque de Balzac.

Pour ce faire, il faut remonter aux années de l'apprentissage de Balzac, entre 1820 et 1824, lorsque les séquelles de la légende noire (Tulard, 1971, p. 51-53) coexistent encore avec le regain de popularité du culte de l'Empereur (Ménager, 1998, p. 189). Même avant la publication du *Mémorial de Sainte-Hélène*, Balzac travaille « dans un Paris fiévreux où les légendes napoléoniennes remplacent l'histoire » (Saint-Paulien, 1979, p. 36), et où la diffusion des pamphlets anti-napoléoniens demeure considérable (Tulard, 2013, p. 47).

S'il est probable que Balzac ait été en contact avec les éléments de la légende noire, il est certain qu'il a connu très tôt la légende dorée : d'abord à Vendôme (Evans, 1951, p. 29), ensuite à travers André Campi (Saint-Paulien, 1979, p. 47), et enfin grâce à Zulma Carraud (Pierrot, 1994, p. 265 ; Saint-Paulien, 1979, p. 62) qui lui permit de connaître « un grand nombre d'officiers ayant fait, avec des fortunes diverses, les guerres de l'Empire » (Guyon, 1951, p. 34), dont le colonel Périolas.

Certes *La Comédie humaine* transformera en mythes la matière contemporaine ; en revanche, l'œuvre de jeunesse de Balzac paraît plutôt extraire « les mythes [que l'époque contemporaine] lui paraît contenir » (Laubriet, 1968, p. 285) pour s'approprier et en réélaborer les repères esthétiques. Encore loin des ambitions sociologiques de la maturité, Balzac est cependant conscient qu'il est impossible de peindre la Restauration sans y insuffler les contrastes entre la morne réalité du temps présent et « les attentes stéréotypées » (Chollet et Vachon, 2012, p. 226) des nostalgiques de l'Empire, ou les chimères de ses antagonistes.

Deux tendances à l'œuvre dans *La Comédie humaine* trouvent ainsi un laboratoire privilégié dans les premiers romans de Balzac. D'une part, l'imaginaire merveilleux de la légende napoléonienne pénètre dans l'écriture du jeune Balzac jusqu'à rendre ses repères emblématiques des manifestations transhistoriques de la Volonté. D'autre part, la légende napoléonienne impose, par contraste, « une impitoyable analyse non tant de la réalité impériale que de ses suites » (Barbéris, 1970b, p. 1042), un contre-discours du réel qui apparaît comme l'antichambre du réalisme de la maturité de l'écrivain.

À travers l'analyse de *Falthurne* et d'*Annette et le criminel*, en passant par *Le Centenaire*, il sera question d'interroger le contraste entre la légende de Napoléon et la misère de ses soldats, entre la grisaille du présent et la gloire du Passé, entre « le principe Honneur » de l'Empire rêvé et « le principe Argent » (*CH*, X, p. 347) qui imprègne l'époque où Balzac écrit.

MATRICANTE ET SAVONATI : SATIRE ET LÉGENDE NAPOLÉONIENNE DANS *FALTHURNE*

Depuis ses premières ébauches littéraires, Balzac entreprend de travailler la distance « entre hier et aujourd'hui » (Déruelle, 2019, p. 106), le passé récent produisant un « double sentiment d'éloignement et de proximité » (*ibid.*) par rapport au temps présent.

En effet, tout en transposant le contexte historique d'*Ivanhoé* en Italie du Sud (Guise, 1972, p. 27), *Falthurne* inscrit le texte de l'abbé Savonati dans un cadre situé juste après la chute de l'Empire. Le pseudo-manuscrit a été récupéré lors des campagnes napoléoniennes par le neveu de Matricante, « caporal au 14e régiment d'infanterie de nos invincibles armées d'Italie » (*OD*, I, p. 677).

D'ailleurs, le savant n'a pas cédé la traduction du texte à un spécialiste parce qu'il connaît des difficultés financières, son neveu se trouvant à la demi-solde (*OD*, I, p. 678). Aux antipodes de la Gloire immortelle que le *Discours sur l'immortalité de l'âme* attribuait à Napoléon (Chollet, 2019, p. 276), le jeune homme apparaît comme le prototype des grognards de l'Empire qui vivront aux marges de la société dans *La Comédie humaine* (Saurel, 1950) : une condition tragicomique, rendue d'autant plus amère par les singeries que Matricante adresse à M. Sophistiquet pour qu'il place « son neveu garçon de bureau au ministère de la Guerre » (*OD*, I, p. 700).

La tentation de Matricante de brûler le manuscrit de Savonati suggère le danger politique du texte (*OD*, I, p. 699). En opposition à l'exactitude et aux longueurs des mémorialistes (*OD*, I, p. 646-647), les manipulations du traducteur feraient du manuscrit de Savonati un éloge indirect de l'Empire. La célébration de la France qui accompagne le débarquement de Robert voile en réalité un apologue de la France impériale, et le profil de Napoléon se dessine lorsque l'on exalte les Français « maîtres du monde, sous un chef digne d'eux, sous un gouvernement capitolien ! » (*OD*, I, p. 707)

La « réalité insupportable » (Ménager, 1988, p. 32) de la Restauration, qui se manifeste dans le premier cadre du récit, serait ainsi rachetée par le merveilleux napoléonien qui imprègne le pseudo-manuscrit, en dressant une résistance moins politique qu'esthétique au temps présent.

Il est aisé de percevoir un rapport de continuité entre le monde de Falthurne, peuplé par les « descendants sans gloire de tant de grands hommes » (*OD*, I, p. 678), et la France de Louis XVIII. D'une part, le texte s'ouvre sur l'amère considération que la Nature efface tout, y compris « des générations, des siècles et des Empires » (*OD*, I, p. 677) ; d'autre part, le mythe du sauveur incarné par Napoléon se prolonge dans la sorcière Falthurne, destinée, comme l'Empereur, à délivrer « l'humanité de ses vieilles chaînes » (*OD*, I, p. 698).

Le lien entre les deux est établi à partir de l'étymologie du mot « Falthurne », qui « voulait dire, soit brillant tyran, soit brillante tyrannie, ou bien la tyrannie de la lumière » (*OD*, I, p. 702). De même que Napoléon, étant à la fois « un autocrate malgré lui ou un libéral sans le savoir » (Guyon, 1967, p. 134), Falthurne synthétise les pôles antithétiques du despotisme et des valeurs illuminées de l'humanisme.

Balzac reproduit ainsi dans ses premières ébauches romanesques l'ambiguïté d'un mythe napoléonien qui est tout à fait « à double face » (Petiteau, 2004, p. 31), sans sacrifier aucune de ses deux facettes. À l'image de Napoléon, Falthurne est ange et démon, résultant de « la fusion de la sorcière de Sommaris et de l'ange du Mont Sarano » (*OD*, I, p. 1532). L'opération témoigne moins d'un engagement politique que du soin « sociologique » de peindre le phénomène dans toute son ambivalence.

Le véritable contraste se mesure moins entre la légende noire et la légende dorée qu'entre la sphère mythique du manuscrit de Savonati et l'ironie amère, désacralisée (« anti-mythique », pour paraphraser Barbéris [1970b]) de Matricante. Qu'elle fasse de Falthurne un ange ou un démon, la légende napoléonienne creuse l'écart entre l'Idéal que l'on attribue au souverain et le réel des sujets, entre le pouvoir sublime de l'Empereur et le grotesque, voire le ridicule, de ceux qui lui ont survécu.

N'étant remarquable que dans *Falthurne* à proprement parler, l'opposition entre l'Empereur de la légende et Matricante paraît s'affirmer en cours de route, pendant que Balzac avance dans la rédaction du texte. Le prétendu transformisme politique du savant (Castex, 1950, p. 15) s'expliquerait par le fait que le temps présent d'*Agathise* est reculé par rapport à *Falthurne*. L'un se situe sous la Restauration, alors que l'autre se déroule sous l'Empire. En effet, contrairement à celui de *Falthurne*, le Matricante d'*Agathise* ne craint aucune censure à cause de son bonapartisme ; au contraire, il revendique l'affiliation de son neveu au 14e régiment d'infanterie et évite de traduire un passage lyrique de Savonati célébrant le « siècle de la féodalité » (*OD*, I, p. 667).

Les « circonstances actuelles » (*OD*, I, p. 667) de la traduction du manuscrit auraient ainsi changé au fil de l'écriture, en modifiant la posture de l'œuvre. La parodie des velléités héroï-comiques de l'Empire dans *Agathise* (printemps 1820) adopte dans *Falthurne* (été 1820) les contours plus sombres d'une compensation romanesque face à un monde qui n'est plus à la hauteur des espoirs des vaincus de la Restauration (Ménager, 1988, p. 56).

La convergence entre Falthurne et l'Empereur s'effectue d'ailleurs par l'adoption de l'iconographie liée à la légende napoléonienne. Sans compter les « proportions gigantesques » (*CH*, VIII, p. 678) que Napoléon prend dans l'imagination de Laurence dans *Une ténébreuse affaire*, Balzac évoque déjà « la prestigieuse image d'un géant de cinq pieds[1] » pour dépeindre Napoléon dans *La Mode* du 2 octobre 1830. Dix ans auparavant, Falthurne affiche une stature « colossale pour une femme » (*OD*, I, p. 691). Cela vaut autant pour le regard de la sorcière : Napoléon est célèbre pour « la flamme » de ses yeux (Jourdain, 2021, p. 94) ; de même, dans ceux de Falthurne une « espèce de flamme paraît y pétiller tant sa prunelle est brillante » (*OD*, I, p. 685). De ses yeux émane une Volonté face à laquelle « l'homme n'a qu'à courber la tête » (*OD*, I, p. 689), et qui s'exerce par une force « au milieu du concert magique des puissances infernales » (*OD*, I, p. 691).

Certes, un tel répertoire infernal est présent dans d'autres œuvres bien connues par le jeune Balzac, dont *Melmoth ou L'Homme errant* (1820) de Maturin. Néanmoins, le roman ne fut traduit qu'en 1821 (*OD*, I, p. 1541). L'évocation des origines infernales du pouvoir de la sorcière paraît renvoyer plutôt au côté satanique de la légende noire, que Jean Tulard fait remonter à l'œuvre de Dubuc de Marentille, *L'Identité de Napoléon et de l'Antéchrist complètement démontrée* (1810) (Tulard, 1971, p. 51-53), et qui trouve des épigones dans le pamphlet de l'abbé Jean Wendel Wurtz, *L'Apollyon de l'Apocalypse ou la Révolution française prédite par Saint-Jean* (1816), et dans l'anonyme *Lamuel ou le Livre du seigneur* [...], *histoire authentique de l'empereur Apollyon et du roi Béhémot* (1816).

Les continuités entre l'imaginaire napoléonien et *Falthurne* sont nombreuses mais elles ne permettent pas d'établir de manière certaine un

1 Cité par Guyon, 1951, p. 32.

rapport de dérivation. Nous allons ainsi analyser comment les éléments cernés par *Falthurne* s'organisent en système cohérent, en relation avec l'imaginaire napoléonien, dans *Le Centenaire ou Les Deux Béringheld.*

TULLIUS ET BÉRINGHELD : L'EMPEREUR ET SON SOLDAT DANS *LE CENTENAIRE*

Falthurne s'articulait autour du contraste entre deux plans narratifs et deux tendances discursives opposées : l'ironie amère de Matricante et le sombre pouvoir de la sorcière. En revanche, *Le Centenaire ou les deux Béringheld* synthétise l'opposition dans le rapport entre Tullius, vicomte qui s'est joint à l'armée napoléonienne, et son *Doppelgänger*, l'ancêtre alchimiste Béringheld.

Les lecteurs familiers du texte ne rencontreront aucune difficulté à percevoir une forme de continuité entre Falthurne et le sorcier du *Centenaire.* Béringheld est d'une taille « gigantesque » (*PR*, I, p. 874) ; il a « une bouche d'une grandeur démesurée » (*PR*, I, p. 872) et des « jambes massives » (*PR*, I, p. 872). Son regard annonce une énergie surhumaine : « la pupille seule brillait solitairement de ce filet de flamme brûlante, sèche et comme flamboyante » (*PR*, I, p. 871).

Malgré le sens philosophique de la représentation de Béringheld (Van Laere, 1968, p. 135-148), le sorcier s'insère dans le devenir de l'Histoire : appartenant plutôt « à la minéralogie qu'à l'ordre animal » (*PR*, I, 871), Béringheld est présenté comme une sorte de monument : « si l'on avait à faire la statue du Destin, il en rendrait à merveille l'inflexibilité » (*PR*, I, p. 871), à la fois symbole de l'écoulement du Temps et de la résistance que les œuvres humaines y opposent.

Les implications politiques du concept de « monument » sont claires : associé aux « pyramides d'Égypte » (*PR*, I, p. 968), Béringheld évoque par analogie la colonne de la place Vendôme, métonymie de l'Empereur et décor habituel dans les représentations des vétérans de la Grande Armée sous la Restauration, dépeints « au pied d'une colonne incomplète – le haut manquait, par prudence » (Vidalenc, 1955, p. 190).

Les lectures politiques du *Centenaire* sont rares, et ne concernent que de manière marginale Napoléon (Martonyi, 1990). *Le Centenaire* serait avant tout un « roman familial », dont le cadre de l'Empire ne réfléchirait que le rapport père-fils (Lorant, 1986, p. 59-60).

Cependant, l'envers paraît également plausible, le rapport père-fils réfléchissant une condition politique plus large. Lucette Besson cite à juste titre la lettre d'Honoré à Laure dans laquelle Bernard-François est associé à une pyramide d'Égypte (Besson, 1997, p. 380), mais cela n'empêche que la figure du père dans *Le Centenaire* soit moins littérale que symbolique. En effet, dans le *Mémoire sur deux grandes obligations à remplir par les Français*, Bernard-François Balzac demandait la construction d'une pyramide plus vaste que celles d'Égypte pour célébrer la gloire de l'Empereur (Saint-Paulien, 1979, p. 19).

Étant donné la stérilité du comte de Béringheld, Tullius est disputé entre deux pères, aussi allégoriques l'un que l'autre : le sorcier, sorte de divinité tutélaire de la lignée aristocratique des Béringheld, et Napoléon.

Bien que Besson considère le vieillard Béringheld comme une transfiguration de Bernard-François (Besson, 1997, p. 379), âgé de soixante-seize ans à la publication du *Centenaire*, n'oublions pas que le contraste entre le pouvoir illimité de Napoléon et la faiblesse du corps de Bonaparte est déjà un *leitmotiv* célèbre parmi les détracteurs de Napoléon (Petiteau, 2004, p. 77), qui intègre toute lecture intime du roman.

Béringheld paraît ainsi une sorte de *Doppelgänger* de l'Empereur, enfin délivré des limites de l'homme Bonaparte. Le sorcier s'adresse aux mortels en les appelant « enfants d'un jour », ce qui évoque les *Nouvelles Messéniennes* (1822) de Delavigne, où l'on dit laconiquement de Napoléon qu'il n'a « régné qu'un jour[2] ». De plus, les deux sont des “vampires”, se nourrissant de l'énergie vitale de leurs victimes. À l'instar de Béringheld, dans *De Buonaparte et des Bourbons* Chateaubriand définit Napoléon comme « un Moloch dévoreur d'enfants » (Petiteau, 2004, p. 50), en donnant une dignité littéraire à un mythe dont les manifestations sont cependant nombreuses (Houdecek, 2022) : déjà dans ses *Mémoires pour servir à l'histoire de France*, Salgues dépeint Napoléon comme « couvert du sang de ses concitoyens[3] ».

2 Cité par Tulard, 2013, p. 32.
3 Cité par Petiteau, 2004, p. 34.

Une distinction si nette pourrait conduire à une dichotomie simpliste, que *Le Centenaire* nuance cependant avec finesse. Béringheld ne représente pas une puissance transhistorique « légitime », opposée à l'Usurpateur. En revanche, il conserve la même duplicité que la synthèse des légendes attribue à Napoléon. Parfois anthropophage, le sorcier est néanmoins ange « vainqueur de la mort » et manifestation d'une « puissance céleste » (*PR*, I, p. 924) : la nécessité de préserver la vie de son descendant le contraint à utiliser ses pouvoirs du côté de la Grande Armée, en sauvant Tullius à Gizeh, à Jaffa, en Espagne.

Les manifestations du pouvoir du Centenaire sont les mêmes que celles que Goguelat attribue à l'Empereur dans *Le Médecin de campagne*, dont la clairvoyance et l'ubiquité. Si le succès de la campagne d'Italie s'est vérifié « comme Napoléon l'avait prédit » (*CH*, IX, p. 522), le départ d'Égypte avait consolidé la croyance en l'ubiquité du général, qui « se transportait en un clin d'œil d'un lieu à un autre, comme un oiseau » (*CH*, IX, p. 524). De la même manière, Béringheld surprend Tullius en se manifestant aux quatre coins de l'Europe pour réaliser ses propres prophéties.

Lors de la campagne de Syrie, Napoléon n'est pas seulement immunisé contre la peste (*CH*, IX, p. 525), mais il assume aussi les mêmes pouvoirs (Chanteranne, 2021) que ceux que Marc Bloch attribuait aux rois thaumaturges et que Gros a peint dans *Les Pestiférés de Jaffa* (1804)[4]. De la même manière, grâce aux interventions de son génie tutélaire, Tullius devient aussi invulnérable que son général, capable de passer à travers « les décharges de mitraille qui nous emportaient comme des mouches, et qui avaient du respect pour sa tête » (*CH*, IX, p. 521).

D'ailleurs, les colloques entre l'officier et son mentor surhumain évoquent les rencontres surnaturelles entre Napoléon et le mystérieux Homme rouge (*CH*, IX, p. 527). L'article « Napoléon » du *Dictionnaire infernal*, que Prioult considère comme une des sources du *Centenaire* (Prioult, 1936, p. 158), attribue un sens néfaste au génie, qui était « apparu à Napoléon Ier pour lui annoncer ses revers » (Collin, 1863, I, p. 340). Au contraire, l'Homme rouge du *Médecin de campagne* paraît plutôt, comme Béringheld, une incarnation de la Volonté, dont Napoléon se sert « pour communiquer avec son étoile » (*CH*, IX, p. 527).

4 Le même épisode revient dans *Falthurne II*, dont la datation est proche de celle du *Centenaire*. Comme Napoléon, Minna n'a aucune crainte des lépreux (voir *OD*, I, p. 896). Le vieillard auprès duquel elle s'approche est d'ailleurs un vétéran revenant de Syrie.

À l'instar de l'Homme rouge, le Centenaire permet à son descendant Tullius de satisfaire tous ses désirs, d'accomplir toutes ses volontés, ce qui va conduire le militaire au désespoir : en « parvenant à ces nouvelles sommités de choses humaines, il tomba dans le dégoût qui le saisissait ordinairement lorsqu'il arrivait à *quelque faîte* » (*PR*, I, p. 974). À travers Béringheld, Tullius fait l'expérience du surhumain que la légende attribue à Napoléon : ses deux pères symboliques ne font plus qu'un. Mais le résultat est loin de l'enthousiasme des vétérans de la Grande Armée. Le passage à la maturité héroïque engendre le dégoût des choses mortelles, de même [que] l'éprouve [le héros] du *Pacte* (1822), lui aussi s'étant glissé, cette fois littéralement, sous la peau de l'Empereur.

Falthurne plaçait l'opposition entre l'Idéal de Napoléon et les *realia* de ses soldats sur deux plans narratifs différents ; au contraire, *Le Centenaire* fait de l'antithèse l'essence même de l'intrigue. Néanmoins, le dernier affrontement de Tullius et Béringheld n'aboutit pas : le contraste entre la Volonté démesurée du sorcier et les forces humaines du jeune officier se dissout sans que le conflit ne voie triompher l'un ou l'autre. Comme le fera Chabert, Tullius et son adversaire s'effacent. La dichotomie qui traverse *Le Centenaire* est destinée à se prolonger dans les romans postérieurs du jeune Balzac, dont *Annette et le criminel*, en se résolvant dans la synthèse d'une nouvelle force historique et littéraire : l'Argent.

ENTRE LA GLOIRE ET L'ARGENT : ARGOW DANS *ANNETTE ET LE CRIMINEL*

Malgré la saisie du *Vicaire des Ardennes*, Balzac veut continuer son « chemin comme par le passé, et, entre nous soit dit, je crois que *le Centenaire* et *la Dernière Fée* l'ont bien prouvé » (*PR*, II, p. 444). La réticence laisse sous-entendre une volonté d'ordre politique, bien que la fréquentation de Laure de Berny et de Jean Thomassy contribue à estomper, dès 1823, son jacobinisme radical (Saint-Paulien, 1979, p. 57-59).

Si *La Dernière fée* utilise l'imaginaire féérique pour développer une satire du temps présent, de même que dans *L'Ogre de Corse* (1814) de Rougemaître, la persistance des reliquats de la légende napoléonienne va cependant s'adapter par la suite aux nouveaux équilibres sociaux inaugurés par la Restauration.

Annette et le criminel s'ouvre par la rencontre de l'héroïne avec le chef d'une bande de brigands, ayant, comme Falthurne et Béringheld, « l'œil plein d'énergie étonnante et d'une assurance prodigieuse » (*PR*, II, p. 470) : il s'agit d'Argow, le pirate du *Vicaire des Ardennes*.

Certes, la figure du brigand ou du pirate constitue l'un des repères principaux du romantisme : songeons, parmi les références culturelles du jeune Balzac, au *Corsaire* (1814) de Byron. Cependant, le thème du hors-la-loi ne constitue ici qu'un biais pour atteindre la légende noire de Napoléon. En effet, de nombreux libelles, dont l'anonyme *Le Brigand corse* [1816-1818], dénoncent les origines criminelles de l'Usurpateur. L'ambiguïté du proscrit romantique serait d'autant plus cohérente avec une légende napoléonienne qui, chez Balzac, mélange les repères de la légende noire et dorée, jusqu'à atteindre le charme et la démesure d'un Prométhée chez Argow.

Le Vicaire des Ardennes associait Argow moins à Napoléon qu'à Cromwell, le pirate se présentant comme « le célèbre protecteur de l'Angleterre, lorsque pour la première fois il parut au parlement » (*PR*, II, p. 229). Le rapport avec Napoléon est aussi indirect que significatif : « en un temps où il était délicat de parler de l'*Autre* » (Tulard, 1971, p. 62), Cromwell est désormais l'emblème de Napoléon, comme le témoigne la prolifération d'ouvrages à ce sujet, dont l'*Histoire de la République d'Angleterre et de Cromwell* de Guizot, le *Cromwell* d'Hugo et celui de Balzac (Lorant, 1983 ; Heathcote, 2019).

En effet, *Cromwell* établit le même rapport entre le merveilleux et le politique que l'on retrouve dans *Falthurne* et *Le Centenaire* : « Le mot de liberté créa tous ces prodiges, / Il fut le talisman dont les brillants prestiges/Faisaient du Parlement triompher les drapeaux » (*OD*, I, p. 924).

Cependant, Balzac se sert ici d'un aspect de la légende noire négligé dans les romans à venir : l'avidité de l'Usurpateur. Dans *L'Ogre de Corse*, Bonaparte est accusé d'avoir tout dévoré lors de la campagne d'Italie : « de la toile, du marbre, de l'or, de l'argent, du bronze » (Rougemaître, 1815, p. 24). De même, le pouvoir de Cromwell se manifeste par l'Argent : « D'un traité si honteux l'argent seul fut le prix/Cromwell, en les payant, prodigua ses mépris » (*OD*, I, p. 926).

Alors que *Le Vicaire des Ardennes* insistait sur le caractère exceptionnel d'Argow en tant que bandit, *Annette et le criminel* lui attribue une nouvelle identité bourgeoise, sans renoncer à la stature surhumaine (et napoléonienne) du personnage.

Après la saisie du *Vicaire*, la crainte de la censure rend l'indentification avec l'Empereur plus opaque. Argow est « comme l'aigle » (*PR*, II, p. 470), et les références napoléoniennes se limitent à l'allusion : « on appliquait à sa figure les idées que l'on conçoit de certains hommes historiques, dont on se trace un portrait idéal » (*PR*, II, p. 471). Néanmoins, en devenant le riche Maxendi, Argow concentre les repères de la légende napoléonienne sur l'Argent, de même que le fera Castanier, ancien dragon de l'Empire, dans *Melmoth réconcilié* (Perron, 1983, p. 42).

Argow est « une image de la puissance sous ses deux formes, la forme temporelle et la forme spirituelle » (Bardèche, 1940, p. 168) : le thème de l'argent comble le creux entre l'époque militaire et industrielle que *De l'esprit de conquête et de l'usurpation* (1814) de Constant envisageait dans la chute de l'Empire (Barbéris, 1970b, p. 1034), en conservant les traits mystiques animant Béringheld et Falthurne.

En effet, l'Argow d'*Annette et le criminel* s'échafaude sur les mêmes repères esthétiques de ses prédécesseurs : il « apparaissait à [l'] imagination comme un monument » (*PR*, II, p. 474) et « l'énergie extraordinaire de son âme brillait comme l'éclair parmi les nuages » (*PR*, II, p. 474). Comme Béringheld, Argow apparaît et disparaît instantanément (*PR*, t. II, p. 480), et manifeste une sorte d'invulnérabilité, en survivant miraculeusement à l'agression de Navardin (*PR*, II, p. 512-514).

D'ailleurs, Annette affiche elle aussi une certaine « disposition à la grandeur » (*PR*, II, p. 458) : en la regardant, Argow « baissa aussitôt ses yeux qu'il sentait exprimer une flamme terrible et jeter du feu » (*PR*, II, p. 525). Couple « napoléonien » transplanté sous la Restauration, Argow et Annette nous permettent de saisir la grandeur héroïque de Napoléon, puisque l'on conçoit « mieux l'immensité par un de ses fragments, l'infini par un immense fini » (*PR*, II, p. 540), de même que la cathédrale de Montivers est une métonymie de la grandeur de Dieu.

Le couple est néanmoins victime de la société de la Restauration, ce qui anticipe le sort des amoureux de *La Vendetta*. C'est l'autre prétendant d'Annette, son cousin Charles Servigné, qui va causer leur perte. Emblème des nouveaux parvenus, Charles est le contraire d'Argow :

avide et désireux de réussir, il craint que l'offre que son oncle a faite de « l'habillement de trois gardes d'honneur à Sa Majesté l'ex-empereur » (*PR*, II, p. 453) puisse compromettre sa carrière. Ironiquement, il sera le seul héritier de la fortune du couple, après avoir causé leur mort (*PR*, II, p. 672).

Charles fait de sorte que « la réalité sociale commence à avoir, dans l'œuvre de Balzac, une place plus importante » (Bardèche, 1940, p. 171), mais celle-ci est d'abord le résultat d'un désenchantement, une forme d'opposition à l'idéalisme napoléonien dont s'imprègne le couple : « *l'envers* de la Gloire » (*Corr.*, I, p. 37) qui tourmentait le jeune écrivain en 1819 finit par intégrer son esthétique romanesque, jusqu'à devenir le moteur même du drame.

L'échec d'Argow et d'Annette ouvre ainsi la voie à une écriture qui, loin de refouler la légende napoléonienne, en conserve la trace en tant qu'envers : le sublime autrefois incarné par les conférences entre Tullius et Béringheld ne fait plus, dans *La Dernière fée*, que l'objet des ragots sur Abel, jeune homme que l'on « voyait quelquefois le soir au clair de la lune, causer avec un revenant qui voltigeait comme une ombre » (*PR*, II, p. 48).

EN GUISE DE CONCLUSION

La fin du cycle Pollet ne fait pas tomber le rideau sur l'imaginaire napoléonien dans l'œuvre de Balzac. Argow constitue une ébauche de Vautrin (Vernière, 1948), dont les qualités surhumaines en font le « Bonaparte » des voleurs (*CH*, III, p. 208). D'ailleurs, le corrupteur de Lucien de Rubempré paraît mettre en scène le commandement que Béringheld adresse à son descendant Tullius, « la vie est *tout* ! » (*PR*, I, p. 1010), lorsqu'il sauve la vie de son 'disciple'.

Cependant, d'autres persistances napoléoniennes plus profondes s'insinuent dans le tissu de *La Comédie humaine*. Dans *La Maison du Chat-qui-pelote*, dont le titre originel était significativement *Gloire et malheur*, M. Guillaume a des « petits yeux verts [qui] flamboyaient » (*CH*, I, p. 44-45) comme ceux de Falthurne ou Béringheld. Sa célèbre affiche ayant pris la place de la colonne Vendôme, monsieur Guillaume garde en germe le merveilleux de ses prédécesseurs, ancré dans les aspects les plus anodins de la vie quotidienne : sa fortune réside en effet dans le fait qu'il fournissait ses draps à la Garde impériale (*CH*, I, p. 62).

L'iconographie napoléonienne sert le succès financier tout autant que la faillite. Dans *La Recherche de l'Absolu*, Claës est tellement obsédé par l'alchimie que « ni la première chute de Napoléon, ni le retour des Bourbons ne le tirèrent de ses occupations » (*CH*, X, p. 746). Certes, l'alchimiste incarne l'échec de la Volonté philosophique, mais celle-ci se mesure toujours à l'épreuve du triomphe de la Volonté historique de Napoléon.

Envers de la déroute humaine, la légende napoléonienne se révèle ainsi le terrain privilégié pour mettre en relief le clivage entre l'Idéal et le Réel. *La Peau de chagrin* nous rappelle que les légendes liées à Napoléon nous permettent de « fuir de désespérantes vérités » (*CH*, X, p. 79) : qui mieux que Hyacinthe Chabert, méconnaissable par les cicatrices qu'il a remportées à Eylau, pourrait témoigner de l'écart qui sépare son corps de celui de l'Empereur (Roulin et Windish, 2012), invulnérable, immortel, divin ? Peut-être seulement Philippe de Soucy, « sec, maigre, nerveux » (*CH*, X, p. 975) après la campagne de Russie dans *Adieu*.

À l'instar de l'épopée chevaleresque dans *Don Quichotte*, Balzac est conscient du contraste opposant le réel et la légende napoléonienne déjà lorsqu'il associe, dans *La Dernière fée*, l'aliénation d'Abel à la folie d'un auditeur auquel Napoléon confie son portefeuille (voir *PR*, II, p. 60). De même, dans *Clotilde de Lusignan* l'Idéal romanesque est associé à un mirage, l'écrivain étant « semblable au soldat français qui, succombant à la fatigue, à la soif, apercevait, au milieu des sables brûlants de l'Égypte des ruisseaux limpides et des ombrages frais produits par le *mirage* » (*PR*, I, p. 755). L'Égypte, la vie militaire et le mirage ne peuvent qu'évoquer *Une passion dans le désert*, en étendant sur *Clotilde de Lusignan* l'ombre des légionnaires de Napoléon : une association d'autant plus étroite si l'on considère que, comme le rappelle *Le Médecin de campagne*, « Napoléon veut dire *le lion du désert* » (*CH*, XI, p. 536).

Peut-être non sans raison, dans *L'Héritière de Birague* l'ivrogne Vielle-Roche roule « dans un ruisseau de deux pieds de profondeur, où il but tant d'eau, qu'il en mourut » (*PR*, I, p. 252). L'allégorie aquatique de *Clotilde de Lusignan* se prolonge sans perdre sa valeur politique : Chanclos et Vielle-Roche se sont battus à côté d'Henri IV, leur « *invincible maître* » (*PR*, I, p. 52) et contrepoint de Napoléon, dont la statue sur la colonne Vendôme a été fondue en 1814 pour réaliser celle d'Henri IV sur le Pont Neuf[5].

Ainsi, l'Idéal peut nous faire mourir de soif ou nous noyer, comme le démontrent nombre d'autres grognards, ridicules mais aimables, dans *La Comédie humaine* (Saurel, 1950). D'autres hommes, comme Charles Servigné, sont comme « l'eau qui se glisse dans toutes les sinuosités d'un rocher en en prenant les formes » (*PR*, II, p. 453). Qu'il s'agisse de ridicules ou d'opposants ambitieux, plusieurs types commencent ainsi à renvoyer, par contraste ou par analogie, à la légende napoléonienne, en démontrant une souplesse de réemploi jusque-là inattendue.

Cela parvient même à brouiller les frontières morales entre le héros et l'anti-héros. Dans *Wann-Chlore*, Landon est un amant inconstant mais est également loin d'être un simple *miles gloriosus* : après avoir perdu sa maîtresse par son absence prolongée lors des campagnes napoléoniennes, il se trouve suspendu entre un « amour d'Empire », Jane, aussi absolu que fatal, et la banalité bourgeoise d'un « amour de Restauration », Eugénie, première ébauche de la plus célèbre Grandet.

Ainsi, les rapports de l'imaginaire napoléonien avec l'œuvre de Balzac paraissent bien plus nuancés que ceux que nous avons tracés. Si Napoléon finit par définir le fondement de tout un roman, comme *Wann-Chlore* le laisse présumer, il faudrait alors prendre à la lettre Mme Vauquer : pour raconter les vicissitudes de ses pensionnaires, il faudrait s'appuyer sur le merveilleux de l'Empereur, dont la légende, par rapport aux soucis ménagers, est « dans l'ordre des choses possibles » (*CH*, III, p. 233).

Michele MORSELLI
Université de Bologne

---

5 Nous pouvons là encore renvoyer au libelle de Bernard François Balzac, l'*Opuscule sur la statue équestre que les Français doivent faire ériger pour perpétuer la mémoire d'Henri IV* (Barbéris, 1970a, p. 218-219).

OUVRAGES ET ÉTUDES CITÉS

Amblard Marie-Claude, 1972, *L'Œuvre fantastique de Balzac. Sources et philosophie*, Paris Marcel Didier.

Barbéris Pierre, 1970a, *Balzac et le mal du siècle. Contribution à une physiologie du monde moderne*, t. I, *1799-1829. Une expérience de l'absurde : aliénations et prises de conscience*, Paris Gallimard.

Barbéris Pierre, 1970b, « Napoléon : structures et signification d'un mythe littéraire », *Revue d'Histoire littéraire de la France*, vol. 70, nº 5-6, p. 1031-1058.

Barbéris Pierre, 1972, *Mythes balzaciens*, Paris Armand Colin.

Bardèche Maurice, 1940, *Balzac romancier : la formation de l'art du roman chez Balzac jusqu'à la publication du* Père Goriot *(1820-1835)*, Paris Plon.

Besson Lucette, 1997, « La figure du père dans les œuvres de jeunesse de Balzac », *AB*, p. 375-392.

Castex Pierre-Georges, 1950, « Étude préliminaire à l'édition de *Falthurne* », dans Honoré de Balzac, *Falthurne, manuscrit de l'abbé Savonati, traduit de l'italien par M. Matricante, instituteur primaire*, texte inédit établi et présenté par Pierre-Georges Castex, Paris José Corti, p. XI-LXXXV.

Chanteranne Philippe, 2021, *Les douze morts de Napoléon*, Paris Passés Composés-Humensis.

Chollet Roland et Vachon Stéphane, 2012, *À l'écoute du jeune Balzac. L'écho des premières œuvres publiées (1822-1829)*, Saint-Denis-Montréal Presses Universitaires de Vincennes-Lévesque.

Chollet Roland, 2019, « L'Homme qui dispose de la pensée », dans *Id.*, *À la lumière de Balzac. Études (1965-2012)*, édition de Marie-Bénédicte Diethelm, Paris Classiques Garnier, p. 275-295.

Collin de Plancy Jacques, [1818] 1863, *Dictionnaire infernal. Répertoire universel*, Paris Plon.

Déruelle Aude, 2019, « Balzac penseur de l'histoire ? », dans Francesco Spandri (dir.), *Balzac penseur*, Paris, Classiques Garnier, p. 101-114.

Déruelle Aude, 2021, « Napoléon », dans Éric Bordas, Pierre Glaudes et Nicole Mozet (dir.), *Dictionnaire Balzac*, Paris Classiques Garnier, t. II, p. 892-893.

Donnard Jean-Hervé, 1963, « À propos d'une supercherie littéraire. Le "bonapartisme" de Balzac », *AB*, p. 123-143.

Evans Henri, 1951, Louis Lambert *et la philosophie de Balzac*, Paris Corti.

Gengembre Gérard, 1988, *À vos plumes citoyens ! Écrivains, journalistes, orateurs et poètes, de la Bastille à Waterloo*, Paris Gallimard.

Guise René, 1972, « Le problème de *Falthurne*. Pour une nouvelle lecture du premier essai romanesque de Balzac », *AB*, p. 3-42.

Guyon Bernard, [1947] 1967, *La Pensée politique et sociale de Balzac*, deuxième édition augmentée, Paris Colin.

Guyon Bernard, 1951, *La Création littéraire chez Balzac. La Genèse du* Médecin de campagne, Paris Colin.

Heathcote Owen, 2019, « La pensée politique de Balzac dans *Cromwell* », *AB*, p. 89-101.

Himmelsbach Siegbert, 1988, *L'Épopée ou la "case vide" : la réflexion poétologique sur l'épopée nationale en France*, Tübingen Niemeyer.

Houdecek François, 2022, « Napoléon, le dévoreur de la jeunesse française », dans Thierry Lentz et Jean Lopez (dir.), *Les Mythes de la Grande Armée*, Paris Perrin, p. 317-330.

Jourdain Annie, 2021, *Napoléon. Héros, Imperator, Mécène*, Paris Flammarion.

Laubriet Pierre, 1968, « La légende et le mythe napoléonien chez Balzac », *AB*, p. 285-301.

Lee Scott, 2002, *Traces de l'excès. La nouvelle philosophique de Balzac*, Paris Champion.

Lorant André, 1983, « De Cromwell à Argow », *AB*, p. 313-317.

Lorant André, 1986, « *Le Centenaire* », *AB*, p. 59-87.

Martonyi Eva, 1990, « L'expression de la peur révolutionnaire dans *Le Centenaire* », *AB*, p. 291-306.

Ménager Bernard, 1988, *Les Napoléon du peuple*, Paris Aubier.

Méra Brigitte, 2004, *Balzac et la figure mythique dans les* Études philosophiques, Paris L'Harmattan.

Pagé Sylvain, 2013, *Le Mythe napoléonien : de Las Cases à Victor Hugo*, Paris Éditions du CNRS.

Perron Paul, 1983, « Désir du sujet/sujet du désir : *Melmoth réconcilié* », *Nineteenth-Century French Studies*, vol. 12, n° 1-2, p. 36-53.

Petiteau Nathalie, [1999] 2004, *Napoléon, de la mythologie à l'histoire*, édition revue par l'auteur, Paris Seuil.

Petiteau Nathalie, 2012, « Le Napoléon des mémorialistes : construction, traces et contestations du mythe », dans *Ead.*, *Écrire la mémoire : mémorialistes de la Révolution et de l'Empire*, Paris Les Indes savantes, p. 183-211.

Pierrot Roger, 1994, *Honoré de Balzac*, Paris Fayard.

Prioult Albert, 1936, *Balzac avant* La Comédie humaine *: 1818-1829, contribution à l'étude de la genèse de son œuvre*, Paris Courville.

Rougemaître de Dieuze C. J., [1814] 1815, *L'Ogre de Corse, histoire véritable et merveilleuse*, Paris Louis.

Roulin Jean-Marie et Windish Colette, 2012, « The return of the undead : the body politic in *Le Colonel Chabert* », *South Central Review*, vol. 29, n° 3, p. 20-35.

Saint-Paulien, 1979, *Napoléon, Balzac et l'Empire de la* Comédie humaine, Paris Michel.

Saurel Louis, 1950, « Les soldats vus par Balzac », *Europe*, vol. 28, n° 55-56, p. 101-104.

Tulard Jean, [1964] 2013, *L'anti-Napoléon. La légende noire de l'Empereur*, nouvelle éd. revue et augmentée, Paris Gallimard.

Tulard Jean, 1971, *Le Mythe de Napoléon*, Paris Colin.

Van Laere François, 1968, « *Les Deux Béringheld* ou la préfiguration des *Études philosophiques* » *AB*, p. 135-148.

Vernière Paul, 1948, « Balzac et la genèse de Vautrin », *Revue d'Histoire littéraire de la France*, vol. 48, n° 1, p. 53-68.

Vidalenc Jean, 1955, *Les Demi-solde. Étude d'une catégorie sociale*, Paris Rivière.

GENÈSE ET EFFET DE L'INTERTEXTE BALZACIEN

Autour d'un bal de Lady Dudley

En 1838, au cours d'une période de création remarquable qui voit naître ou aboutir de nombreux projets d'écriture, Balzac entreprend la rédaction d'une œuvre devant s'intituler *Les Amours forcés*. Rapidement mise de côté, cette ébauche devient plutôt le point de départ de deux nouveaux romans : *Une fille d'Ève*, qui paraîtra en feuilleton dans *Le Siècle* du 31 décembre 1838 au 14 janvier 1839, et la première partie de *Béatrix*[1], qui s'échelonnera dans la même revue du 13 avril au 19 mai 1839[2]. Ces deux œuvres se partagent un premier matériel génétique puisque dans l'une comme dans l'autre seront intégrées des pages de l'ébauche initiale[3], le verso servant même à la rédaction de *Béatrix*. Outre cette conception jumelle, *Une fille d'Ève* et *Béatrix* se distinguent surtout du reste de la production balzacienne par une pratique intertextuelle marquée par la réutilisation non signalée de textes de Théophile Gautier ayant déjà fait l'objet d'une publication. Pour l'élaboration de trois personnages féminins de *Béatrix*, Balzac choisit de reprendre des bribes tirées de portraits de femmes célèbres dressés par Gautier dans la *Galerie des belles actrices* du *Figaro* d'octobre à décembre 1837. Dans le cas de deux passages d'*Une fille d'Ève*, c'est dans la nouvelle *Onuphrius* de Gautier que Balzac trouve son inspiration. Le présent article propose d'analyser l'intégration graduelle des éléments intertextuels dans l'œuvre de Balzac en positionnant d'abord ce phénomène dans le vaste champ des pratiques intertextuelles de l'auteur pour ensuite se pencher sur *Une*

1 Le roman portant maintenant ce titre est en effet composé de deux parties distinctes rédigées à environ six années d'intervalle : *Béatrix ou les Amours forcés* et *Les Petits Manèges d'une femme vertueuse* ou, selon l'édition originale, *La Lune de miel*.

2 Avec une pause du 27 avril au 9 mai.

3 Voir sur ce point le travail de Maurice Regard dans son édition de *Béatrix* parue chez Garnier Frères (1962).

fille d'Ève et en tirer une étude de cas singulière : celle de la scène de bal chez Lady Dudley. À partir d'une analyse génétique de ce passage, nous suivons d'abord le parcours des choix d'écriture de Balzac afin de prendre pleinement conscience du réseau intertextuel qui le sous-tend pour finir par en déterminer les principaux effets.

Avant de présenter notre étude de cas, il convient donc de la replacer dans le cadre plus large de nos recherches sur les pratiques intertextuelles chez Balzac[4] visant à définir la construction de l'acte d'écriture autour de ou à partir d'un premier texte, qui plus est un texte exogène. La nature des intertextes présents dans toute œuvre varie grandement et peut être orientée, nous inspirant en partie des catégories établies par Gérard Genette, en considérant leur emplacement sur deux axes aux pôles opposés : de l'implicite à l'explicite et du littéral à l'allusif. Genette définit le plagiat comme un « emprunt non déclaré, mais encore littéral » (Genette, 1982, p. 8) partageant la qualité implicite de l'allusion qui, pour sa part, est une forme « moins littérale » qui elle-même s'oppose à la citation, « forme la plus explicite et la plus littérale » (*ibid.*). L'attrait de la trace tangible d'un emprunt qui n'est pas signalé par l'auteur est en partie dû à sa qualité à la fois matérielle et secrète, rappelant l'artefact enfoui ou, pour conserver les termes de Genette, le palimpseste. C'est à ce niveau que peuvent désormais espérer intervenir les outils numériques[5], rassemblant et comparant une quantité de texte que la mémoire humaine ne peut égaler. Une fois l'intertexte repéré, on peut délimiter l'ampleur de la coocurrence, la percevoir aisément comme une entité distincte du texte qui l'entoure et dont elle fait à la fois partie. Ainsi isolé, ce concentré sémantique s'active en deux temps : il a sa signification propre, donnée par la première main ; signification détournée, nuancée ou renouvelée par son nouvel environnement. Grâce à eux, les effets herméneutiques se multiplient et de nouvelles voies d'interprétations s'ouvrent aux lecteurs.

L'intérêt de la mise au jour de ces intertextes ne consiste pas en une simple quête de sources, moins encore en une tentative de dévaloriser

4 La présente étude permet de revoir et présenter quelques pistes d'analyses figurant dans notre thèse doctorale inédite, *Écriture romanesque, intertextualité et genèse chez Balzac : l'exemple de deux romans des années 1838-1839*, Béatrix *et* Une fille d'Ève.

5 Voir, entre autres, les outils développés dans le cadre du projet eBalzac, dirigé par Andrea Del Lungo, Jean-Gabriel Ganascia et Pierre Glaudes, pouvant être consultés sur le site internet du même nom.

l'œuvre en en soulignant son manque d'originalité, mais bien de pouvoir suivre le cours du développement créatif de l'écriture et de reconstituer minutieusement le contexte de la genèse du roman. Les traces intertextuelles implicites occupent une place différente des intertextes explicites puisqu'elles ne peuvent garantir une orientation immédiate de la lecture, invitant à faire au passage des liens avec d'autres textes, à replacer l'œuvre dans le paysage littéraire. L'implicite peut révéler l'influence (consciente ou non) de la bibliothèque balzacienne tissant tout un réseau intertextuel sous-jacent à son œuvre, mais surtout les dessous de certaines étapes de la création romanesque et les enjeux stylistiques la façonnant.

Dans le cas qui nous occupe, l'existence de passages recelant un intertexte implicite avait déjà été signalée par la critique[6], sans toutefois que leur dénombrement ait été exhaustif, ni que les effets résultants en aient été systématiquement étudiés. Afin de brosser les grandes lignes d'une poétique intertextuelle de Balzac pour pouvoir la confronter à ses pratiques d'écriture, nous avons d'abord recensé tous les intertextes explicites et leur moment d'apparition (ou de disparition) au cours des différentes étapes de rédaction et de publication de *Béatrix* et d'*Une fille d'Ève*, avant d'explorer la place occupée par les emprunts à Gautier dans ces mêmes œuvres. Pour ce faire, il faut prendre en compte l'aspect génétique des romans en dépouillant autant que possible les divers états du texte, du manuscrit à la publication des éditions dites du « Furne corrigé », en passant par les épreuves en vue de publication dans *Le Siècle*, pour pouvoir examiner la présence et l'évolution du plagiat à travers l'écriture et les corrections subséquentes[7]. L'analyse des avant-textes disponibles est incontournable : ce sont là des étapes décisives dans le (re) maniement du texte qui n'est pas encore exposé aux yeux des lecteurs. L'étude génétique retrace l'histoire du passage d'une main à l'autre et nous apporte de précieuses indications quant à la logique de ce nouveau texte hybride dont l'élément exogène est en voie de s'intégrer pleinement.

6 Voir d'abord Fournel, 1876 puis Ambrière, 1987 ; Berthier, 1971 et Brua, 1972.

7 Les travaux récents de Takayuki Kamada ont souligné l'ampleur de l'entreprise d'une analyse génétique de l'œuvre balzacienne qui constitue un « ensemble hypertophique […] aux frontières en partie indéterminées » (Kamada, 2021, p. 10) mais dont l'étude, même à l'échelle « microgénétique », peut révéler des pistes interprétatives importantes puisque « la masse des dossiers de genèse recèle d'innombrables traces d'intervention à parcourir, ceci en vue de lire sous un jour nouveau le texte de l'œuvre » (*ibid.*, p. 49).

C'est ensuite que nous sommes en mesure de constater à quel point ces intertextes peuvent orienter la lecture et l'interprétation, et la façon dont ils contribuent à la construction du roman et à la caractérisation de son personnel.

Revenons maintenant à *Une fille d'Ève* et à la nature des emprunts issus de *l'Onuphrius* de Gautier, nouvelle publiée six ans avant la parution en feuilleton du roman de Balzac. Deux passages de ce dernier recèlent des phrases puisées dans le texte de Gautier : le premier correspond à la description physique du personnage de Raoul Nathan, tandis que le second est la description d'une scène de bal chez lady Dudley. Ce cas se distingue de tous les autres passages repris de Gautier que nous connaissons à ce jour qui, d'ordinaire, concernent tous des personnages. Autre particularité, c'est le seul passage dont nous avons peut-être une preuve de la nature collaborative ou, du moins, de l'approbation de Gautier pour sa reprise dans l'œuvre de Balzac. En effet, dans une lettre que Roger Pierrot croit être de mars 1839, alors que Balzac doit corriger les épreuves du roman en vue de sa publication originale, il écrit à Souverain : « Je verrai Gautier pour le bal. » (*Corr.*, III, p. 578) De plus, il le relance le 17 mars de la même année en disant : « J'ai vu M. Gauthier [*sic*] qui ne sait ce que veut dire ce que v[ous] lui avez envoyé, car v[ous] ne lui avez envoyé que le ch[apitre] du *Bal*, et il n'y comprend rien. Envoyez-moi donc au plus tôt un exemplaire de bonnes feuilles, et il le lira et ne demande qu'une journée pour arranger les corrections. » (*Corr.*, III, p. 579) À l'évidence, si Gautier est chargé des corrections de la scène de bal d'*Une fille d'Ève*, il ne peut ni ignorer ni condamner la présence de ses propres mots dans le roman de son ami. Soulignons toutefois que l'intertexte tiré d'*Onuphrius* est présent dès le manuscrit d'*Une fille d'Ève* et figurait donc déjà dans l'édition en feuilleton du *Siècle* sans que nous ayons une preuve de la collaboration directe de Gautier au premier jet ou à tout autre moment avant les corrections en vue de l'édition chez Souverain.

Ainsi, le manuscrit est bel et bien entièrement de la main de Balzac et, grâce aux hésitations révélées par les ratures, on conçoit aisément que l'écrivain ait pu avoir une version du texte de Gautier sous les yeux durant sa rédaction. Dans un article paru dans *L'Année balzacienne* de 1971, Patrick Berthier avance qu'il est possible que Balzac ait « remarqué une œuvre parmi les plus originales de son cadet, et qu'il ait mis dans ses cartons cette page descriptive dans la pensée de l'utiliser un jour pour l'un de ces "morceaux poétiques" qui lui donnaient tant de soucis » (Berthier, 1971, p. 285). Quoique ce soit possible, une telle méthode, une telle préméditation, aurait vraisemblablement donné lieu à plusieurs autres cas similaires d'emprunt à ses contemporains, alors que cette pratique reste relativement restreinte et qu'elle ne prend cette ampleur que dans la période et les romans qui nous intéressent. De plus, la nature des passages concernés ne peut guère être qualifiée de « morceaux poétiques ». Ils ne sortent pas non plus entièrement des ornières de la facture ordinaire balzacienne. Au contraire, ils touchent l'un des aspects les plus typiques (et typifiés) de l'écriture de Balzac : la description. Ceci tend à bousculer l'idée reçue du romancier posé en observateur fidèle de son environnement pour plutôt faire intervenir Balzac lecteur, frappé d'une image formée mentalement à partir du texte d'un autre et qui prendra désormais le rôle de référent.

Pour mieux saisir les mécanismes de l'intégration du texte de Gautier dans celui de Balzac, nous reproduisons ici la transcription du passage de la scène de bal en question. À gauche, le texte d'*Onuphrius* et à droite, celui du manuscrit d'*Une fille d'Ève*, avec les ratures et ajouts trouvés en marge (indiqués par <<…>>). Les mots repris de manière exacte sont en italiques, incluant ceux qui ont été raturés. Le passage est marqué par plusieurs énumérations dont nous avons numéroté les éléments chez Gautier afin de pouvoir suivre la manière dont Balzac les répartit dans son propre texte.

Description d'une scène de bal : *Onuphrius*, dans *Les Jeunes-France* (p. 109-110)	Description du bal de lady Dudley : manuscrit d'*Une fille d'Ève*[8]
La soirée était des plus *brillantes. Un coup d'œil* magnifique ! cela *reluisait, chatoyait, scintillait*[1] ; cela bourdonnait, papillonnait, tourbillonnait. *Des gazes comme des ailes* d'abeilles[2], *des tulles*[3], *des crêpes*[4], *des blondes*[5], *lamés*[6], *côtelés*[7], *ondés*[8], *découpés*[9], *déchiquetés*[10] à jour ; *toiles d'araignée*[11], l'air filé, *brouillard*[12] *tissu*[13] ; de *l'or* et de *l'argent*[14], *de la soie*[15] et du velours, des paillettes, du clinquant, *des fleurs*[16], *des plumes*[17], *des diamants*[18] et *des perles*[19]. *Tous les écrins vidés*, le *luxe* de tous les mondes à *contribution*[20]. Un beau *tableau* sur ma foi ! les girandoles de cristal étincelaient comme des étoiles, des gerbes de lumière, des iris prismatiques s'échappaient des pierreries ; *les épaules* des femmes, *lustrées, satinées*, trempées d'une molle sueur semblaient des agates ou *des onyx* dans l'eau, *les yeux* papillotaient, les gorges battaient la campagne, les mains s'étreignaient, les têtes penchaient, les écharpes allaient au vent, c'était le beau moment ; *la musique* étouffée par les voix, *les voix* par *le frôlement des* petits *pieds sur le parquet* et le frou-frou *des robes*, tout cela formait *une harmonie de fête*, un *bruissement* joyeux à enivrer le plus mélancolique, à rendre fou tout autre qu'un fou.	C'était la première ~~gra~~ solennité du grand monde en 1833, car elle eut lieu dans le mois de janvier. ~~*Un coup d'œil*~~ Les salons offraient ~~un~~ à l'*œil* un spectacle magique : *des fleurs*[16], *des diamants*[18], des chevelures *brillantes* ; ~~*tous*~~ *les écrins vidés*, ~~les~~ ~~*1 mot*~~ les ressources de toilette mises *à contribution*[20], tout *reluisait, scintillait, chatoyait*[1] ; *des gazes* ~~*comme des*~~ peintes ou blanches *comme les ailes des* plus jolies libellules[2], *des crêpes*[4], des dentelles, *des blondes*[5], *des tulles*[3] variés comme l~~a~~es ~~nature~~ fantaisies de la nature entomologique : *découpés*[9], *ondés*[8], dentelés, ~~fins~~ ~~com~~ du vent *tissu*[13], des ~~*toiles d'araignée*~~ ~~*d*~~ fils d'aranéide[11] en *or*, en *argent*[14], des *brouillards*[12] aurore, *de la soie*[15], ~~*du lamé*~~[6], ~~*des*~~ à *fleurs*, ourdies par les fées ou peintes par des génies en prison, *des plumes*[17] ~~ar~~ colorées par les feux du tropique ~~*3 mots*~~ en saule pleureur au-dessus ~~d'une t~~ des têtes orgueilleuses, *des perles*[19] ~~en~~ tordues en nattes, des étoffes *lamées*[6], *côtelées*[7], *déchiquetées*[10] comme ~~si l'o~~ le génie du moyen âge avait ~~fait~~ conseillé l'industrie moderne, et ce *luxe* en harmonie avec les plus belles *épaules* les unes d'une couleur d'ambre, les autres d'un ~~*1 mot*~~ *lustré* qui faisait croire à la pression d'un cylindre, celles-ci *satinées*, celles-là ~~d'un b~~ mates ~~et palpa~~ et grasses comme ~~la une~~ si Rubens en avait préparé la pâte << enfin toutes les nuances ~~qui~~ trouvées par l'homme dans le blanc, >> des yeux étincelant comme des *onyx* ou des turquoises, bordées de velours noir ou de franges blondes ; *l~~a~~es* ~~*musique*~~ *bruissements* des plus douces *voix* ~~*2 mots*~~ ~~la musique, le frôle~~ *le frôlement des*

8 Manuscrit d'*Une fille d'Ève*, conservé à la Bibliothèque de l'Institut de France, *Lov. A 232, fos 21-22*.

	robes les le murmure de la danse, les chocs de la valse, rivalisant avec la musique ; enfin une sorcellerie étouffante, *une harmonie de fête*, et de parfums, les lumières irisées ~~des lus~~ dans les cristaux, de les pétillements des bougies, les *tableaux* multipliés par les glaces, les profils élégants, fins, corrects des nobles, les moustaches fauves, les figure graves des anglais, les visages gracieux de l'aristocratie française << tous les ordres de l'Europe ~~*1 mot*~~ scintillant sur les poitrines, pendus au cou, en sautoir et sur la hanche et >>, les jolis *pieds* ~~*sur le parquet*~~ glissant sur *le parquet*, des regards malicieux échangés, de blanches jeunes filles étourdies et curieuses, des méchancetés dites sous l'éventail, des compliments exagérés, enfin la société parée, frisée, musquée, un tutti complet, enivrant, ~~qui~~ une folie *de fête* qui portait au cerveau comme ~~le vin~~ une fumée capiteuse.

À l'aide de cette numérotation, un premier constat s'impose : la description balzacienne est parsemée d'emprunts quelque peu pêle-mêle. L'auteur réorganise le texte, en dressant la mise en scène comme il l'entend, éparpillant les différents items trouvés chez Gautier à travers cette nouvelle salle de bal. Ainsi le début de la série d'énumérations de Balzac (« des fleurs, des diamants », etc.) reprend-elle d'abord les éléments 16, 18 et 20 de Gautier avant d'enchaîner avec le premier (« reluisait, scintillait, chatoyait »). Déjà chez Gautier, l'énumération était à l'honneur dès la seconde phrase du passage et les éléments les constituant formeront la base de l'intertexte. Cette phrase introduisant l'énumération, débutant par « Un coup d'œil magnifique », Balzac a d'abord envie de la reproduire telle quelle avant de se raviser et rayer pour écrire plutôt « Les salons offraient un à l'œil un spectacle magique[9] » ce dernier adjectif étant manifestement influencé par le « magnifique » de Gautier,

9 Notons au passage la tentation de Balzac de retourner au « un » original, ce qui aurait exigé le réemploi de la formule « un coup d'œil ».

du fait de ses consonances rapprochées. À plusieurs reprises[10], les ratures révèlent ainsi des remaniements stylistiques qui, sans gommer tout à fait la formule initiale de Gautier, peuvent en brouiller la présence ou en réduire l'importance. Sans ces preuves additionnelles[11] de la présence d'un hypotexte, on pourrait être tenté de ne voir dans ce texte que des lieux communs propres à la description romanesque de cette époque.

D'ailleurs la réutilisation de ces listes descriptives peut sans doute étonner un lectorat averti. L'accumulation typiquement balzacienne est bien connue et, en 1838, sa pratique était déjà bien rodée. Est-il possible de concevoir l'auteur en manque d'inspiration devant la (relative) nécessité de dresser une liste des beautés à contempler lors d'un bal ? Et si Balzac avait conservé dans ses cartons cette scène *d'Onuphrius* non pour « ces morceaux poétiques qui lui donnaient tant de soucis », pour reprendre la formule de Patrick Berthier évoquée plus haut, mais plutôt parce qu'il en appréciait les éléments listés et que, en les reprenant, il participait à un jeu intertextuel déjà mis en abyme dans l'œuvre de Gautier ? Le texte repris de ce dernier consiste essentiellement en deux listes séparées par une phrase (« Un beau tableau sur ma foi ! »), exclamation faisant ressortir l'esthétisme pictural de la première pour introduire la seconde. Dans une étude portant sur « Les tentations balzaciennes de l'énumération », Alexandre Péraud souligne la nature intertextuelle de cette pratique chez Balzac (avec, à sa source, Rabelais et Sterne) dont l'auteur « imite la verve satirique et burlesque » (Péraud, 1999, p. 96). *Onophrius*, dont il faut rappeler le sous-titre, « ou les vexations fantastiques d'un admirateur d'Hoffmann », est une nouvelle elle-même placée explicitement sous le sceau intertextuel d'une façon tout à fait ludique.

La scène de bal en question a pu marquer l'esprit d'un lecteur tel que Balzac par sa peinture d'une atmosphère luxueuse, celle reprise dans *Une fille d'Ève*, qui basculera toutefois rapidement dans le registre d'un fantastique quasi-frénétique, illustrant le point d'orgue de la folie du

10 Voir dans le manuscrit : « des gazes comme des », « des toiles d'araignée », « du lamé », « laes musique bruissements », « pieds sur le parquet ».

11 Dans l'introduction à son premier volume de *Balzac, fictions génétiques*, Pierre Laforgue évoque des « disfonctionnements » du texte qui ne sont « pas dépourvus de sens » puisqu'ils « contribu[ent] à leur façon à projeter un éclairage sur l'œuvre où ils se laissent repérer » (Laforgue, 2017, p. 12). Laforgue propose une typologie de quatre cas possibles dont les raisons sont « la plupart du temps d'ordre génétique » (*ibid.*, p. 14). Nous pourrions considérer l'ajout d'un autre cas, celui de l'impression de « déjà-lu » menant au repérage plus ou moins facile de la source textuelle implicite selon les compétences du lectorat.

personnage éponyme qui se croit être devenu la proie d'une entité malveillante ayant pris la forme d'un dandy. À la fin de la soirée, Onuphrius est sommé de réciter ses vers et, alors qu'il s'exécute, le démoniaque dandy s'empresse de les attraper au vol grâce à un filet puis de les remplacer dans la bouche même du jeune homme en lui y enfournant « une substance mousseuse et rosâtre » (Gautier, 1833, p. 114) faite de vers tirés de poètes anciens. C'est ainsi que :

> Les pensées neuves, les belles rimes d'Onuphrius, diaprées de mille couleurs romantiques, se débattaient et sautelaient dans la résille comme des poissons dans un filet ou des papillons sous un mouchoir.
>
> Le pauvre poëte était à la torture, des gouttes de sueur ruisselaient de ses tempes. Quand tout fut fini, le dandy prit délicatement les rimes et les pensées d'Onuphrius par les ailes et les serra dans son portefeuille. (*Ibid.*, p. 115-116)

L'œuvre de Gautier met dès lors elle-même en scène, certes de façon humoristique et satirique, l'angoisse et les enjeux reliés à la nouveauté, à l'originalité, à l'influence et autres questions propres à la production textuelle artistique faisant toutes parties des théories sur l'intertextualité depuis l'apparition du terme chez Kristeva à la fin des années 1960. Onuphrius est aux prises avec une situation de nature peut-être surnaturelle, mais son désarroi complet en voyant ses mots s'envoler de sa bouche pour être immédiatement interceptés puis rangés par un autre dans un portefeuille avant qu'ils ne puissent atteindre l'oreille du public est, pour sa part, bien réel. Ce désarroi impuissant fait écho à une scène cauchemardesque préalable dans laquelle l'artiste constate avec rage que la paternité de son œuvre a été usurpée par l'un de ses amis qui rencontre un grand succès. Bien entendu la créature de Gautier ne sait pas que son existence même est mise sous la tutelle de l'influence hoffmannienne, façonnée par une foule de codes, d'images et de discours balisant le champ littéraire dans lequel vient s'inscrire le texte de la nouvelle. Que des passages de cette œuvre se soient retrouvés par la suite dans les cartons de Balzac (ou aient été suggérés par Gautier) pour reparaître dans l'un de ses propres romans est un jeu de miroirs qui nous apparaît comme un sourire complice. De plus, les comparaisons naturelles évoquées pour incarner les « pensées neuves, les belles rimes [...] diaprées de mille couleurs romantiques » de son personnage, c'est-à-dire des poissons ou papillons, appartiennent à un réseau sémantique déjà présent dans la description du bal durant lequel le subterfuge démoniaque se produit. Ce réseau sous-tend la scène et sa réappropriation et sa réactivation dans le texte balzacien et, en en suivant le fil, on peut rendre compte de la proche parenté entre les deux textes et appuyer l'hypothèse selon laquelle Balzac n'a pas seulement un souvenir approximatif de celui de Gautier, mais choisit au gré de la plume de le modifier sans toutefois en évacuer l'idée générale.

Ces transformations révèlent souvent des préférences stylistiques de la part de Balzac, mais elles dévoilent aussi l'importance de certains principes guidant sa propre démarche romanesque. L'attrait des sciences naturelles et de ses méthodes sur la pensée et la poétique de Balzac est reconnu. En effet, le parallèle possible entre les conditions animales et humaines, ainsi que les diverses théories scientifiques élaborées pour les représenter, est riche de possibilités romanesques et est la première ligne directrice énoncée dès l'« Avant-propos » de *La Comédie humaine* visant à en expliquer le système : « Cette idée vint de la comparaison entre l'Humanité et l'Animalité » (*CH*, I, p. 7[12]).

Une telle comparaison se trouve donc déjà en germe dans le portrait brossé par les deux descriptions qui nous occupent. En examinant en premier lieu le champ lexical ayant trait aux insectes chez Gautier (« bourdonnait, papillonnait, tourbillonnait », « ailes d'abeilles », « toiles d'araignées » et, plus loin, les papillons colorés représentant les vers volés du protagoniste) on constate que le manuscrit de Balzac reprend le thème moyennant quelques modifications. D'abord, des deux couplets jumeaux constitués principalement de verbes (« cela *reluisait, chatoyait, scintillait* ; cela bourdonnait, papillonnait, tourbillonnait ») Balzac ne conserve que le premier, omettant ainsi ceux qui introduisaient pourtant la thématique. Ces verbes d'action sont écartés au profit de ceux mettant en valeur l'aspect visuel et brillant, insistant sur la peinture vive d'une image mentale du « spectacle magique » que le lecteur est invité à se représenter.

Une deuxième transformation mineure touche la comparaison aux ailes d'abeilles (« *Des gazes comme des ailes* d'abeilles ») qui deviennent « *des gazes* ~~*comme des*~~ peintes ou blanches *comme les ailes des* plus jolies

12 Plus loin, Balzac prenant appui sur l'exemple des travaux du naturaliste Buffon, insiste : « Il a donc existé, il existera donc de tout temps des Espèces Sociales comme il y a des Espèces Zoologiques. » (*CH*, I, p. 8)

libellules » chez Balzac. On suit aisément le fil de la pensée de l'écrivain qui ici aussi avait, dans un premier élan, suivi la comparaison pour en fin de compte la reporter plus loin. Les gazes se divisent pour multiplier les effets de couleur : les premières sont maintenant peintes tandis que les autres deviennent blanches et sont rattachées à la comparaison entomologique désormais enjolivée par l'image des libellules, plutôt que celle des abeilles.

Si ce remplacement nous semble être encore motivé par des considérations esthétiques, certains autres viennent renforcer la fonction éthique du texte, témoignant d'une connaissance naturaliste spécialisée plus approfondie. En effet, les « toiles d'araignée » de Gautier apparaissent sous une rature manuscrite qui est immédiatement suivie de deux termes manifestement de la même famille, « des ~~*toiles d'araignée d*~~ fils d'aranéide ». Si *araignée* était et demeure un vocable courant, apparaissant d'ailleurs à 24 reprises dans *La Comédie humaine*, *aranéide* n'est recensé pour sa part qu'en 1803 dans le *Dictionnaire universel* de Boiste et est directement rattaché à la classification des araignées capables de tisser des toiles, popularisée par la *Zoologie analytique* de Duméril en 1805. Balzac ne réemploiera le mot qu'à une autre reprise dans *La Comédie humaine*, cette fois dans sa forme adjectivale, pour une nouvelle description vestimentaire[13] figurant dans *Béatrix* dont la période de rédaction coïncide et se mêle à celle d'*Une fille d'Ève*.

C'est ainsi qu'*aranéide*, nom à la fois plus rare et plus savant, renforce l'ethos du romancier observateur des espèces. Dans le même ordre d'idée, Balzac ajoute au simple « tulles » de Gautier cette observation : « *des tulles*[3] variés comme l~~a~~es ~~nature~~ fantaisies de la nature entomologique ». Ce dernier adjectif est tiré du substantif *entomologie*, maintenant répandu, mais qui n'est introduit qu'en 1745 dans le *Traité d'insectologie* de Bonnet et ne remplacera que graduellement le terme d'insectologie. Si *entomologie* se trouve ailleurs dans *La Comédie humaine* à cinq reprises, *Une fille d'Ève* contient la seule occurrence d'*entomologique*. Ce mot se distinguant encore par une qualité plus érudite (et inédite) va servir à l'introduction d'une comparaison plus développée entre production humaine et naturelle.

---

13 « Ce fut une pèlerine en guipure d'une finesse aranéide » (*Béatrix*, *CH*, II, p. 918). En guise de comparaison, araignée, pour sa part, apparaît à 27 reprises dans *La Comédie humaine*.

À partir du quatrième jeu d'épreuves pour *Le Siècle*, étape à laquelle Balzac fait bon nombre de modifications supplémentaires, il poussera plus loin en ce sens la métaphore naturelle en avançant que « [l]e salon pouvait se comparer à l'une des serres coquettes où de riches horticulteurs rassemblent les plus magnifiques raretés » et que « [l]'industrie humaine semblait aussi vouloir lutter avec les créations animées » (*CH*, II, p. 310). Dans la même veine, Balzac garde aussi l'aspect minéral rattaché aux épaules chez Gautier (« les épaules des femmes [...] semblaient des agates ou *des onyx* dans l'eau, les yeux papillotaient ») pour plutôt les attribuer aux yeux « étincelant comme *des onyx* ou des turquoises ».

Ce dernier passage est un excellent exemple du phénomène d'amplification du texte à l'œuvre ici. Car si la description du bal de Gautier est contenue en 188 mots, celle de Balzac, dès le manuscrit, comporte 338 mots et ne cessera d'augmenter au fil des différentes étapes de la rédaction. Suivons de plus près cette pratique en examinant d'abord le texte source de Gautier : « *les épaules* des femmes, *lustrées, satinées*, trempées d'une molle sueur semblaient des agates ou des *onyx* dans l'eau, *les yeux* papillotaient ». Ce qui devient chez Balzac :

> les plus belles *épaules* les unes d'une couleur d'ambre, les autres d'un ~~*1 mot*~~ *lustré* qui faisait croire à la pression d'un cylindre, celles-ci *satinées*, celles-là ~~d'un b~~ mates ~~et pulpe~~ et grasses comme ~~la une~~ si Rubens en avait préparé la pâte << enfin toutes les nuances ~~qui~~ trouvées par l'homme dans le blanc, >> des *yeux* étincelant comme des *onyx* ou des turquoises, bordées de velours noir ou de franges blondes [...]

Entre crochets se trouvent les mots inscrits en marge du manuscrit, dénotant que, même au premier jet, Balzac ajoute des précisions à son texte ou, dans ce cas, y revient pour inclure un élément visuel qu'il n'avait pas su placer dans la phrase initiale, ce blanc qui l'avait d'abord tenté, à en croire les lettres visibles sous la rature (« d'un b »...). À partir de trois éléments trouvés chez Gautier (les épaules, les pierres fines et les yeux), le romancier construit un texte qui, sémantiquement, diffère déjà quelque peu de celui de son cadet. Les épaules demeurent « lustrées » et « satinées », mais elles se rangent dorénavant dans l'une ou l'autre de ces catégories qui, elles aussi, ont droit à une description. Balzac fait intervenir non seulement des contrastes de couleurs, entre l'ambre et le blanc, mais aussi de textures : d'un côté la netteté mécanique du cylindre et, de l'autre, la production artistique humaine de la pâte. Puis, il reprend les yeux, suivant les « onyx » et « agates » qui, dans le texte de Gautier, se rapportent aux épaules. De façon plus réaliste, ce sont donc les yeux qui, pour Balzac, évoquent des gemmes colorées. Au lieu des agates du texte original, on trouve dès lors les turquoises qui, on le sait, sont l'une des pierres fétiches de l'écrivain et qui ont l'avantage de représenter une couleur à la fois plus nette et plus vive, un bleu contrastant les iris ou prunelles noires comme l'onyx.

Dans ce même passage, Balzac reprend aussi l'élément pictural de Gautier évoqué plus haut qui rapproche la scène des arts visuels (« Un beau tableau, sur ma foi ! ») et choisit de renchérir en faisant intervenir l'art de Rubens dans la description des épaules « mattes et grasses » des dames, insistant sur le fait que ces épaules représentent « toutes les nuances trouvées par l'homme dans le blanc ». Faire intervenir un référent aussi important que Rubens permet d'incorporer une dimension matérielle encore plus précise pour le lecteur qui est désormais en mesure de faire appel à sa mémoire visuelle (ou de consulter directement les tableaux du maître flamand) afin de se recréer une image mentale de la scène et, surtout, de toutes les chairs qui y sont fièrement exhibées. Balzac intensifie et varie les couleurs, les textures, les contrastes, les référents. L'hybridité textuelle s'allie au sujet pour créer un effet prismatique, une expérience immersive mobilisant tous les sens du lecteur.

En un mot, le texte produit l'effet escompté. La finale de la scène de Gautier est une « harmonie de fête », expression réutilisée par Balzac qui évoquera aussi plus loin une « folie de fête ». Le passage de l'harmonie à la folie s'explique en partie par le souci de complétude dont l'amplification du texte rend compte[14]. Chez Gautier, le bal produit déjà « un bruissement joyeux à enivrer le plus mélancolique, à rendre fou tout autre qu'un fou » et qui ne touche donc guère Onuphrius affligé par ses démons. Cette idée plait manifestement à Balzac qui compare d'abord les effets du bal à une « sorcellerie étouffante » avant de se lancer dans une description des invités pour enfin résumer le tout en annonçant qu'il s'agit d'« un tutti complet, enivrant, ~~qui~~ une folie *de fête* qui portait au cerveau comme ~~le vin~~ une fumée capiteuse ». À partir du quatrième jeu d'épreuves, il ajoutera à la suite cette phrase : « Il semblait que de tous les fronts,

14 Madeleine Ambrière (1987, p. 18) parle ainsi du « besoin irrésistible d'enchâsser la variété dans l'unité » d'un Balzac à la tendance globalisante.

comme de tous les cœurs, il s'échappât des sentiments et des idées qui se condensaient et dont la masse réagissait sur les personnes les plus froides pour les exalter. » Cet ajout, qui servira à expliquer pourquoi la sage épouse de Félix de Vandenesse, Marie, se sent autant attirée par Raoul Nathan[15] à ce moment précis, rappelle aussi l'idée première de Gautier selon laquelle les pouvoirs du bal opèrent même sur les « plus mélancoliques ». L'allusion à la folie, directement reliée à la condition mentale d'Onuphrius, est retirée.

À chaque retrait, à chaque ajout, à chaque modification, Balzac opère dans le sens d'une logique : celle propre à son texte. Au fil des épreuves, l'intertexte initial parvient à être homogénéisé pour bien se fondre dans la trame de la nouvelle œuvre. Le champ sémantique à teneur naturaliste est développé puis intégré dans le système balzacien qui s'y prête déjà si bien parce qu'il rejoint la poétique du romancier telle que décrite dans l'« Avant-propos ». Les contrastes sont renforcés et les énumérations sont raffinées de sorte à former l'image ultime recherchée, celle de la serre aux fleurs rares, métaphore naturaliste pour cette salle de bal où s'amasse une tranche de la société à même d'être observée, dénombrée, analysée. Dans cette optique et dès le premier jet, Balzac « historien des mœurs » ajoute une date précise à la scène pour qu'elle situe exactement le récit. Il y insère de plus des personnages masculins (de façon plus nette, il ajoutera dans le troisième jeu d'épreuves que « [c]ette assemblée des plus jolies femmes et des plus jolies toilettes se détachait sur la masse noire des hommes » [*CH*, II, p. 311]) ainsi que des précisions quant à la société formée par ce bal (des anglais, des aristocrates français, des dignitaires de l'Europe, des jeunes filles « étourdies et curieuses »). En somme, il fait de la simple description énumérative de Gautier la représentation d'un bal suivant les troubles de juillet 1830, brossant le portrait hétéroclite et contrasté d'une « assemblée remarquable par la réunion de plusieurs personnages du drame politique très étonnés de se retrouver ensemble » (*CH*, II, p. 310). L'addition de ces personnages et de ce qu'ils représentent pour la société de l'époque est ce qui démarque véritablement le texte de Balzac de celui de Gautier, d'une telle façon que les emprunts finissent par ne représenter qu'un pourcentage relativement restreint

15 La description physique de ce personnage de journaliste prétendument poète porte d'ailleurs la trace d'autres emprunts à la nouvelle de Gautier, ce qui le rapproche de l'excentrique Onuphrius à certains égards.

de la description et ne se rattachent qu'à des éléments esthétiques de celle-ci. Balzac explicite d'ailleurs sa volonté de démontrer une scène de société vivante dans cet ajout figurant dès le troisième jeu d'épreuves : « En examinant ce monde, il ne présentait pas seulement les brillantes couleurs de la parure, il avait une âme, il vivait, il pensait, il sentait. Des passions cachées lui donnaient une physionomie » (*CH*, II, p. 311). C'est précisément ce que Balzac a pu réaliser après être entré dans ce jeu intertextuel : à travers ses remaniements d'une scène d'abord habilement peinte par les brillantes couleurs de Gautier, il réussit à l'animer afin qu'elle soit à même de remplir sa fonction réaliste dans un nouveau système romanesque.

Tania Duclos
St. Thomas More College
Université de la Saskatchewan

OUVRAGES ET ÉTUDES CITÉS

Ambrière Madeleine, 1987, « Balzac du réel à l'imaginaire, le document et ses métamorphoses », *Romans d'archives*, Raymonde Debray-Genette et Jacques Neefs (éd.), Paris Presses Universitaires de Lille, p. 11-37.

Balzac Honoré de, [1839] 1962, *Béatrix*, Maurice Regard éd., Paris Garnier.

Berthier Patrick, 1971, « Balzac lecteur de Gautier », *AB*, p. 282-285.

Boiste Pierre-Claude-Victor, 1803, *Dictionnaire universel de la langue françoise*, Paris Desray.

Bonnet Charles, 1745, *Traité d'insectologie ou Observations sur les pucerons*, Paris Durand.

Brua Edmond, 1972, « Gautier aide de Balzac », *AB*, p. 381-384.

Duméril Constant, 1805, *Zoologie analytique*, Paris Allais.

Fournel, Victor, 10 décembre 1876, « Les œuvres et les hommes », *Le Correspondant*, Paris V.-A. Waille.

Gautier Théophile, 1833, *Les Jeunes-France, romans goguenards*, Paris Renduel.

Genette Gérard, 1982, *Palimpsestes*, Paris Éditions du Seuil.

Kamada Takayuki, 2021, *Balzac, Multiples genèses*, Paris Presses universitaires de Vincennes.

Kristeva Julia, 1969, *Séméiotikè, Recherches pour une sémanalyse*, Paris Éditions du Seuil.

Laforgue Pierre, 2017, *Balzac, fictions génétiques*, Paris Classiques Garnier.

Péraud Alexandre, 1999, « Les tentations balzaciennes de l'énumération », *« Balzacien ». Styles des imaginaire*, Éric Bordas (éd.), Presses Universitaires de Bordeaux, p. 95-105.

« LE DÉBITEUR EST PLUS FORT QUE LE CRÉANCIER »

Balzac, la dette et la morale dans la société post-moderne

Dans *Il Fronteggiatore : Balzac e l'insurrezione del romanzo*, un livre-conversation avec Antonio Moresco, Susi Pietri observe l'une des caractéristiques communes à la relation changeante et complexe établie, au cours de deux siècles d'histoire littéraire, entre *La Comédie humaine* et ses « grands lecteurs » – de Baudelaire à Proust, de Stevenson à Oscar Wilde, de Brecht à Pasolini :

> tout en accordant la place nécessaire à la contextualisation historique, il faut toujours lire les œuvres balzaciennes *au présent*, comme si elles n'appartenaient pas à une histoire littéraire plus ou moins lointaine, comme si elles étaient constamment actives, incandescentes dans leur virulence, *ici et maintenant* (Moresco-Pietri, 2017, p. 29[1]).

La réflexion est susceptible d'être généralisée. Le pouvoir cognitif des romans de Balzac réside dans leur capacité à amener chaque lecteur à se poser ses propres questions, car, comme tout classique, son œuvre

> n'est pas l'énonciation d'une chose disparue, elle n'est pas le simple témoignage d'une autre chose qui a encore besoin d'être expliquée, mais elle s'adresse à chaque présent comme un discours qui lui est spécifiquement destiné (Gadamer, 1986, p. 294[2]).

C'est donc précisément en raison de cette « vérité intérieure [...] qui ne coïncide que pour un moment en mille points secondaires avec la réalité éphémère » (Hofmannsthal, [1908] 2019, p. 44), que les pages de Balzac peuvent être utilement lues par les juristes – mais également par tous

1 Les italiques sont dans le texte : nous traduisons.
2 Nous traduisons.

les spécialistes des sciences sociales (Brugnolo, 2021, p. 171) – comme base de leurs analyses : non seulement parce que ces pages peuvent servir à la compréhension historique des origines de certaines solutions normatives, mais aussi et surtout parce qu'elles permettent, en tant qu'expression d'un réalisme pourtant toujours visionnaire, d'identifier précisément *ici et maintenant* les problèmes vitaux de la société moderne auxquels le système juridique doit s'efforcer d'apporter une réponse. Problèmes constants que les juristes ne cessent de débattre aujourd'hui encore. Ainsi, l'avertissement que Giovanni Macchia adressait aux écrivains-lecteurs de Balzac, son invitation à pénétrer et à se perdre dans le « grand labyrinthe » de *La Comédie humaine* sont encore valables pour le lecteur-juriste sachant qu'un tel exercice ne peut jamais conduire à des erreurs (Macchia, [1985] 1997, p. 1597).

Parmi les nombreux sujets pour lesquels semble valable la considération de Macchia, l'un de ceux qui suscitent à mon sens le plus de réflexion chez le lecteur-juriste contemporain se plongeant dans l'œuvre de Balzac est le rôle que joue le rapport entre le crédit et la dette, et plus précisément le rôle que joue la dynamique de l'endettement. Il s'agit d'ailleurs d'un aspect qui a depuis longtemps attiré l'attention des critiques littéraires, sur lequel il existe une vaste littérature et à propos duquel Alexandre Péraud a donné l'une des contributions les plus importantes (Péraud, 2012). Ce dernier a approfondi le rôle du crédit, et, inévitablement, de la dette – puisque dans la dynamique de la relation obligatoire, le premier ne peut être pensé séparément du second – en tant qu'institution de la société bourgeoise libérale, caractérisée par l'essor irrésistible de l'économie de marché et du système capitaliste.

Cet ouvrage propose une réinterprétation suggestive de la centralité même de l'argent dans l'œuvre de Balzac et souligne son importance non pas en tant que tel, mais en tant que simple *support* à travers lequel se manifestent les phénomènes du crédit et de la dette, devenant ainsi l'authentique moteur du système social et du mécanisme narratif (Péraud, 2012, p. 72 *sqq.*). L'auteur déploie en outre une reconstruction extrêmement précise du rôle joué par les codifications napoléoniennes pour assurer la force contraignante du crédit et donc la suprématie du créancier sur le débiteur. Dans le sillage de ce travail, on peut se demander comment le lecteur-juriste de *La Comédie humaine* peut approfondir la question.

Reste en vérité à analyser et à interroger la capacité de Balzac à offrir une vision toujours *plurielle* de la réalité observée[3], c'est-à-dire une vision multiforme qui, en mettant en valeur ses aspects extrêmes, permet à l'auteur d'interpréter les signes de la modernité, et donc également d'anticiper, dans une certaine mesure, son évolution.

Comme beaucoup d'auteurs l'ont observé (Stimilli, 2015), l'endettement représente la caractéristique principale de l'expérience économique contemporaine. Depuis le début du troisième millénaire – mais d'une certaine manière, le phénomène est encore plus ancien, puisqu'il remonte aux années 70 du XXe siècle – la tendance à la consommation, surtout pour la classe moyenne, n'est plus corrélée aux revenus perçus sur la base du travail. Le recours systématique à l'endettement est donc aujourd'hui généralisé à tous les niveaux : il concerne aussi bien les entrepreneurs, les professionnels, les consommateurs, qui tous ont recours à une multitude d'instruments – qu'il s'agisse des nombreux types d'opérations de crédit à la consommation ou des opérations d'achat de biens et de services caractérisées par des paiements différés – qui permettent aujourd'hui de satisfaire tous les besoins – qu'ils soient liés à l'exercice des activités économiques ou aux besoins individuels.

Or ce recours massif à l'endettement n'est pas toujours, et même presque jamais, corrélé à une capacité adéquate de remboursement. La réalité qui nous entoure montre donc, de plus en plus fréquemment, des situations de débiteurs incapables, dans l'immédiat ou même simplement dans le futur, de rembourser régulièrement leurs dettes, de sorte qu'il faut reconnaître que le véritable mal frappant la société contemporaine est bien « le levier financier, la dette induite », que « le véritable ennemi est l'emprunt [qui] constitue un billet sûr, sans retour, pour la faillite[4]. »

Face à un phénomène « systémique, malin et global, comme un cancer » (d'après les mots du financier imaginaire de *Wall Street*), la réponse commune tendancielle en Europe se caractérise par le dépassement progressif de la tradition des pays dits *de droit civil* basée sur le principe de l'universalité de la responsabilité patrimoniale du débiteur.

3 À ce propos, voir Gambino, 2022, p. 169 *sqq.*, bien que son étude se déploie à partir de l'analyse d'une œuvre peu canonique de Balzac (*L'Art de payer ses dettes et de satisfaire ses créanciers, sans débourser un sou ; enseigné en dix leçons, ou Manuel de Droit Commercial*).

4 Pour reprendre les mots de Gordon Gekko dans *Wall Street : Money Never Sleeps* d'Oliver Stone, deuxième chapitre d'une des représentations cinématographiques les plus efficaces du système capitaliste contemporain.

C'est-à-dire sur le principe, consacré par l'article 2092 du Code civil de 1804, puis repris ensuite par les codes subséquents apparus en Europe continentale entre le XIXe et le XXe siècle, tous directement ou indirectement influencés par la codification napoléonienne, selon lequel

> [q]uiconque s'est obligé personnellement, est tenu de remplir son engagement sur tous ses biens mobiliers et immobiliers, présents et à venir[5].

Ce principe, accepté par les législations représentatives de l'essor du système capitaliste, et configurant une responsabilité patrimoniale potentiellement perpétuelle, surtout lorsque les montants des dettes sont tels qu'ils dépassent toute perspective raisonnable de remboursement même par les revenus futurs du débiteur, est apparu, d'après la vision influencée par les postulats du *law and economics*, comme un frein au développement même de l'économie de marché. Le danger d'un assujettissement patrimonial perpétuel – transfiguration moderne de l'assujettissement personnel qui caractérisait le rapport d'obligation dans les sociétés anciennes – est un facteur qui, en présence de ressources financières limitées, peut inciter chaque individu à ne pas recourir à l'endettement, déterminant une stagnation de la consommation mais aussi dissuadant d'entreprendre des initiatives entrepreneuriales qui pourraient être rentables et utiles à la communauté (Stanghellini, 2004, p. 440). D'où la déformation progressive, dans la plupart des systèmes juridiques européens, des principes et des règles relatifs à l'exécution forcée du rapport d'obligation, qui avait aussi été imaginé pour être au service de l'idéologie capitaliste. Les disciplines conçues dans l'intérêt premier des créanciers, et qui devaient servir à maximiser leur satisfaction, sont remplacées par des disciplines de plus en plus orientées, non seulement vers la minimisation de la charge du débiteur[6], mais aussi vers l'abandon de la même perspective postulant la « culpabilité » du débiteur défaillant au profit d'une perspective totalement opposée, cette dernière tendant au contraire à favoriser le plus rapidement possible son désendettement.

---

5 Et que l'on retrouve, en France, dicté par l'article 2284, tel que modifié par l'Ordonnance n° 2006-346 du 23 mars 2006 relative aux sûretés. Pour un principe identique, en Italie, voir l'article 2740 du code civil.

6 Il suffit de penser, par exemple, à l'attention croissante portée à la maîtrise des coûts du crédit, assurée par l'imposition de règles impératives et l'interprétation extensive proposée par la Cour de justice de l'Union européenne.

Le changement de perspective adoptée surtout à l'égard de ce que l'on appelle le débiteur civil, c'est-à-dire la personne surendettée qui n'exerce pas d'activité entrepreneuriale, est certainement significatif (Modica, 2024, p. 253). Toutefois, il serait faux de considérer le changement progressif de la position du débiteur – son passage « de la prison à la libération[7] » – comme l'expression d'une plus grande attention aux instances solidaires, visant à rééquilibrer un rapport que l'idéologie capitaliste considère comme structurellement inégalitaire (Cardilli, 2022, p. 42). Au contraire, le changement de paradigme reste au service d'une auto-préservation du système (Modica, 2024, p. 259).

Car dans un contexte historique où les revenus diminuent et où les classes moyennes s'appauvrissent progressivement, il est nécessaire, afin que l'économie de marché fonctionne, que la dette soit reproduite en permanence. Si « l'endettement planétaire s'avère être l'un des engrenages de l'économie mondiale » (Stimilli, 2015, p. 152), pour que ce mécanisme continue à fonctionner, il est donc nécessaire d'introduire des dispositifs rendant possible sa reproduction continue. Il est donc nécessaire, sinon d'éliminer, du moins *d'atténuer la règle de la responsabilité patrimoniale perpétuelle*, car cette disposition, en soumettant non seulement les biens présents mais aussi les biens futurs à un cercle spécifique de créanciers, risque de limiter la prise en charge de nouvelles dettes, finissant par bloquer l'engrenage susmentionné. Le système d'économie de marché dans ce moment historique n'a donc pas tant besoin d'un appareil répressif qui privilégie la coercition à l'accomplissement, comme cela avait été envisagé à terme avec l'avènement de la nouvelle société bourgeoise ; c'est exactement le contraire qui est nécessaire, à savoir développer des mécanismes facilitant la décharge du débiteur. En effet, ce n'est que si les dettes passées sont annulées à un certain moment que les conditions sont créées pour que de nouvelles dettes voient le jour.

La mise en valeur des procédures de règlement des dettes, clairement exprimée dans la législation de source européenne la plus récente[8] et concernant tant les entrepreneurs en crise ou insolvables que les

7 Tel est le titre expressif du numéro monographique consacré, en 2004, par la revue *Analisi Giuridica dell'Economia*, au thème de l'insolvabilité des débiteurs civils.

8 Il suffit de penser à la directive UE no. 1023/2019 visant à « augmenter l'efficacité des mesures de restructuration, d'insolvabilité et de remise de dettes ».

consommateurs surendettés, mise en valeur qui façonne le système de la société post-moderne et qui continue à orienter les systèmes juridiques capitalistes, semble donc renverser complètement les postulats qui caractérisaient son essor au début du XIXe siècle, ceux-là mêmes que Balzac a esquissés de manière si efficace. La règle bourgeoise du « tu dois » n'est donc plus « absolue » (Péraud, 2012, p. 76), on ne peut pas dire qu'elle représente un fondement de la morale sociale et qu'elle constitue une règle que « tout débiteur intériorise » (*ibid.*). Au contraire, la possibilité pour le débiteur de recourir facilement au désendettement permet de relativiser cette règle, et l'atténuation des pouvoirs du créancier d'obtenir la pleine satisfaction sur les biens du débiteur[9] renverse de façon décisive le sens du rapport. Le véritable pouvoir n'est plus entre les mains du premier mais entre celles du second, qui peut même rejeter moralement cette règle et qui, grâce à la possibilité d'obliger ses créanciers, c'est-à-dire à leur accorder une remise partielle de ses dettes, peut d'autant plus facilement s'entêter dans son propre comportement *d'endettement irresponsable* : cette faute, dans une inversion de la logique traditionnelle, est alors attribuée au créancier[10]. En minimisant les conséquences de la dette contractée même au moment où il n'y avait pas de capacité réelle de la rembourser, on finit donc par favoriser ce que l'on appelle le *moral hazard* du débiteur.

Dans la société contemporaine, le système capitaliste se réapproprie ainsi certains principes qui avaient caractérisé les sociétés anciennes (Graeber, 2011, p. 67), et perduré jusqu'au XVIIIe siècle où, comme on

9 Un exemple symptomatique de ce phénomène est d'ailleurs le choix opéré par la directive européenne n° 1023/2019, citée, lorsqu'elle permet aux systèmes juridiques nationaux de surmonter, dans le cadre des procédures de restructuration des entreprises insolvables visant à assurer la poursuite de l'activité, la règle dite de la « priorité absolue » – c'est-à-dire la règle qui exige que les actifs du débiteur soient répartis entre tous les créanciers en respectant le rang de leurs créances – en la remplaçant par la règle dite de « priorité relative ». Cette règle signifie que même en l'absence de satisfaction complète des créances de rang supérieur, il est désormais possible de payer quelque chose aux créances de rang inférieur, et même – au moins dans les entreprises organisées comme des sociétés – de réserver une partie des valeurs futures dérivant de la poursuite de l'activité aux actionnaires eux-mêmes.

10 Voir en ce sens les dispositions de la directive européenne n° 2225/2023 sur le crédit à la consommation, dont le « considérant 53 » prévoit que les États membres doivent surveiller le comportement des prêteurs, et éventuellement adopter des mesures de sanction à l'encontre de ces derniers s'ils accordent un crédit de manière « *irresponsable* », c'est-à-dire en faveur d'une personne qui n'est pas en mesure de rembourser la dette. Dans cette perspective, ce n'est donc pas le débiteur qui demande un crédit de manière irresponsable qui est sanctionné, mais seulement celui qui l'accorde.

l'a vu (Péraud, 2012, p. 78), la dette pouvait encore être exceptionnellement annulée et le remboursement suspendu ou négocié[11] ; mais cela ne se fait plus au nom d'une nécessité supérieure de cohésion sociale, comme dans ce lointain passé, mais parce qu'il est toujours nécessaire de maintenir actif le régime du marché libre, cette possibilité obéissant elle aussi, en fin de compte, à un principe de rationalité économique.

Malgré ce changement radical de scénario, du moins d'un point de vue idéologique[12], les pages de Balzac sur la dynamique de la dette sont néanmoins « constamment actives », toujours « incandescentes » (Moresco-Pietri, 2017).

Si, comme l'écrivait Balzac lui-même, « l'âme de l'artiste est un miroir dans lequel l'univers entier est susceptible de se réfléchir » (*OD*, II, p. 713), nous pouvons dire que grâce à cette « vue intérieure, qui pénètre tout » – théorisée aussi dans *Séraphîta* (*CH*, XI, p. 794) – ce miroir « où vient se réfléchir la nature morale, avec ses causes et ses effets » lui a permis de « devine[r] l'avenir et le passé », confirmant ainsi que la réflexion sur la société de son temps est à la fois « prophétique et passéiste » (Mazzacane, 2014, p. 212). Elle est passéiste, parce que l'attention, même excessive (Péraud, 2012, p. 118), réservée aux débiteurs les plus impénitents qui, à l'image de Maxime de Trailles, considèrent comme « une escroquerie » toute initiative prise par un créancier « pour se faire payer immédiatement » (*CH*, VII, p. 780), représente une opposition quelque peu anachronique aux règles du capitalisme triomphant et à la morale bourgeoise[13]. Mais elle est aussi prophétique, précisément parce

11 Cependant, cette mesure a été exceptionnellement appliquée par la société bourgeoise de l'époque de Balzac. Le 20 mars 1848, au lendemain de la révolution de février, le gouvernement provisoire adopte un décret suspendant pour trois mois le droit des créanciers d'agir en recouvrement des créances impayées (Vause, 2018, p. 234). Balzac fait ainsi implicitement référence à cette mesure dans sa lettre à Mme Hanska du 10 juillet 1948 (*LH*, II, p. 896).

12 Sur le plan factuel, on peut cependant souligner une forte analogie entre la réalité actuelle et celle observée par Balzac : l'endettement généralisé, conséquence de la grave pénurie de liquidités, est en effet un trait historiquement caractéristique de la monarchie orléaniste (Péraud, 2005, p. 151 *sqq.*).

13 Pour ceux qui partagent l'idée que Francesco Orlando se fait de la littérature (Orlando, 1993, *passim*), l'accentuation de ce phénomène peut être considérée comme l'expression d'un « retour du refoulé », en ce sens qu'elle témoigne « des rejets et des résistances que les hommes opposent aux règles et aux exigences des sociétés auxquelles, peu ou prou, ils se soumettent » (Brugnolo, 2013, p. 3 : nous traduisons). Pour cette approche, et en

que cet éloge de l'endettement, puis de son défaut systématique, qui, pour l'idéologie prévalant dans le moment historique où Balzac écrit, peut en effet apparaître comme l'expression d'une logique déformante et déviante, voire obscène (Péraud, 2012, p. 118), finit par anticiper ce qui, « *ici et maintenant* », semble au contraire constituer, d'une certaine manière, la norme.

Il me semble que, non seulement dans *La Comédie humaine* mais plus généralement dans l'ensemble de l'œuvre de Balzac[14], on trouve de nombreux exemples de cette anticipation intuitive selon laquelle « la vie […] est un emprunt perpétuel », ainsi que l'observe Mercadet (Balzac, 2012, p. 47) et de la transformation que le rapport crédit-débit allait subir avec le temps dans le système économique capitaliste, et de la façon dont « la bataille incessante [que se] livrent les créanciers et les débiteurs » (*CH*, VII, p. 778) était destinée, en définitive, à se résoudre très souvent en faveur de ces derniers – ce qui justifie l'affirmation de Bixiou concernant cette « vérité pécuniaire […] écrite nulle part », à savoir que « [l]e débiteur est plus fort que le créancier » (*CH*, VI, p. 391[15]).

À propos du problème de la gestion et du traitement du surendettement dans l'entreprise, la stratégie du père Grandet pour faire face à l'insolvabilité de son frère semble emblématique, lui qui agit toujours encore dans le cadre de la morale bourgeoise et de sa conception de l'inexécution de l'obligation comme culpabilité ainsi que de la faillite

particulier en ce qui concerne la signification que cette conception peut avoir dans la perspective de l'utilisation des textes littéraires par les chercheurs en sciences sociales, voir aussi Brugnolo, 2021 p. 174.

14 Le thème du rôle de la dette, puis de la lutte incessante entre créanciers et débiteurs, est en fait également au centre du *Faiseur* où les deux conceptions de la dette discutées dans le texte sont représentées de manière extrêmement efficace. D'une part, il y a celle de la morale bourgeoise, incarnée de manière exemplaire par le personnage de Mme Mercadet, qui à la conviction de son valet de chambre selon laquelle « les créanciers […] sont la cause de tout le mal » et qu'il serait bon de connaître « quelque bon tour à leur jouer » réplique que « le meilleur, ce serait de les payer » (Balzac, 2012, p. 41), et qui agit donc tout au long de la pièce pour que « tous les créanciers de monsieur Mercadet [soient] satisfaits » (Balzac, 2012, p. 151). D'autre part, il y a celle, précisément prophétique, de l'éloge de la dette (Balzac, 2012, I, p. 47 *sqq.*) et surtout de sa non-réalisation systématique, exprimée par le protagoniste qui considère l'initiative de sa femme comme « un coup de probité bête » (Balzac, 2012, p. 151).

15 Une assertion qui rappelle également celle de Mercadet (Balzac, 2012, p. 47) à propos de « supériorité » du débiteur sur ses créanciers. Sur la relation de continuité thématique substantielle entre *Le Faiseur* et *La Comédie humaine*, et plus généralement sur la transversalité de la poétique balzacienne entre scène et roman, voir Spandri, 2020, p. 267.

comme rituel de dégradation[16]. La décision qui consiste à recourir à l'instrument de la liquidation des biens de Victor par un règlement à l'amiable avec les créanciers, afin de « se moquer des Parisiens, [...] les tordre, les rouler, les pétrir, les faire aller, venir, suer, espérer, pâlir ; pour s'amuser d'eux » (*CH*, III, p. 1105), est en fait connotée comme extrêmement moderne. La stratégie adoptée rappelle non seulement les caractéristiques souvent tortueuses de la procédure de formation de certains des instruments actuels de résolution des crises d'entreprise, lorsqu'ils sont régis par l'autonomie privée, mais permet également au père Grandet, en exploitant les *biais* cognitifs et émotionnels des créanciers[17] et leur tendance à la désorganisation, de désactiver leurs créances résiduelles – au moins jusqu'au moment de sa mort : Eugénie, éduquée à la morale bourgeoise, sera orientée différemment.

Mais non moins significatives me semblent les techniques de gestion de crise et d'insolvabilité, réelles ou simulées, qui nous sont présentées dans *La Maison Nucingen*. Dans ce cas également, la stratégie du banquier alsacien consiste à « payer ses créanciers » avec « un petit pâté pour un louis d'or » (*CH*, VI, p. 370), ne leur assurant ainsi qu'une satisfaction minimale et partielle de leurs créances (Roney, 2021, p. 206). Une stratégie qui exploite donc aussi, dans ce cas, la naïveté des créanciers – « grands enfants qui, comme les petits enfants d'autrefois, préfèrent le pâté à la pièce, sans savoir qu'avec la pièce ils peuvent avoir deux cents pâtés » (*CH*, VI, p. 370) – et qui lui permet, finalement, de liquider l'entreprise et de repartir, comme dans la logique du *fresh star* prônée aujourd'hui par le droit européen. Mais cette reprise se fait, comme toujours, essentiellement aux dépens de cette dernière.

Cette capacité de *La Comédie humaine* à illustrer la nature problématique de la mise en œuvre de la relation obligatoire, et à développer

16 « Faire faillite [...] c'est commettre l'action la plus déshonorante entre toutes celles qui peuvent déshonorer l'homme » (*CH*, III, p. 1094). Sur ce thème, qui trouve son expression la plus aboutie dans *César Birotteau*, voir Carrillo, 2013, p. 313.

17 « Le créancier », souligne Balzac avec une surprenante anticipation des études d'économie comportementale, est « une sorte de maniaque. Aujourd'hui prêt à conclure. Demain il veut tout mettre à feu et à sang ; plus tard il se fait ultra-débonnaire. Aujourd'hui sa femme est de bonne humeur, son petit dernier a fait ses dents, tout va bien au logis, il ne veut pas perdre un sou ; demain il pleut, il ne peut pas sortir, il est mélancolique, il dit oui à toutes les propositions qui peuvent terminer une affaire ; le surlendemain, il lui faut des garanties, à la fin du mois il prétend vous exécuter, le bourreau [...]. Grandet avait observé les variations atmosphériques des créanciers, et ceux de son frère obéirent à tous ses calculs » (*CH*, III, p. 1143-1144).

une représentation capable de communiquer avec force et efficacité, au lecteur d'hier comme à celui d'aujourd'hui, le renversement des relations de pouvoir entre débiteur et créancier, apparaît encore plus clairement si l'on s'attarde sur les événements concernant le surendettement individuel – qu'il s'agisse de celui des familles ou de celui des consommateurs. Même dans le monde de Balzac, malgré l'ample appareil répressif de l'inexécution de l'obligation prévu par le système juridique, le créancier est tout de même dépourvu d'instruments véritablement orientés vers l'obtention de la pleine satisfaction de sa créance, de sorte que c'est presque toujours le débiteur qui commande le jeu.

De ce point de vue, me paraît peu convaincante l'observation de ceux qui ont souligné que dans la société mise en scène dans *La Comédie humaine*, la sévérité des règlements, voulue par Napoléon[18], profite aux créanciers en leur offrant le moyen de « contraindre les 'petits' débiteurs » à payer, et en permettant même « des possibilités infinies de 'farces' » à leur détriment (Péraud, 2012, p. 91). Si l'application de la loi constitue une source d'injustice, ce n'est pas parce que son appareil répressif est réellement au service de la raison du crédit, mais parce que le monde de Balzac est régi par le principe de l'*homo homini lupus* (Luckács, 1951, p. 40) et que dans la guerre de tous contre tous qui s'y déroule, ce sont simplement les plus faibles qui sont destinés à succomber, étant indifférent qu'ils jouent le rôle de créancier ou de débiteur.

Cela est tout d'abord éloquemment démontré, me semble-t-il, par le fait que la réflexion de Balzac sur les deux principes qui animent l'action de Grandet – à savoir « l'amour propre et l'intérêt » – illustrant aussi bien une manifestation de l'« exercice de la puissance humaine » que l'expression d'une « supériorité réelle » au détriment d'autrui (*CH*, III, p. 1104), est significativement formulée à propos d'une affaire dans laquelle il assume le rôle de débiteur, et où « ceux qui, trop faibles, se laissent ici-bas dévorer » (*CH*, III, p. 1105) sont précisément ceux qui assument la position de créanciers. Mais cela est également démontré, à y regarder de plus près, par le fait que l'application de la plus sévère des mesures coercitives destinées à protéger le crédit, à savoir la *contrainte par*

18 Sur le rôle de Napoléon dans les décisions concernant le renforcement des sanctions contre le débiteur, et en particulier pour la confirmation de la disposition prévoyant la *contrainte par corps* en cas de non-paiement des lettres de change et pour le commerçant déclaré en faillite, voir Padoa Schioppa, 1992, p. 89 *sqq*.

corps, est le plus souvent appliquée à des personnes – il suffit de penser à David dans *Illusions perdues* ou à Esther dans *Splendeurs et misères des courtisanes*, pour citer les cas les plus connus – qui n'assument même pas réellement le rôle de débiteurs, la falsification de leur signature sur les lettres de change étant le fruit d'une machination orchestrée contre eux.

Ainsi, même dans la société balzacienne les instruments de protection du crédit finissent par manquer d'efficacité (Botrel, 2012, p. 178). L'emprisonnement pour dettes est inutile, car même une fois appliqué, le débiteur défaillant

> en sort sans avoir payé ses dettes, il est vrai, car il n'est plus contraignable que par sa conscience qui le laisse toujours en repos (*CH*, VII, p. 113-114).

Mais les mesures d'expropriation typiques de la procédure d'exécution – à supposer que le créancier trouve quelque chose à saisir dans les biens du débiteur, ce qui est rare, du moins en ce qui concerne les plus astucieux, comme l'illustrent bien Maxime de Trailles, qui, en fait, « ne possédait rien, sa voiture, ses chevaux étaient loués » (*CH*, VII, p. 780) et Michonnin, « garçon [...] élégant » selon la définition qu'en donne *Le Faiseur*, « un débiteur introuvable [...] qui a ses meubles sous le nom d'un ami » (Balzac, 2012, p. 124, 119-120) – ne sont pas plus attrayantes ni rémunératrices. Ceci est particulièrement frappant si l'on considère, d'une part, les coûts élevés de cette procédure – comme l'explique clairement l'avocat Desroches dans *Un homme d'affaires* (*CH*, VII, p. 791) – et, d'autre part, le risque même de perte de valeur des biens attachés au cours du processus d'exécution, comme le souligne directement Balzac dans *César Birottteau* (*CH*, VI, p. 277), dans une longue digression sur l'« Histoire générale des faillites[19] ». C'est alors que s'explique le choix des créanciers, qui, comme Ragon, finissent par considérer comme une « grande perte de temps » le fait de se précipiter pour initier les actes d'exécution, et qui finissent donc par considérer « le maigre et incertain dividende » possiblement obtenu

> comme amplement regagné par l'emploi du temps qu'on ne perdait point à aller, venir, faire des démarches et courir après les excuses de l'improbité. (*CH*, VI, p. 79)

19 C'est le titre choisi par Balzac pour le chapitre 14 de l'édition originale publiée en 1837 chez Boulé (*CH*, VI, p. 1130).

Comme dans la société contemporaine, le créancier dans la société de Balzac ne dispose donc pas de beaucoup de leviers pour obtenir le paiement intégral de ce qui lui est dû, et le débiteur peut même se permettre de décider de payer, ou non, selon son bon plaisir – « Je ne payerai cette créance qu'à ma fantaisie » déclare effrontément Maxime de Trailles à Cérizet (*CH*, VII, p. 784) – sans même avoir à recourir aux subterfuges et aux mensonges auxquels Mercadet est encore obligé de recourir (Bordas, 2020, p. 205 *sqq.*). Puisqu'il n'est plus possible de faire appel aux principes de l'éthique bourgeoise et de la culpabilité morale du débiteur – ces principes qui poussent encore César Birotteau à s'acquitter de la dette même lorsqu'elle n'est plus due et dont, dans une sorte de sacrifice rituel comme celui des sociétés anciennes (Graeber, 2011, p. 134 *sqq.*), il paiera le prix avec sa vie –, dans un contexte où celui qui s'acquitte intégralement de sa dette n'est rien d'autre qu'un « [b]rave homme, mais bête » (*CH*, VI, p. 360), le seul véritable moyen offert aux créanciers de ne pas succomber à la « vérité pécuniaire » décrite par Bixiou est simplement, aujourd'hui comme hier, de savoir inventer, à l'instar de Cérizet dans la nouvelle balzacienne, des « *roueries* » plus efficaces face aux moyens désormais légaux que les débiteurs peuvent utiliser pour ne pas payer.

Giuseppe GUIZZI
Université de Rome Tor Vergata

OUVRAGES ET ÉTUDES CITÉS

Balzac Honoré de, 2012, *Le Faiseur*, présentation, notes et bibliographie par Philippe Berthier, Paris Flammarion (« GF »).

Bordas Éric, 2020, « *Le Faiseur* et ses mensonges », dans Éric Bordas et Agathe Novak-Lechevalier (dir.), *Le Théâtre de Balzac. Splendeurs et misères d'un parent pauvre*, Paris Classiques Garnier p. 205-215.

Botrel Émilie, 2012, « Le droit de l'exécution forcée », dans Nicolas Dissaux (dir.), *Balzac. Romancier du droit*, Paris LexisNexis.

Brugnolo Stefano, 2013, « Desiderio e ritorno del represso nella teoria di Francesco Orlando », *Between*, n° 5, p. 1-23.

Brugnolo Stefano, 2021, « Sull'uso dei testi letterari come documenti storici : il caso di Balzac », dans *Balzac Politico*, Cristina Cassina (éd.), Pise Edizioni ETS, p. 171-186.

Cardilli Riccardo, 2022, *Obbligazione e diseguaglianza (Per una lettura critica dell'obbligazione in Friedrich Karl von Savigny)*, Bologne Il Mulino.

Carrillo Gennaro, 2013, « Morte a credito », dans *Il borghese fa il mondo*, Francesco de Cristofaro et Marco Viscardi (dir.), Rome Donzelli Editore, p. 303-313.

Fiorentino Francesco, 1989, *Introduzione a Balzac*, Bari Laterza.

Gadamer Hans-Georg, 1960, *Wahrheit und Methode*, C. B. Mohr Tübingen.

Gambino Francesco, 2021, « Le verità del credito tra diritto e letteratura », dans *LawArt*, p. 373-389.

Gambino Francesco, 2022, « Balzac et les tensions narratives du crédit », *The Balzac Review / Revue Balzac*, n° 5, p. 169-183.

Graeber David, 2011, *Debito. I primi 5000 anni*, Milan Il Saggiatore.

Guizzi Giuseppe, 2020, *Il « caso Balzac ». Storie di diritto e letteratura*, Bologne Il Mulino.

Hofmannsthal Hugo von, [1908] 2019, *La fanciulla dagli occhi d'oro, con altri due scritti su Balzac*, Cristiano Bianchi et Giuseppe Grasso (éd.), Chieti Solfanelli.

Luckács György, 1951, *Balzac und der französische Realismus*, Berlin Aufbau-Verlag.

Macchia Giovanni, [1985] 1997, « Nella città del romanzo : il ritorno a Balzac », publié pour la première fois dans *Le rovine di Parigi*, et ensuite dans *Ritratti, personaggi, fantasmi*, Milan Arnoldo Mondadori Editore, p. 1597-1601.

Mazzacane Aldo, 2014, « Diritto e romanzo nel secolo della borghesia. *Le Colonel Chabert* di Honoré de Balzac », *Giornale di storia costituzionale*, n° 28, p. 187-213.

Modica Lara, 2024, « Disciplina generale dell'obbligazione e sovraindebitamento », *Rivista del diritto commerciale e del diritto generale delle obbligazioni*, I, p. 247-274.

Moresco Antonio-Pietri Susi, 2017, *Il Fronteggiatore : Balzac e l'insurrezione del romanzo*, Florence-Milan Bompiani.

Orlando Francesco, 1993, *Gli oggetti desueti nelle immagini della letteratura*, Torino Einaudi.

Padoa Schioppa Antonio, 1992, « Napoleone e il Codice di commercio », dans *Saggi di Storia del diritto commerciale*, San Donato Milanese Edizioni LED, p. 89-112.

Péraud Alexandre, 2005, « La construction de l'identité du débiteur : des physiologies au récit balzacien », dans *Balzac et la crise des identités*, Emmanuelle Cullmann, José Luis Diaz, Boris Lyon-Caen (dir.), Saint-Cyr sur Loire Christian Pirot.

Péraud Alexandre, 2012, *Le Crédit dans la poétique balzacienne*, dont sont extraites les citations figurant.

Roney Kristina M., 2021, « A Tale of two Bankruptcies. *César Birotteau* and *La Maison Nucingen* », *The Balzac Review / Revue Balzac*, n° 4, p. 197-213.

Spandri Francesco, 2020, « *Le Faiseur* ou les interférences entre roman et théâtre », dans Éric Bordas et Agathe Novak-Lechevalier (dir.), *Le Théâtre de Balzac. Splendeurs et misères d'un parent pauvre*, Paris Classiques Garnier, p. 267-283.

Stanghellini Lorenzo, 2004, « "Fresh Start" : implicazioni di "policy" », *Analisi Giuridica dell'Economia*, n° 2, p. 437-454.

Stimilli Elettra, 2015, *Debito e colpa*, Rome Futura Editrice.

Vause Erika, 2018, *In the Red and in the Black : Debt, Dishonor and Law in France between the Revolutions*, Charlottesville University of Virginia Press.

RUBRIQUES/*COLUMNS*

RECHERCHES BALZACIENNES

SOUTENANCES DE THÈSES

Alexandra Grand, *Représentations romanesques du vieillard dans les œuvres d'Honoré de Balzac et George Sand*[1]

George Sand et Balzac représentent deux pôles en leur siècle. Encensés tout autant que critiqués, ils marquent indéniablement leur époque de leur empreinte. Leur contribution romanesque est considérable. Leurs contemporains les ont généralement opposés et aujourd'hui encore l'enseignement scolaire traduit ce clivage. Quant à la figure du vieillard, elle devient émergente au XIXe siècle. Or, la représentation de ce personnage récurrent s'avère être un puissant révélateur de l'aspect artificiel de la dichotomie supposée entre les deux romanciers. En outre et surtout, le vieillard, forme représentative et symbolique de la vieillesse dans toutes ses dimensions, apparaît comme un prisme, un miroir grossissant de la société et de l'homme en général au sein de leurs œuvres romanesques. Une approche essentiellement sociopoétique mais qui ne dédaigne pas des éclairages provenant de l'ethnocritique est mise en avant dans cette étude.

Le vieillard est un personnage aux multiples facettes. Sa représentation prend toute sa dimension au XIXe siècle, période durant laquelle il naît véritablement, tant au niveau sociétal que romanesque. Type social marginalisé, il est foncièrement un être de la marge et du seuil qui se joue dans

1 Thèse de l'Université Clermont Auvergne préparée sous la direction de P. Auraix-Jonchière et soutenue le 7 novembre 2024 à l'Université de Clermont Auvergne. Jury : J. Anselmini (Université de Caen), P. Auraix-Jonchière (Université Clermont Auvergne), B. Didier (ÉNS Ulm), A. Montandon (Université Clermont Auvergne), C. Masson (Wellesley College).

l'hésitation et l'incertitude. Aux yeux de leurs contemporains, Honoré de Balzac et George Sand paraissent figurer deux pôles contradictoires : l'un le réalisme, l'autre l'idéalisme. L'un s'emploierait à décrire fidèlement la réalité, l'autre à la transposer pour en exposer les meilleurs aspects. La figure du vieillard s'avère être une figure emblématique permettant de canaliser les particularités des poétiques de ces deux auteurs. À sa lumière, les différences s'estompent, des clarifications se font jour.

Son entrée en scène participe souvent du théâtre cher au deux auteurs, en particulier Sand. Isolé, tant au niveau sociétal que géographique, sa représentation se résout souvent dans une notion de type. De plus, sa catégorisation l'éloigne de l'espèce humaine. Ainsi, il apparaît comme un être volontiers métaphorique dont la nature puise autant dans le règne animal que végétal, quand il n'est pas réifié. Il est également essentiellement l'avare et le père, montrant ainsi les profondes mutations familiales de la société de l'époque. Essentiel tant au niveau diégétique que dramatique, il est marqué par l'ambivalence. Il se révèle serviteur, révélateur ou guide. Sa place dans la diégèse est essentielle. Monomane, il est également celui qui rejoint l'enfance, nouveau paradoxe inhérent à sa nature composée d'absolus contraires. Son traitement s'inscrit ainsi dans les importantes recherches et avancées médicales et psychiatriques du XIXe siècle. Être « hors norme », il se voue entièrement à une passion qui prend les allures d'obsession et qui conduit alors sa vie. Dans tous les cas, il demeure ainsi cet être d'exception si important pour Balzac comme pour Sand qui désirent s'affranchir des caractères ternes ou médiocres. Il ne permet pas moins que de réfléchir aux limites entre la vie et la mort. Aux portes de la mort, parfois véritable cadavre ambulant, il est l'être empli de vie et dotée d'une force considérable. Sous de nombreux aspects, il dépasse la simple condition humaine. Sa position privilégiée, comme être liminaire, lui permet d'interroger spécifiquement la société. Figure du Sens, il allie les postulations contraires. À travers lui se résorbent vérité et sournoiserie, sagesse et folie. Source de vérité, il s'avère également représenter la tromperie et le mensonge. Figure fantastique, volontiers allégorique, qu'elle soit politique ou plus métaphysique, le vieillard peut représenter Dieu ou le Diable. Il est toujours figuré par les extrêmes, ces derniers existant tour à tour ou coexistant même en la représentation de sa personne. Sa figuration côtoie celle de l'alchimiste et du savant obnubilé par ses recherches. Il atteint toutes les dimensions, de la plus prosaïque à la plus éthérée. Il figure ainsi profondément la transgression et s'assimile parfois à la Mort elle-même. Vieillard épousant de très jeunes femmes, empli d'un désir que la société réprouve à son âge, concupiscent, et auquel on associe de nombreux vices, il représente également ce beau vieillard aux cheveux blancs auréolé de sagesse, figuration de l'expérience, dont l'âme est trempée par les principes antiques et où se mêlent visions stoïciennes et épicuriennes de l'existence. Finalement, le tout se résout dans sa dernière et plus symbolique figuration : le visionnaire et le prophète. Figure surréelle – dans le sens où, d'un personnage idéal, il devient idéel puis transcende encore cet état pour montrer la réalité transfigurée par l'art, plus réelle que la réalité même – il ouvre la voie à la transcendance et l'absolu. Personnage ambigu et complexe, mystique, il échappe à toute volonté de le définir aisément, tel un « vieux sphinx » impénétrable mais profondément significatif.

La mise en scène des hommes âgés est certes conforme aux représentations sociales de l'époque, mais elle dépasse également ce cadre car la vieillesse est porteuse de valeurs et de symboliques pérennes. Le vieillard permet de mieux appréhender la société, d'en percevoir toutes les aspérités, tous les manquements. Finalement le vieillard présente pour les deux auteurs la figure idéale et idéelle de l'artiste, de l'ermite, du savant, de celui qui pouvait regénérer le monde, présenter au mieux leurs visions respectives. Le vieil homme devient alors prophète ou mystique rapprochant ainsi les deux auteurs. Une étude actuelle sur des écrits récents pourrait permettre de percevoir si les dimensions oxymoriques de ce personnage et l'incertitude qui le détermine demeurent tout aussi fortes. Car la nouvelle réalité de la vieillesse induit des changements d'optique qui pourraient effacer en partie l'ambivalence inhérente à cette figure et certaines dimensions qui lui étaient intrinsèquement liées.

*

* *

Elisa Puntarello, *Le Républicain de Juillet : anamorphoses littéraires d'un type politique (1830-1848)*[2]

Qu'ont en commun le Michel Chrestien d'*Illusions perdues* et le Ferrante Palla de *La Chartreuse de Parme*, le du Bousquier de *La Vieille Fille* et l'Enjolras des *Misérables* ? En empruntant une métaphore picturale qui renvoie aux jeux d'optique chers à la peinture baroque, chacun de ces personnages peut être considéré comme l'*anamorphose* littéraire d'un type répandu : celui du Républicain de Juillet. Par ce dernier syntagme, la présente étude désigne l'image sociale et littéraire du partisan de la république telle qu'elle se répand au lendemain des Trois Glorieuses, alors que les caricaturistes et les romanciers, les pamphlétaires et les dramaturges puisent dans un même répertoire de traits reconnaissables et récurrents afin de donner vie à des représentations du républicain *spécifiques* à l'époque de la monarchie de Juillet.

Cette thèse étudie l'émergence et l'affirmation du type du Républicain de Juillet dans le discours social de la période, en interrogeant un vaste corpus qui inclut, entre autres, des articles de journal, des illustrations de presse, des physiologies, des brochures politiques, des romans et des pièces de théâtre de tout positionnement idéologique. L'étude, organisée en trois parties, retrace les origines d'un imaginaire typisé du républicain sous Louis-Philippe, aborde ensuite la caractérisation physique et morale de cet opposant, et explore enfin les rôles récurrents qui lui sont attribués au sein de la fiction littéraire. Fidèle à une perspective sociocritique, l'enquête se focalise sur les spécificités des réécritures littéraires du Républicain de Juillet, mettant au jour l'entreprise de resémantisation ou de déconstruction du type engagée – entre autres – par Balzac, Stendhal, Sand, Musset, Nerval, Hugo, Félix Pyat.

« [P]ersonnage qui résume en lui-même les traits caractéristiques de tous ceux qui lui ressemblent plus ou moins » – selon la définition qu'en donne Balzac dans la préface d'*Une ténébreuse affaire* –, le type possède

2 Thèse en cotutelle internationale, préparée sous la direction d'O. Bara (Université Lumière Lyon 2) & A. Silvestri (Università degli Studi di Salerno) et soutenue le 11 décembre 2024 à l'Université Lumière Lyon 2. Jury : O. Bara (Université Lyon 2), X. Bourdenet (Université de Rennes 2), P. Perazzolo (Université de Vérone), P. Petitier (Université Paris Cité), A. Silvestri (Université de Salerne), F. Spandri (Université Roma Tre), J.-C. Yon (EPHE, Paris).

avant tout une vocation épistémologique, puisqu'il simplifie et offre au déchiffrement une réalité complexe : en l'occurrence, l'échiquier politique brouillé de la monarchie de Juillet. D'où les oppositions binaires qui juxtaposent point par point, au physique comme au moral, des types censés incarner les deux extrêmes du spectre politique. C'est à ce manichéisme apparemment anodin que semble souscrire Balzac lorsqu'il oppose le républicain du Bousquier au légitimiste chevalier de Valois. Or, Balzac ne semble céder à des abstractions simplistes que pour mieux en faire ressortir les limites : les ambigüités que trahissent les personnages de *La Vielle Fille* encouragent le lecteur à se méfier de toute lecture à clé.

En tant que type politique, le Républicain de Juillet est investi d'une charge idéologique puissante ; Balzac, dans ce contexte, n'est que l'un des nombreux auteurs qui font de ce personnage un monstre assoiffé de sang, imitateur médiocre et passablement ridicule de ses idoles, les Jacobins. Mais si le Publicola Masson des *Comédiens sans le savoir* se réclame explicitement des républicains de la Terreur, le Desroys des *Employés* n'a jamais l'occasion de prendre la parole pour confirmer ou pour démentir sa réputation diabolique. De quoi semer le doute à l'égard du fondement réel d'une image typisée largement nourrie par la propagande monarchique.

Malgré son légitimisme affiché, l'auteur de *La Comédie humaine* ne manque pas de puiser dans le discours idéalisant pro-républicain pour détailler le portrait de Michel Chrestien, l'un des esprits d'élite du Cénacle de la rue des Quatre-Vents. Tué lors de l'insurrection de juin 1832, Michel Chrestien rejoint les rangs des martyrs dont les plumes républicaines de la monarchie de Juillet exaltent l'héroïsme tragique. Foudroyé sur les barricades, le militant de 1832 incarne un idéal irréalisé – donc à l'abri de l'épreuve du réel. Plus tard, Victor Hugo donnera vie, dans *Les Misérables*, aux Amis de l'ABC – dont le chef, Enjolras, est en partie inspiré de Michel Chrestien –, martyrs bienheureux puisqu'ils ne connurent pas la tragédie de la république en juin 1848. Les jeunes combattants de 1832 « ne virent jamais, jamais, ce que nous vîmes », s'exclame encore Verlaine dans un poème de 1872, confirmant la fascination tragique que le Républicain de Juillet continue d'exercer sur l'imaginaire littéraire au lendemain de la Commune.

Ainsi que le suggèrent ces quelques exemples, le Républicain de Juillet catalyse une pluralité d'enjeux sociaux, culturels, littéraires et politiques. Étudier l'imaginaire qui gravite autour de ce type, et relire les œuvres littéraires à l'aune d'un arsenal de représentations partagées circulant dans le discours social permet de saisir ces enjeux, et d'éclairer même les textes les plus connus d'une lumière nouvelle.

MANIFESTATIONS SCIENTIFIQUES

Séances du Cercle des études balzaciennes de Tokyo :

27 mars 2024 (Université Komazawa) : Saori Osuga, « *Séraphîta* et l'"esprit" dans la littérature romantique »
14 décembre 2024 (Université Sophia) : Mayu Tanizawa, « L'épouse et la courtisane dans *La Comédie humaine* » ; Takayasu Oya, « Les chercheurs balzaciens peuvent-ils lire *Volupté* de Sainte-Beuve avec objectivité ? »

Séances du Cercle des études balzaciennes d'Osaka :

22 mars 2024 (Université Kindai) : Izumi Iwamura, « L'empathie dans *La Peau de chagrin* : entre loi naturelle et loi sociale » ; discussion autour du livre de Kyoko Murata, *Lire la littérature française à travers la mode* – présentation par Takashi Sakuma.
31 août 2024 (sur Zoom) : « En hommage à Yuko Nishikawa » – intervenants : Takao Kashiwagi, Hiroko Otake, Kyoko Murata, Hiroshi Matsumura ; Yoshié Oshita, « Balzac, une création théâtrale 1839-1848 : autour des sources et des archives de mise en scène (1) »
26 décembre 2024 (Université Kindai) : Yoshié Oshita : « Balzac, une création théâtrale 1839-1848 : autour des sources et des archives de mise en scène (2) »

Cercles (réunis) des études balzaciennes de Tokyo et d'Osaka :

1er juin 2024 (Université Meiji) : Tatsunosuke Azuma : « Lire la nouvelle traduction de *La Rabouilleuse* en classe : ce que révèlent les interrogations et réflexions des étudiants » ; Izumi Iwamura : « *La Rabouilleuse* : la prolepse comme technique narrative » ; Kaoru Hakata : « Le temps dans *La Rabouilleuse* : autour des animaux (empaillés) et de la peinture »

Publications :
Michiaki Tanimoto, *Études balzaciennes à la carte. Du conte au roman*, Shumpusha, 2024 [en japonais].

Mieko Yoshinouchi, *Étude sur Balzac,* La Peau de chagrin *: une conception complexe à la lumière de Dante et Rabelais*, Suiseisha, 2024 [en japonais].

*

Le colloque annuel de *Nineteenth Century French Studies* s'est tenu les 19-21 septembre 2024 à l'Université de Duke ; sujet : *Producing and Receiving the Nineteenth Century.* Sur Balzac :
Derek Lake Berghuis (The Graduate Center, CUNY) : "Romanticizing the Historical. Context in Literature : The narrative as a platform for fantasizing in George Sand's *Nanon* and Honoré de Balzac's *Les Chouans*"
Emma Bielecki (King's College London) : "An Evening with Balzac and Vidocq"
Thomas Briggs (Independent Scholar) : "Balzac, 'Littérature industrielle' and the Creation of the Modern Novel"
Tadas Bugnevicius (Columbia University) : "Fanaticized Through the Reading of *La Comédie humaine*" : A History of the balzaciens 1890–1960"
Mary Jane Cowles (Kenyon College) : "Producing Copy, Producing a Name : Lucien's Impressions in *Illusions Perdues*"
Pierre Forfert (Yale University) : "Balzac's Poplar Trees : The Economy of Silviculture in *Eugénie Grandet*"
Basma Jaafar (University of North Carolina, Chapel Hill) : "Pouvoir, désir mimétique, et espace intime dans *La Duchesse de Langeais* de Honoré de Balzac"
Theodore Kellogg (Cornell University) : "Modes of Literary Production and the 19th-Century French Novel : Balzac, Flaubert, and Zola"
Judith Lyon-Caen (EHSS) : "Transmettre « Balzac », une histoire politique ?"

Eleanora Mancuso (Boston University) : "Producing Disability in *Madame Bovary* and *Le Colonel Chabert*"
Armine Kotin Mortimer (University of Illinois, Urbana-Champaign) : "Producing Paper in the Restoration France of Balzac"
Roger Navas-Sole (University of Oxford) : "The Quixotic Pursuit of Cultural Capital in *Illusions perdues*"
Karen Quandt (Wabash College) : "Paper Ecology in Balzac's *Illusions perdues*"
Courtney Sullivan (Washburn University) : "'Achetez, achetez toujours plus' : Consumerism, Prostitution, and the Press in Xavier Giannoli's *Illusions perdues* (2021)"
Christine Tchamabo (University of Oklahoma) : "Inflexion esthétique ou trajectoire des déprimés en proie à la société dans *René*, *Le Rouge et le Noir*, *Indiana*, *Le Curé de Tours* et *Madame Bovary*"
Pauline de Tholozany (Clemson University) : "Trivial Objects, Human Feelings : Balzac and Flaubert on the Material Effects of Impatience"
Paul Young (Georgetown University) : "'L'effet d'un simple mécanisme' : Balzac, the Guillotine and the Production of the Nineteenth-Century"

*

Le séminaire du Groupe International de Recherches Balzaciennes à l'Université de Paris Cité (CERILAC) en 2024-2025 a pour sujet « Le faux », sous la direction de Jacques-David Ebguy & Kathia Huynh :

27 septembre 2024 : Kathia Huynh (Lethica/POLEN) : « Faiblesse du vrai, puissances du faux »
22 novembre : José-Luis Diaz (Paris Cité) : « Blagueurs, faiseurs, charlatans : Balzac face à l'emprise du faux sur le monde "intelligentiel" »
31 janvier 2025 : Loïse Lelevé (Paris Nanterre) : « Faut-il excuser les fautes du copiste (et de ses dupes) ? Ontologies du faux et cristallisation de la figure du faussaire chez Balzac »
4 avril : Nathalie Solomon (Université de Perpignan Via Domitia) : « La *Comédie* des dupes : fausses pistes et autres mystifications balzaciennes »
Journée d'études le 20 juin 2025 à la Maison de Balzac.

*

Les 17 et 18 octobre 2024 s'est tenu à l'École Normale Supérieure de Lyon le colloque international *Balzac : lire les Contes drolatiques*, organisé par l'ÉNS de Lyon, le Labex Comod, l'IHRIM (UMR 5317), le CSLF (EA 1586) et le CÉRÉdl (UR 3229) ; responsables : Vincent Bierce & Éric Bordas (ÉNS Lyon & IHRIM) :

Éric Bordas (ÉNS Lyon) & Vincent Bierce (CPGE Lyon) : introduction
Takeshi Matsumura (Université de Tokyo) : « Pourquoi une nouvelle édition des *Contes drolatiques* ? »
Silvia Baroni (Universités de Bologne et Vérone) : « Dessiner, voir, interpréter : Gustave Doré illustre les *Contes drolatiques* »
Joëlle Ducos (Sorbonne Université) : « Les *Contes drolatiques* et les *Cent nouvelles nouvelles* ou l'intertextualité en acte »
Michèle Clément (Université Lyon 2) : « Un autre rabelaisianisme : *Le Moyen de parvenir* de Béroalde de Verville dans les *Contes drolatiques* »
Jean-Claude Mühlethaler (Université de Lausanne) : « Jeux parodiques entre chronique et satire : des "comiques joyeusetez" médiévales aux *Contes drolatiques* et retour »
Lucien Derainne (Université Jean Monnet de Saint-Etienne) : « L'observateur face au "metteur en lumière" des *Contes drolatiques* »
Marie-Ange Fougère (Université de Bourgogne) : « "Il n'y a pas de iouissance qui vaille un bon cas." Le rire scatologique des *Contes drolatiques* »
Laurent Susini (Sorbonne Université) : « "Madame la Vierge" : culbutes mariales dans les *Contes drolatiques* »
Julie Anselmini (Université de Caen Normandie) : « Les *Contes drolatiques*, un art d'aimer ? »
Agnese Silvestri (Université de Salerne) : « L'exercice de la violence et ses enjeux dans les *Contes drolatiques* »
Anne-Marie Baron (Société des Amis de Balzac) : « L'occulte drolatique »
Tim Farrant (Pembroke College, Université d'Oxford) : « Contes drolatiques, comédie drolatique »
Alain Vaillant (Université Paris Nanterre) : « Les *Contes drolatiques*, ou *Louis Lambert* en farce »
Sylvain Ledda (Université de Rouen-Normandie) : « Les *Contes drolatiques*, ou la contre-culture selon Balzac »
Dominique Massonnaud (Université de Haute Alsace) : « Les *Contes drolatiques* : une écriture anti-académique »

Philippe Desan (Université de Chicago) : « “Absous par son talent” ou Balzac par les mœurs qui courent »
Mickaël Savchenko (Paris) : « Traduire la langue des *Contes drolatiques* »
Hervé Plagnol (Société des Amis de Balzac) : « Un trésor d'inspirations pour les illustrateurs »

*

Le séminaire du Groupe d'Études Balzaciennes à l'École Normale Supérieure de la rue d'Ulm en 2024-2025 a pour sujet « Balzac, contes et nouvelles », sous la direction de Thomas Conrad & Bernard Gendrel :

18 octobre 2024 : Émile Pézard : « Les nouvelles de Balzac en contexte. Une lecture des *Deux Rencontres* et d'*El Verdugo* »
22 novembre : Tim Farrant : « Quoi de neuf sur la nouvelle ? »
13 décembre : Isabelle Mimouni : « La nouvelle : entrer dans *La Comédie humaine* par la porte étroite »
7 février 2025 : Éric Bordas : « Les *Contes drolatiques*, l'œuvre (concentrique) dans l'œuvre »
14 mars : Andrea Del Lungo : titre non précisé
28 mars : Chantal Massol : titre non précisé
4 avril : Xavier Bourdenet : « Nouvelle et mythe : Stendhal, Mérimée et Don Juan »
11 avril : Mariane Bury : titre non précisé

*

Les 8 et 9 novembre 2024 s'est tenu à l'Université Gustave-Eiffel et à la Maison de Balzac le colloque international *Le Merveilleux médical chez Balzac et ses contemporains*, organisé par l'équipe Littératures, Savoirs et Arts et le Groupe d'Études Balzaciennes ; responsable : Christelle Girard :

Christelle Girard (Université Gustave-Eiffel) : introduction
Sophie Vanden Abeele-Marchal (Sorbonne Université) : « Le Docteur-Noir dans *Stello* d'Alfred de Vigny »
Kathia Huynh (Université Polytechnique Hauts-de-France) : « Poudres de perlimpinpin chez Balzac, Flaubert et Maupassant : charlatanisme médical et merveilleux artificiel »

Julie Müller (Université de Hambourg) : « L'Antéchrist revisité : premières représentations du malade alcoolique chez Balzac et ses contemporains »
Romain Enriquez (Sorbonne Université) : « *Le Roman d'un géologue* de Xavier de Reul : la première "étude sur l'hystérie" »
Sabine Le Hir (EPHE) : « Hector Berlioz et la médecine, entre discours scientifiques et récits fantastiques : résonances et dissonances avec Balzac »
Dana Vuckovic (Université d'Oxford) : « Le duo/duel psychologique entre Stéphanie de Vandières et Philippe de Sucy : la dimension scientifique et romanesque de la folie dans *Adieu* »
Shane Lillis (Université de Nantes) : « L'image de l'âme à travers le prisme de la médecine chez Balzac et ses contemporains »
Audrey Millet (Université de Caen) : « L'accouchement-catastrophe dans *L'Enfant maudit* (1837) de Balzac et *Une histoire sans nom* (1882) de Barbey d'Aurevilly »
Tim Farrant (Université d'Oxford) : « Balzac, Gall et Lavater, merveilles médicales et merveilles romanesques »
Marie-Hélène Dumot (Université de Göttingen) : « Merveilleux médical et discours idéologique : le médecin porte-voix d'Eugène Sue dans la série *Le Diable médecin* (1854-1856) »
Anne-Marie Lefebvre (Université Toulouse II – Jean-Jaurès) : « Les superpouvoirs de la métaphore médicale chez Balzac »
Olivier Laurini (GHU Paris, Sainte-Anne) : « *La Recherche de l'Absolu* de Balzac : merveilleux, délire ou addiction ? »
Anne-Marie Baron (Société des Amis d'Honoré de Balzac) : « Miracle de la médecine balzacienne : *imitatio Christi* ou performances para-psychiques ? »
Mokhtar Belarbi (Université de Meknès) : « Le merveilleux médical dans *Le Médecin de campagne* de Balzac »

Rubrique coordonnée par
Éric BORDAS

ARCHIVES

Riccardo Bacchelli, « Balzac » (1950)

> et vous, ô Honoré de Balzac, vous le plus héroïque, le plus singulier, le plus romantique et le plus poétique parmi tous les personnages que vous avez tirés de votre sein[1] !

Dans le monde de la critique littéraire, il arrive souvent que l'intérêt pour un écrivain et son œuvre s'amplifie et se renouvelle à l'occasion de certains anniversaires particulièrement importants. Dans le cas de Balzac, nous nous référons spécifiquement à l'année 1950, correspondant au centenaire de sa mort. Au-delà des célébrations académiques rituelles et des témoignages journalistiques de circonstance, certaines interventions ont apporté, à l'intelligence critique de l'auteur, de nouveaux éclairages et, dans certains cas, des ouvertures révélatrices sur des aspects ou des thèmes fondamentaux jusque-là mal explorés de son œuvre.

À partir des années qui suivent immédiatement la Seconde Guerre mondiale, on assiste, même en Italie, à une véritable renaissance des études balzaciennes. De ce regain d'intérêt et de la manière dont il s'est concrétisé par la publication d'essais critiques conçus avec une rigueur scientifique et méthodologique rarement rencontrée jusque-là, le plus grand mérite revient à quelques personnalités d'excellence de la culture dite universitaire. Cependant, il serait restrictif de méconnaître voire d'ignorer l'apport de certains écrivains, qui, en revenant sur Balzac dans leur célébration, ont reconnu en lui un *exemplum* et un modèle de référence permanent[2].

1 Charles Baudelaire, *Salon de 1846. De l'héroïsme de la vie moderne*, dans *Curiosités esthétiques*, Paris, Michel Lévy Frères, Libraires Éditeurs, 1868, p. 198.

2 Pour un examen des travaux critiques produits en Italie à l'occasion du centenaire balzacien, voir Paolo Russo, *Primo inventario della fortuna di Balzac in Italia (Introduzione a*

À l'occasion de la cinquième Journée mondiale de l'Unesco, Riccardo Bacchelli (Bologne, 1891-Monza, 1985) a tenu à Florence, le 14 juin 1950, dans la salle des Cinq-Cents du Palazzo Vecchio, une conférence commémorative à la mémoire de Balzac, dont le texte a été publié quelques mois plus tard dans les pages de la revue florentine « Il Ponte ». À notre connaissance, ce texte n'a jamais été inclus dans aucun recueil d'écrits critiques de Bacchelli publiés après 1950[3].

Lorsqu'un écrivain écrit à propos d'un autre écrivain, nous apprend Susi Pietri[4], nous sommes toujours confrontés à une expérience exceptionnelle. Autrement dit, il s'agit d'un exercice raffiné de « réflexivité autoréflexive » qui insère « l'expérience présente du travail d'autrui dans un rapport essentiel et incontournable, qui se tisse au fil du temps entre la construction critique de la lecture, la recherche insatisfaite, peut-être utopique, de l'“auteur” idéal […] et le projet incessant de se forger *sa propre identité d'écrivain* – une identité à sonder, redéfinir, remettre chaque fois en question[5] ».

Près de quarante ans après sa première et totale expérience de lecture de la *Comédie humaine*, alors que dans aucune de ses précédentes études littéraires il ne s'était jamais occupé spécifiquement de Balzac, l'écrivain italien, désormais reconnu et arrivé à sa pleine maturité d'artiste, établit avec lui un dialogue à distance extrêmement ouvert et dynamique : un dialogue qui, dans le cas du texte que nous présentons ici, se développe et se prolonge dans un tissu de réflexions suggestives sur les implications d'une expérience intime et prolongée avec *La Comédie humaine* et strictement liée à la formation de son individualité artistique.

Après les débuts bolonais de Bacchelli en tant que journaliste, en mai 1912 déjà, on voit apparaître sa signature dans la revue florentine « La Voce ». Après avoir abandonné les études universitaires, (il avait

---

una bibliografia critica 1948-1957), « Belfagor », Florence, A. XIV, N. 5, 30 septembre 1950, p. 551-561 et Marco Stupazzoni, *Echi italiani del bicentenario balzachiano*, Moncalieri, CRIER-CIRVI, 2001, p. 21-28.

3 Voir notamment, Mario Saccenti, *Bacchelli. Memoria e invenzione*, Florence, Le Lettere, 2000, p. 173.

4 Voir *L'Invention de Balzac. Lectures européennes*, Saint-Denis, Presses Universitaires de Vincennes, 2004 et *L'Opera inaugurale. Gli scrittori-lettori della* Comédie humaine *I*, Milan-Udine, Mimesis, 2009.

5 Susi Pietri, *L'Opera inaugurale*, *op. cit.*, p. 29.

eu, comme professeur, à Bologne, Giosuè Carducci), dans les quinze premières années du XXe siècle c'est Florence qui devient pour lui le pôle d'attraction culturelle privilégié. Après l'expérience « vocienne » et dans une perspective diamétralement opposée, Bacchelli sera, avec Bruno Barilli, Antonio Baldini, Emilio Cecchi, Giuseppe Raimondi et Vincenzo Cardarelli, le fondateur de la revue « La Ronda » (avril 1919-novembre 1922), devenant le porte-parole de la nécessité d'un retour à l'ordre après les tentatives d'expérimentation expressive prônées par les Avant-gardes. À partir des années 1920, on assiste, en Italie, à un renouveau, à une véritable relance de l'écriture fictionnelle. Chez Bacchelli, l'élargissement des horizons du roman est explicitement lié à la tradition européenne du roman historique du XIXe siècle (Manzoni, Nievo, Tolstoi) : l'érudition manifestée dans la reconstitution de grandes fresques historiques et son talent stylistique permettent à Bacchelli, en tant qu'auteur, d'utiliser des formes, des modèles et des genres passés pour revendiquer son autonomie d'artiste et pour créer de nouveaux styles et une nouvelle élégance expressive. C'est ce que l'on observe dans son premier roman véritablement représentatif : *Il diavolo al Pontelungo* [*Le diable au Pontelungo*] (1927), centré sur la figure et le séjour à Bologne de Mikail Bakùnin et sur la révolte anarchiste d'Imola en 1874 ; et plus encore dans son chef-d'œuvre narratif certainement le plus connu et le plus apprécié du grand public : *Il mulino del Po* [*Le moulin du Pô*] (1938-1940), qui raconte l'histoire de trois générations d'une famille de meuniers établis près de Ferrare dans la plaine du Pô et s'étend sur une période comprise entre l'expédition napoléonienne en Russie (1812) et la fin de la Première Guerre mondiale (1918[6]).

6 Parmi les œuvres qui composent l'immense production poétique, fictionnelle et critique de Bacchelli, nous signalerons, avant 1927, l'édition des *Poemi lirici* [*Poèmes lyriques*] (1914) et du conte de fables : *Lo sa il tonno* [*Le thon sait*] (1923) ; ensuite, à partir de 1930 : *Una passione coniugale* [*Une passion conjugale*] (1930), *Il pianto del figlio di Lais* [*Le cri du fils de Lais*] (1945), *Lo sguardo di Gesù* [*Le regard de Jésus*] (1948), *Il figlio di Stalin* [*Le fils de Staline*] (1953), *I tre schiavi di Giulio Cesare* [*Les trois esclaves de Jules César*] (1957), *Non ti chiamerò più padre* [*Je ne t'appellerai plus mon père*] (1959), *Il coccio di terracotta* [*L'éclat de faïence*] (1966). Parmi les derniers textes narratifs : *Rapporto segreto* [*Rapport secret*] (1967), *L'Afrodite* [*L'Aphrodite*] (1969), *Il progresso è un razzo : un romanzo matto* [*Le progrès est une fusée : un roman fou*] (1975), *Il sommergibile* [*Le sous-marin*] (1978) et *In grotta e in valle : romanzo preistorico* [*Dans la grotte et dans la vallée : roman préhistorique*] (1980). Bacchelli a rédigé aussi une biographie critique de Rossini (1954) et de nombreux textes pour le théâtre. Une bibliographie détaillée des écrits de l'auteur a été établie par Maurizio Vitale : *Bibliografia degli scritti di Riccardo Bacchelli. 1909-1970*, Milan-Naples, éditeur

Fortifiée par l'historicisme idéaliste de Hegel et de Benedetto Croce, la poétique du roman de Bacchelli place l'omniscience de l'auteur au centre d'un lien étroit et fidèle avec la tradition. Cependant, il serait trompeur, voire carrément insultant, de penser que, pour Bacchelli, la réalité de la littérature et, en particulier, celle du roman – genre littéraire impur, pluriel, imprévisible, dont personne n'a jamais fixé les règles – se limite à assumer de manière acritique des conventions préétablies ou héritées de schémas et de modèles appartenant au passé. Et cela parce que le roman, écrit Baudelaire, est, par sa nature même, « un genre bâtard dont le domaine est vraiment sans limites » et qui, contrairement à la poésie et à l'histoire, « ne subit d'autres inconvénients et ne connaît d'autres dangers que son infinie liberté[7] ».

Dans un écrit de 1932, Bacchelli aborde, à cet égard, la question du caractère substantiellement paradoxal du roman[8]. L'écrivain italien conçoit l'art narratif, et plus généralement la littérature, comme une création capable d'exister sous une forme autonome, c'est-à-dire étrangère et rebelle à tout type de lois, de normes et de catégories critiques imposées ou appliquées de l'extérieur. Le roman, écrit Bacchelli, est « une invention vraisemblable. Une contradiction. Celle-ci est constitutive du roman et, si l'on peut dire, de l'art moderne, conformément à la philosophie qui réduit tout concept, et donc aussi le beau, au réel concret. Lorsqu'une dialectique s'établit entre les deux termes opposés et qu'elle se déploie dans l'âme et dans l'esprit de l'artiste, la synthèse naît avec l'œuvre d'art[9] ».

En quoi consiste donc le paradoxe du roman ? Dans le fait que, au roman, « l'auteur et le lecteur doivent demander de paraître vrai en ce qu'il a de plus proprement inventé, et inventé là où il est le plus proprement vrai ». C'est dans cette tension entre idée de beau et idée de vrai que le roman est contraint et poussé à « se déterminer dans une pluralité formelle riche, inquiète, dynamique, très vive,

---

Ricciardi, 1971 complétée par Claudia Masotti pour les années 1971-1985 (*Uno scrittore nel tempo*, Florence, Le Lettere, 2001).

7 Charles Baudelaire, *Théophile Gautier* (« L'Artiste », 13 mars 1859), dans *Balzac*, préface et notes de Stéphane Vachon, Paris, Presses de l'Université Paris-Sorbonne, 1999, p. 247.

8 Riccardo Bacchelli, *Paradosso del romanzo* [*Paradoxe du roman*], « La Cultura », A. XI, N. 4, octobre-décembre 1932, p. 680-688, publié ensuite dans *Saggi critici* [*Essais critiques*], Milan, A. Mondadori, 1962 (« Tutte le opere », XIX).

9 Riccardo Bacchelli, *Paradosso del romanzo*, dans *Saggi critici*, *op. cit.*, p. 48.

illusoire, mais d'une illusion vitale[10] » qui est la marque distinctive de la modernité.

Illusion vitale et modernité : deux forces qui, selon Bacchelli, semblent s'imprimer et se répandre dans cette scène prodigieuse de fictions, *La Comédie humaine*, qui ne serait autre que la projection figurative, intime et profonde, d'une immense personnalité créatrice d'exception : celle de Balzac.

Lire Balzac, *étudier le romancier qui entre tous excelle et se distingue par la faculté combinatoire de sa surabondante fantaisie inventive, le prince des inventeurs d'intrigues et de cas extraordinaires*, présuppose, selon Bacchelli, *l'abandon total de l'esprit critique* : cela signifie, en d'autres termes, qu'il faut plonger, s'immerger dans son œuvre *corps et âme, à corps perdu et les yeux fermés* et se laisser séduire par la violence *captivante et captieuse* que ses représentations exercent sur nos sens et sur notre esprit[11]. C'est comme si, en lisant les romans de *La Comédie humaine*, on était d'abord frappés par cette violence puis suspendus et oscillants, dans une dimension de souvenirs et d'impressions dont la charge onirique, par son caractère vague, lointain et fugace, reste imprimée dans notre mémoire comme le faible reflet d'une éclipse solaire ou comme la lueur d'une aurore boréale. Cette trace de *mémoire éclipsée*, qui se nourrit et se colore des inventions de l'imaginaire balzacien, accueille, assemble et recompose l'ensemble des données concrètes observées et restituées, dans les romans, avec la plus grande précision réaliste (que Bacchelli conçoit comme simple *pratique technique de représentation*), mais qui, en réalité, sont façonnées et transfigurées par le pouvoir visionnaire de l'auteur, par *l'état permanent de frénésie imaginative* dans laquelle l'écrivain se trouve, héroïquement, éternellement et dramatiquement seul. Au terme de cette opération mémorielle, suscitée et habitée par l'imaginaire de Balzac, il ne reste donc que la présence vivante et obsédante du romancier. Et c'est précisément cette présence qui constitue pour Bacchelli, comme déjà pour Baudelaire et pour Gautier, le seul et unique critère de jugement de son œuvre : celui qui *rend tous les autres superflus*. Dans sa voracité imaginative et expressive, dont le style est *l'expression passionnée et sensible*, Balzac ne se borne pas à inventer et à peindre ses fables : comme l'*Alexandre le Grand*

10 *Ibid.*, p. 50.

11 Nous citons en italique, ici comme dans les pages qui suivent, les passages tirés de la conférence de Bacchelli de 1950.

de la légende médiévale, il les vit, c'est-à-dire qu'il *les subit, les endure ou en jouit* entraîné par le tourbillon de *son impérieuse vitalité, de son humeur dense et sanguine*, de *sa force d'imagination et de représentation qui s'apparente à celle des rêves, hallucinée et hallucinante*[12].

On s'imagine le voir, Balzac, en train de créer ses *fantômes* pour ensuite les observer avec une participation enthousiaste et, avec son regard de dompteur (comme le définit Gautier[13]), diriger à distance la mise en scène de ce « carnaval de fantoches extravagants et réels[14] », qu'est *La Comédie humaine*. Nous avons l'impression, nous dit Bacchelli, avant tout de l'entendre, de percevoir sa voix de *Souffleur* invisible caché dans le trou ou dans les coulisses de la scène qui, comme le Dieu biblique, insuffle la vie à ses créatures. On croirait entendre la *voix nocturne et souterraine* de Vautrin, le génial détenteur des secrets les plus indéchiffrables, l'impitoyable manipulateur des âmes et des destins qui, tout en inoculant ses poisons à Lucien de Rubempré, lui murmure : « Je suis l'auteur, tu seras le drame ; si tu ne réussis pas, c'est moi qui serai sifflé[15] ».

Dans ce destin d'analogie et de cohérence entre Balzac et son double littéraire, dans cette fureur de l'écriture et de l'action si impérieusement liée au corps et à la terre, dans cet enfer des passions, des besoins humains, des leurres, des injustices et des illusions, est-il possible, se demande Bacchelli, d'entrevoir la lumière de la poésie ?

Arrivé presque à la fin de sa conférence, Bacchelli nous dit entendre le murmure d'une autre voix de Balzac : c'est la voix de son âme d'homme ou de dieu miséricordieux, presque un cri étouffé de douleur dans un élan de pitié et de compassion profonde pour les victimes et les bourreaux de cette condition de souffrance morale universelle qui est la marque indélébile de notre destin humain. Ce sentiment *de la cruauté fatale de l'existence et des besoins humains et terrestres, dans tous les ordres de choses, est*

---

12 Dans la même perspective critique que celle de Bacchelli se situe un autre écrivain italien de la seconde moitié du XXe siècle, Guido Piovene. Celui-ci se fait le porte-parole, sous l'égide de Balzac, d'une idée de littérature et de critique détachée de toute forme de rigorisme : il considère, en effet, Balzac comme « un grand halluciné, dont la vision est porteuse de vérité, comme dans les rêves fiévreux » (*La città dei misteri* [*La ville des mystères*], « Corriere della Sera », Milan, 5 mars 1950 et dans *Madame la France*, Milan, Mondadori, 1966, p. 226).

13 Théophile Gautier, *Honoré de Balzac*, Paris, Poulet-Malassis et De Broise, 1859, p. 8.

14 *Ibid.*, p. 106.

15 Voir *Splendeurs et misères des courtisanes*, *CH*, VI, p. 504.

intense et tragique chez Balzac, et il le traduit par une pitié profonde et intime pour les victimes et leurs oppresseurs, pour les victimes et ceux qui en font des victimes, et pour ceux qui sont victimes d'eux-mêmes, comme nous tous.

Il ne s'agit pas, croyons-nous, d'une banale attention compatissante envers ceux qui, victimes (comme Louise et Renée des *Mémoires de deux jeunes mariées*) ou bourreaux (comme Vautrin), se retrouvent perpétuellement suspendus dans le cours inexorable et douloureux de l'histoire, entre la vie et la mort. Pourtant, le héros balzacien, qu'il soit l'incarnation du bien ou l'incarnation du mal, n'est pas la victime passive d'un destin tout tracé. Souvent il exprime, de manière voilée mais insistante, un sentiment intérieur de liberté : il a conscience de sa propre responsabilité. Le lecteur sent en lui le poids de la solitude, de l'inquiétude ou de l'enthousiasme face à l'obligation d'opérer des choix et d'assumer la responsabilité de ces choix. Un nouvel espace de liberté surgit alors dans le récit, au sein duquel ces créatures, dans les veines desquelles circule « un véritable sang au lieu de l'encre[16] », gagnent en humanité et en grâce.

Si ces « fantômes » sont en réalité des créatures de chair et de sang, les fils bien-aimés auxquels Balzac a imposé les commandements de son imagination, nous pensons qu'il est permis de supposer que, s'il existait une fonction éthique du roman, elle consisterait à conserver, pour ces « ombres vivantes », une trace dans la mémoire des lecteurs, à travers une opération de sauvetage qui naît de l'empathie de l'auteur à leur égard : une mystérieuse tension spirituelle entre auteur, personnage et lecteur qui engage le lecteur lui-même dans une participation convaincue de l'âme et qui s'inscrit dans le texte romanesque en tant que champ d'action privilégié. C'est ainsi seulement que le lecteur pourra personnellement assumer, cristalliser et accueillir avec son *assentiment le plus vif et le plus confiant* ces « illusions » que Balzac a prises comme lois et fins de son art et participer aux douleurs et aux orages de leurs misères. Ainsi, écrit Bacchelli, personne ne peut prétendre avoir lu et compris Balzac *s'il n'a été une heure durant, ou un an, balzacien, éperdument balzacien.*

*

16 Théophile Gautier, *Honoré de Balzac*, *op. cit.*, p. 39.

Mesdames et Messieurs,

Quelles étranges illusions provoquent dans la mémoire les innombrables bouleversements qu'a subis notre vie au cours de ce siècle !

Lorsque j'ai eu l'honneur d'être invité à commémorer dans ce Congrès le centenaire de la mort de Balzac, mon premier souvenir, l'embryon de ma réflexion, a été que j'avais lu Balzac avant 1914, la funeste année 1914. Parfois, lorsque viennent à l'esprit de semblables considérations chronologiques, nous sommes saisis par le doute d'avoir rêvé, mais quand ? Nous ne saurions le dire. Ce que nous avons vécu et connu avant cette date fut-il un rêve, ou avons-nous rêvé tout ce qui est venu ensuite ?

Je me suis surpris alors à penser : – Est-ce possible qu'un siècle seulement se soit écoulé depuis la mort de Balzac ? Est-ce possible que tant de temps se soit déjà écoulé depuis que j'ai lu Balzac ?

Remontant à ces jours lointains, j'ai l'impression qu'ils sont sortis du temps sensible et qu'ils appartiennent à un temps révolu, passé à l'histoire, alors que ma mémoire par ailleurs les ressuscite si vivants et si présents que je me surprends aussi à penser : – Est-ce possible qu'un siècle soit déjà passé depuis que Balzac est mort ; que de ces cent ans j'en aie vécu plus de la moitié, et qu'au moment où je l'ai lu à peine plus de cinquante ans se soient écoulés depuis sa mort ?

Cela signifie, avant tout, que la lecture de *La Comédie humaine* est de celles qui s'impriment dans la mémoire avec la couleur et le ton des jours et des heures où nous les avons faites, avec les sensations et les sentiments qu'elles ont produits tandis que nous les faisions, lectures qui demeurent liées au souvenir de la saison, des lieux, du livre même avec ses pages et ses caractères imprimés.

Je vous prie de m'accorder, Mesdames et Messieurs, un peu d'indulgence : la vivacité d'un tel souvenir me presse d'en faire ici le récit. J'espère que celui-ci ne vous paraîtra pas, après coup, tout à fait inutile. Du reste, le grand romancier est si généreux et si minutieux en matière de couleurs et de détails qu'il encourage et peut-être autorise, si vous le voulez bien, une brève licence narrative et descriptive. Un jour de l'été 1913, saison de grand soleil, parti à l'aube de Bologne, je parcourais en automobile la Toscane quand, à l'heure torride de midi, après bien des arrêts forcés, j'arrivai à Pescia dans la Valdinievole, l'estomac de mes vingt ans criant famine et la soif me tourmentant après toutes ces heures de chaleur, de fatigue et d'agacement autour du moteur et des pneus.

Soyez patients Mesdames et Messieurs. Parlant d'un auteur si savoureux et si chaleureux en matière de mets et de boissons, parlant d'un maître éminent comme Balzac quand il s'agit de goûts gastronomiques et œnologiques mais aussi de tout l'éventail des passions et des appétits sensuels, il ne me semble pas déplacé, vous en conviendrez, de vous raconter qu'à Pescia, ce jour-là, dans l'ombre fraîche d'une taverne aux effluves de saine cuisine et de bonne cave, je m'attablai devant un plat typique où excelle la cuisine toscane et une fiasque d'excellent vin.

Ces détails de l'aventure nous mettent dans un climat balzacien, comme le voudrait le style descriptif tellement dense de Balzac. C'est pourquoi j'insiste et précise qu'il s'agissait d'un poulet frit, grésillant d'huile bouillante et, comme on dit, doré. Quant au vin, c'était bien sûr du Chianti, robuste et charnu, sec en bouche et chatouillant la langue, un Chianti aristocratique et paysan, rustique et aimable, sec et parfumé, très invitant, qui comble sans lasser, grise sans peser.

Ainsi donc, dans la taverne où je vous ai emmenés, un verre en appelle un autre, et, avant le dernier, beaucoup d'avant-derniers. Alors, reviennent la gaieté et l'entrain, tandis que s'éclipse tout à fait le bon sens dont nous n'étions d'ailleurs pas trop pourvus mon compagnon de voyage et moi. En outre, tandis que nous reprenions notre route, voilà que le sort malicieux ranime aussi de vibrante allégresse notre moteur. Nous nous sommes mis alors à poursuivre avec fougue et à dépasser hardiment toutes les automobiles que nous rattrapions, jusqu'au moment où, dans l'épais nuage de poussière qui à cette époque couvrait les chemins, nous avons percuté le véhicule d'un innocent et sobre automobiliste qui venait en sens inverse.

À l'hôpital, je vous le dis tout de suite, je fus le seul à être emmené, si bien que j'ai la satisfaction, grâce à Dieu et à la fortune, de n'avoir sur la conscience ni morts ni blessés. Je fus le seul à m'y retrouver, comme je le méritais, et très cabossé, si bien que j'eus tout le temps et le loisir de lire les œuvres complètes de Balzac, et de le lire, comme il convient de le faire, tout entier et d'un seul trait.

Voilà donc le concours de circonstances fortuites qui me fournit l'occasion d'étudier le romancier qui entre tous excelle et se distingue par la faculté combinatoire de sa surabondante fantaisie inventive, le prince des inventeurs d'intrigues et de cas extraordinaires[17]. Bien sûr, je

17 Cette appréciation de Bacchelli est aux antipodes du jugement exprimé à propos de l'écrivain français par Pietro Paolo Trompeo lorsqu'il précise : « à coup sûr, chez Balzac,

ne prétends pas qu'il faut pour le lire de fond en comble une combinaison de hasards finalement aussi catastrophiques, mais cela demande bien plus de temps et de liberté qu'on n'en dispose ordinairement.

En outre, le grand Honoré est un tel héros de la plume, un tel intempérant de l'écriture que le lire exige un certain héroïsme de lecteur et une bonne dose de ce que, dans un moment de pessimisme pénétrant, le talent raffiné d'un sobre écrivain et gourmand lecteur comme Valéry Larbaud a appelé vice impuni, la lecture[18].

Le fait est qu'il me semble encore avoir sur le pupitre de mon lit d'hôpital et sous les yeux les colonnes serrées et les milliers de pages de l'édition – en peu de volumes massifs et épais des œuvres complètes – dans laquelle j'ai lu *La Comédie humaine* durant ce repos forcé.

Je ne sais jusqu'à quel point relève uniquement de mon expérience personnelle ce que je m'apprête à vous dire. Je vous le livre pour ce que cela peut valoir. De la lecture de Balzac est très vif en moi le souvenir extérieur, mais tout aussi vif est le souvenir intérieur des impressions qu'elle a produites. Dans l'ensemble toutefois, ce souvenir m'apparaît comme nimbé d'une lumière d'éclipse solaire ou d'aurore boréale. Ce sont mille sensations en une, une impression en mille, si bien que je suis tenté de dire que du plus fécond inventeur de situations, de personnages et de détails que l'histoire du roman ait connu demeure dans ma mémoire une image innombrable, fourmillante et cependant presque abstraite, changeante et toujours égale, qui comprend toute l'œuvre et d'une certaine manière l'annule, avec toute son immense variété.

Voilà que la figure dominante, le héros de l'aventure, le personnage, unique dirais-je, de cette foule, de cette population dont il a été dit qu'elle faisait concurrence à l'état civil, voilà que ce héros, est le grand, l'extraordinaire, l'énorme, l'inégalable Honoré.

Tandis que le souvenir est braqué sur des centaines de ces milliers de situations, de lieux, de rencontres, de visages, de noms et de discours, si la réflexion veut condenser un jugement, formuler une synthèse, elle doit sortir de l'œuvre d'art concrète pour se concentrer, presque en dehors d'elle, sur la figure plus imaginée que rigoureuse, de l'auteur de cette œuvre.

---

le peintre des lieux, le portraitiste, le moraliste et l'historien laissent loin derrière eux le narrateur-inventeur : autant celui-ci est maladroit ou brouillon, autant les premiers sont vigoureux, intelligents et profonds » (voir *L'Omero della borghesia* [*L'Homère de la bourgeoisie*], « La Fiera letteraria », Rome, A. V, N. 34, 3 septembre 1950, p. 5).

18 Voir *Ce vice impuni, la lecture*, Paris, A. Messein, 1925.

Mon observation semble d'autant plus paradoxale que l'œuvre prétend être (et est certainement en un certain sens) extrêmement réaliste comme pratique technique de représentation. Paradoxale, elle l'est aussi pour une autre raison : si je fais appel au souvenir de toutes les œuvres narratives que j'ai lues, y compris, en trop petit nombre, les œuvres orientales et asiatiques, je suis forcé de reconnaître que ce caractère de mémoire éclipsée est un trait unique et propre à la mémoire qui m'est restée de l'œuvre balzacienne.

Si je cherche la raison de ce paradoxe, il me semble qu'elle réside dans le fait que lire Balzac signifie et exige que l'on plonge en se laissant submerger aussi longtemps que dure l'entreprise, corps et âme, à corps perdu, et les yeux fermés, avec un abandon total de l'esprit critique[19], dans ce répertoire infini d'événements, d'histoires différentes et égales. Cela signifie s'abandonner à cette unité, ou mieux à cette monotonie de ton, au milieu d'une infinie variété de couleurs changeantes et éclatantes ; cela signifie céder à la captivante et captieuse violence, à l'évidence exaspérée et exaspérante, à la séduction irrésistible qu'exerce la représentation balzacienne sur les cinq sens, sur les papilles gustatives, sur la peau, habile comme elle l'est à transformer en sens et passion les images et les figures de la fantaisie et de la langue. Il y a dans l'œuvre de Balzac une incessante délectation, une volupté, une soumission à l'expression et à la fantaisie prises pour elles-mêmes qui captivent, passionnent, et finalement séduisent.

C'est le style de Balzac, luxuriant et sophistiqué, puissant et frelaté, prodigieux et artificiel qu'il faut prendre tel qu'il est, hors de toute règle et de toute mesure : on le subit ou on s'y refuse.

---

19 Dans son étude sur le romancier français, publiée en première édition dans le quotidien « La Stampa » (*Balzac e il romanzo sociale* [*Balzac et le roman social*] ; *Luci ed ombre di un grande artista* [*Ombres et lumières d'un grand artiste*], Turin, 27 mai et 2 juin 1921) reprise ensuite, revue et corrigée, dans le volume : *Poesia e non poesia. Note sulla letteratura europea del secolo decimonono* [*Poésie et non poésie. Notes sur la littérature européenne du* XIX*e siècle*] : *Balzac* (Bari, Gius. Laterza, 1923, p. 240-251), Benedetto Croce fustige avec vigueur les critiques et les intellectuels (Taine et Brunetière, en tête) qui, dominés par « cet esprit intellectualiste et dogmatique qui fait obstacle à la compréhension de l'art » (p. 240 de l'édition en volume), ont considéré Balzac comme un homme de science observateur, comme « narrateur du livre d'observation sociale objective » (p. 244). Croce reconnaît que dans l'œuvre de Balzac certaines observations « jaillissent fulgurantes » ; mais ce ne sont que des éclairs, « non une lumière diffuse et également distribuée », ce sont plutôt des « suggestions de questions que des réponses à des questions » (*ibid.*).

Ainsi, si nous voulons évoquer une similitude, Baudelaire, dans les *Paradis artificiels*, nous décrit un Balzac refusant une drogue stupéfiante parce qu'elle n'aurait pu agir sur son cerveau[20] capable par ailleurs de supporter sans en être embué les plus robustes vins de Bourgogne. Je dirais que ce vigoureux cerveau était constamment dans un tel état d'ivresse imaginative qu'aucune autre n'aurait pu y pénétrer.

Opulence de style rappelant l'éloquence asiatique, dira Sainte-Beuve, avec une perfide malice dictée par son excellent goût, tandis qu'il en fait remarquer les traits récurrents de mollesse voluptueuse[21]. Le goût raffiné et classique, de même que le tempérament de l'auteur de *Volupté*, qui en matière de volupté s'y entendait jusqu'à la goûter mortifiée et contrite, étaient bien de nature à pénétrer ce style et à le rejeter. Ceci m'amène à dire que Sainte-Beuve, loin de l'ignorer, repousse la grandeur propre à Balzac.

Le fait est qu'il ne faut pas le lire avec un esprit critique et averti. Je dirais même que le jugement, à l'égard de l'œuvre balzacienne, advient dans l'ajournement et la suspension de l'examen et de la réflexion, si bien qu'à un certain moment ce jugement même apparaît superflu. Pour mieux dire, un jugement se forme dès la première page ; ensuite il est de ceux que nous nous faisons au sujet des personnes pleines de qualités les plus disparates mais dominées par une puissante et impérieuse vitalité,

---

20 « Balzac pensait sans doute qu'il n'est pas pour l'homme de plus grande honte ni de plus vive souffrance que l'abdication de sa volonté. Je l'ai vu une fois, dans une réunion où il était question des effets prodigieux du haschisch. Il écoutait et questionnait avec une attention et une vivacité amusantes. Les personnes qui l'ont connu devinent qu'il devait être intéressé. Mais l'idée de penser malgré lui même le choquait vivement. On lui présenta du dawamesk ; il l'examina, le flaira et le rendit sans y toucher. La lutte entre sa curiosité presque enfantine et sa répugnance pour l'abdication se trahissait sur son visage expressif d'une manière frappante. L'amour de la dignité l'emporta. En effet, il est difficile de se figurer le théoricien de la *volonté*, ce jumeau spirituel de Louis Lambert, consentant à perdre une parcelle de cette précieuse *substance* » (voir *Les Paradis artificiels*, chronologie et introduction par Marcel A. Ruff, Paris, Flammarion, « GF », 1966, p. 69).

21 Bacchelli reprend ici certaines expressions métaphoriques employées par Sainte-Beuve pour caractériser le style de Balzac : « J'aime de son style – écrit Sainte-Beuve – dans les parties délicates, cette efflorescence [...] par laquelle il donne à tout le sentiment de la vie et fait frissonner la page elle-même. Mais je ne puis accepter, sous le couvert de la physiologie, l'abus continuel de cette qualité, ce style si souvent chatouilleux et dissolvant, énervé, rosé, et veiné de toutes les teintes, ce style d'une corruption délicieuse, tout asiatique comme disaient nos maîtres, plus brisé par places et plus amolli que le corps d'un mime antique » (*M. de Balzac*, « Le Constitutionnel », 2 septembre 1850 et dans *Causeries du lundi*, Paris, Garnier Frères, 1858, p. 449).

par une humeur dense et sanguine qui les mettent en deçà et au-delà du bien et du mal, du vrai et du faux. Il serait injuste de les juger comme si elles étaient – ou en prétendant qu'elles puissent être – pleines de pondération et de maîtrise d'elles-mêmes. Car dans cet état permanent de frénésie imaginative, dans cette tension extrême de chaque parole proférée, dans chaque fait ou personne qu'il invente, résident la force et la vocation, la grandeur et le destin de Balzac. C'est ce que Baudelaire, avec une infaillible intuition, a bien saisi quand il dit que reprocher à Balzac l'exagération, c'est méconnaître et lui reprocher sa grandeur. Alors, l'opération de la mémoire, qui durant la lecture s'abandonne aux mille impressions et se laisse habiter par les mille inventions de l'imagination balzacienne pour ne se souvenir finalement que d'un seul personnage, Balzac lui-même, cette opération-là de la mémoire m'apparaît comme le jugement le plus adéquat, le plus exhaustif, en regard duquel tous les autres sont superflus.

Le plus réaliste des réalistes, le plus vériste des véristes, est en tant qu'artiste le plus romanesque des romanciers. L'art du roman, qui consiste à tout réduire à la dimension du réel et du vrai, il le traite toujours et en tout avec la démesure de l'héroïque et du sublime, en tout et toujours infernal ou paradisiaque, en tout et toujours extraordinaire. Il ne représente pas ses fables, et même il ne les invente pas à proprement parler : il les vit[22] en ce sens qu'il les subit, les endure, ou en jouit[23]. De cette propension, son style, plus que le témoignage et l'instrument poétique, est l'expression passionnée et sensible. Si aucun roman n'est invraisemblable et incroyable comme le sont ceux de Balzac, il est vrai aussi que personne n'a jamais cru en l'inventaire aussi fermement que

22 On se souvient des premières pages de *Facino Cane* où Balzac, dans l'acte d'« observer les mœurs du faubourg, ses habitants et leurs caractères », transforme l'observation en une action imaginative d'une extraordinaire puissance hyperbolique qui lui permet, écrit Balzac, de « vivre de la vie de l'individu sur laquelle elle s'exerçait, en me permettant de me substituer à lui » (*CH*, VI, p. 1019). Gautier, lui-aussi, dans son magnifique *Honoré de Balzac* (*op. cit.*), nous rappelle la confiance démesurée qu'avait Balzac quant à la force de l'imagination : sa lucide « conscience de cette puissante faculté d'intuition » lui permettait de vivre dans la vie et dans la vie même de ses personnages. Balzac, écrit Gautier, « possédait le don d'*avatar* c'est-à-dire celui de s'incarner dans des corps différents et d'y vivre le temps qu'il voulait. [...]. Il ne les copiait pas, il les vivait idéalement » (p. 38-39).

23 Balzac, nous dit Croce, « a le goût des passions poussées à l'extrême, des contrastes nets et intransigeants, des entreprises colossales, des ruses les plus astucieuses, des escroqueries diaboliques, des succès mirobolants, et il jouit de ces inventions, les intensifie pour en jouir plus largement » (voir *Balzac*, *op. cit.*, p. 248).

lui, qui nous insuffle sa foi à un point tel qu'aucun lecteur, aussi longtemps qu'il lit, ne croit à un roman autant que le lecteur de Balzac. Sa force d'imagination et de représentation s'apparente à celle des rêves, hallucinée et hallucinante[24].

Faire le procès de son goût ou de son contenu est aussi injuste que de s'en prendre à ses illusions de mystique ou de physiologiste philosophant, de politique tenant de toutes les écoles, d'historien, de moraliste, d'homme encyclopédique. Il faut dire plutôt que ces illusions, elles aussi, entrent, pour une bonne part, dans l'attraction sympathique qui fait que le lecteur donne à Balzac son assentiment le plus vif et le plus confiant justement au moment où il est le plus tenté de le lui refuser au nom du discernement, de la raison et du goût. Personne ne peut dire qu'il a lu Balzac s'il n'a été une heure durant, ou un an, balzacien, éperdument balzacien.

Assurément, comme je l'ai déjà dit, il fait concurrence à l'état civil, si l'on est bien d'accord toutefois qu'il s'agit du recensement d'une population de fantômes. Il est vrai aussi que l'historien aurait tort de croire qu'il connaît la France de la Révolution et de l'Empire, de la Restauration et de Louis-Philippe, voire l'Europe du XIXe siècle s'il n'a pas fréquenté l'œuvre de Balzac, et cela non parce qu'elle représente ces diverses époques mais bien plus parce qu'elle est enracinée dans la vie, l'humeur, les mœurs, la fantaisie, les vices de ces temps-là.

Sur l'empire de Balzac non plus, le soleil ne se couche jamais, mais parce qu'il s'agit d'un empire chimérique ; l'énergie de conquérant, de législateur, de magicien avec laquelle il domine, embrasse, pénètre et fouille cet empire me fait venir à l'esprit cette pensée de Pascal : Jules César était trop mûr pour caresser le projet de conquérir le monde, plus propre à fasciner le jeune et fascinant Alexandre le Grand. Allant plus loin, on pourrait ajouter que le Macédonien fut une force barbare autant qu'exaltée par la culture hellénique, qui avec lui s'est acheminée vers la somptueuse décadence hellénistique, à moins que l'on ne veuille m'imposer une autre comparaison. Tel cet Alexandre le Grand de la légende médiévale qui, parvenu aux confins de la terre, languit du désir de conquérir la lune, il me semble voir l'inégalable Balzac dans son empire de rêves, conquérant et conquis, se consumant en rêve et en chimère.

---

24 « Tous ces personnages – écrit Baudelaire dans son essai sur Gautier (*op. cit.*, p. 248) – sont doués de l'ardeur vitale dont il était animé lui-même. Toutes ses fictions sont aussi profondément colorées que les rêves ».

Pour en revenir à l'artiste, sa luxuriance et sa minutie, toutes deux prodigieuses, ont l'évidence obsédante et la logique implacable de ce mélange stupéfiant de lucidité imaginative et de fièvre cérébrale, d'exactitude extrême et de mégalomanie inventive, de vigueur stylistique et de graphomanie, de vertu et de virtuosité, qui fait l'étoffe et la singularité de son génie littéraire, un génie qui exerce sur nous une influence comparable à celle d'une comète des ciels fabuleux de l'astrologie, et irradie en nous une lumière illusoire et irrésistible comme celle d'une aurore boréale.

Je m'aperçois, Mesdames et Messieurs, que je me répands en métaphores, mais c'est l'influence de la comète balzacienne. S'il n'était l'inimitable que l'on sait, l'homme serait dangereux, car il montre que l'on peut violer toute règle, aller à l'encontre de toute règle, de la mesure, du bon sens, de la raison, et s'affirmer, non malgré cela mais justement à cause de cela, comme génie et héros littéraire : d'autorité, triomphalement, *sit pro ratione voluntas*, compte tenu de son talent.

Il est juste alors, me semble-t-il, de rappeler également que la vocation et le destin de Balzac se manifestent aussi dans les tracas, les soucis de ses journées angoissées, de ses nuits terribles et laborieuses, avec à sa porte les créanciers, l'huissier, le coursier de la typographie. Ils se manifestent dans l'étrange et indubitable logique de ses folies, de ses nombreuses faillites et de ce projet de conquête du monde, qui, finalement, en se transposant en chimère et en épreuves d'imprimerie, lui a même réussi.

Pour en revenir à un jugement critique et technique, c'est un fait que Balzac romancier possède une vertu qui tient de la toute-puissance et de l'infaillibilité, car chez lui aucune particularité, aucune figure, aucune remarque ne demeure intentionnelle, velléitaire, non aboutie, approximative. Sa puissance de création, si on la prend pour elle-même et en elle-même, est absolue, elle ne se laisse réduire à aucun critère de comparaison si ce n'est par rapport à elle-même, mais tout autre critère l'altère, la détruit. Pour lui appliquer une de ces expressions où il sait condenser toute une saturation de faits et de passions, comme un simple titre (disons par exemple : *La femme de trente ans*) eh bien, cette vertu est sa *Grandeur et Misère.*

La misère, au sens philosophique, est bien celle d'un homme à qui il est donné d'atteindre la grandeur, d'accomplir son œuvre, seulement dans la mesure où il est contraint d'y consumer, dans les limites de celle-ci, toute conscience critique et tout jugement rationnel.

Toutefois, l'ayant intitulée Comédie, c'est-à-dire représentation d'une fiction, involontairement et sans le savoir, Balzac lui-même ouvre la voie à une définition critique de son œuvre. Exactement comme une scène de théâtre à regarder avec une participation enthousiaste mais limitée, intense mais fugitive, *La Comédie humaine* est une œuvre prodigieuse. Et je la vois comme une scène grouillante d'innombrables personnages et masques, inertes jusqu'au moment où s'allument les feux de la rampe et où ils prononcent les paroles qui leur sont insufflées[25]. Ce qui illumine la scène, ce qui encore avant cela insuffle une animation secrète et irrésistible, une impatience universelle de vivre et de parler à ces masques et personnages, c'est la voix de Balzac souffleur. Et il me semble que je l'entends, pareille à celle de Vautrin quand il rentre à la nuit tombée dans la célèbre pension[26] ; – *C'est moi, maman.* C'est une voix nocturne et souterraine, venant de son trou de souffleur imaginaire, vigoureusement asthmatique, avec une puissante inflexion sardonique, qui met en mouvement, presse, anime, agite la scène jusqu'au tomber de rideau. Et il est bon que les spectateurs que nous sommes rentrent chez eux sans monter sur la scène, sans découvrir la tristesse des lumières éteintes, des machines, des décors en trompe-l'œil, des masques et des costumes pendus au clou.

Mais alors, à cette immense œuvre imaginative du prodigieux, du transcendantal romancier manquerait-il les ailes de la légère et simple poésie, qui seule rend immortelles les œuvres d'art ?

La poésie dans l'œuvre de Balzac, je la sens lorsqu'en elle et venant d'elle parle une autre voix qui est aussi celle de Balzac. C'est celle qui, en décrivant, incarne et tout à la fois juge et justifie et condamne et déplore l'irrémissible, la fatalité des passions et de l'abus.

Cette voix, je ne l'entends pas, et je ne crois pas qu'on l'entende, lorsque Balzac s'applique à exprimer des vues morales plus ou moins cyniques, des sentiments mystiques plus ou moins transcendantaux. Je la perçois dans un accent involontaire et constant de compassion profonde allant

25 Croce fait encore remarquer : « Balzac, imprimant une impulsion capricieuse à ses créations, fait en sorte que ses personnages tournoient rapidement sur eux-mêmes et croissent dans une spirale vertigineuse, devenant toujours plus fous d'eux-mêmes, et parfois, au sommet où ils sont parvenus, il fait en sorte qu'ils se métamorphosent dans le contraire de ce qu'ils étaient ou révèlent de manière inattendue d'autres qualités, contradictoires ou discordantes par rapport aux précédentes » (*Balzac*, *op. cit.*, p. 248).

26 Il s'agit de la Pension Vauquer dans *Le Père Goriot*.

jusqu'à la pitié, qui anime et vivifie l'implacable machine figurative et exemplaire : pitié pour la substance tragique qui est celle des passions, et de notre vie, celle de nos injustices et de nos équités, de nos erreurs et de nos vérités, celle de notre destin humain lié à la terre. Le sentiment de la cruauté fatale de l'existence et des besoins humains et terrestres, dans tous les ordres de choses, est intense et tragique chez Balzac, et il le traduit par une pitié profonde et intime pour les victimes et leurs oppresseurs, pour les victimes et ceux qui en font des victimes, et pour ceux qui sont victimes d'eux-mêmes comme nous tous. C'est dans cet accent de l'âme que je sens la poésie de Balzac, présente justement comme accent profond, dans toute la *Comédie*, exprimée d'une voix claire et chantante par plus d'une figure. Chacun peut élire et préférer celle qu'il veut parmi ces figures annonciatrices de pitié dans l'œuvre de Balzac. Pour moi, les deux anges poétiques sont les deux femmes inoubliables des *Mémoires de deux jeunes mariées* : Louise et Renée[27].

Présentation et notes par
Marco STUPAZZONI[28]

---

27 De tous les romans de la *Comédie humaine*, *Mémoires de deux jeunes mariées* était l'œuvre préférée de Bacchelli. Dans un article publié dans « La Stampa » le 21 octobre 1928 et intitulé : *Canapa e altre cose* [*Chanvre et autres choses*] (repris ensuite dans *Italia per terra e per mare* [*Italie par terre et par mer*] en 1952), Bacchelli, évoquant la fierté des femmes émiliennes, écrit : « Si j'avais une épouse, je voudrais la prier de faire elle-même notre lit, non seulement pour les délicates raisons que l'on peut lire dans les lettres des deux "Jeunes Mariées", le roman de Balzac que je préfère, mais aussi parce que dans les tâches féminines, la femme, grande artiste, est des plus charmantes ».

28 Je voudrais exprimer ici ma profonde gratitude à Mme Françoise Capette, avec qui j'ai pu discuter la traduction de ce texte.

RÉSUMÉS/ABSTRACTS

Göran BLIX and Andrea GOULET, "Introduction. Balzac and New Critical Ecologies"

Recent ecocritical approaches allow us to read *La Comédie humaine* anew. Our contributors trace the Balzacian poetics of city and nature in the early industrial age, of human time in the geological sublime, of entanglements with animal and arboreal others, of affective ecologies and material economies in what is now called the Anthropocene. Balzac's fluid, capacious exploration of energy as a vital force, irreducible to human economic terms, reframes him as a prescient ecological writer.

Keywords: ecocriticism, ecologies, energy, Anthropocene, nature.

Göran BLIX et Andrea GOULET, « *Introduction. Balzac et la nouvelle pensée écocritique* »

À la lumière de nouvelles approches écocritiques, les articles de ce volume dessinent une poétique balzacienne de la ville et de la nature à l'ère industrielle, tout en interrogeant nos rapports avec l'autre animal, végétal ou géologique. L'exploration balzacienne de l'énergie comme force vitale, irréductible à la pensée économique humaine, fait de l'auteur de La Comédie humaine *un écrivain écologique avant la lettre.*

Mots-clés : écocritique, écologies, énergie, Anthropocène, nature.

Dominique BAUER, "Deep Time in an Age of Traces. Modern Temporality in Balzac's *Le Colonel Chabert* and *La Peau de chagrin*"

This essay studies and contextualizes the idea of deep time in Balzac, referring in particular to *Le Colonel Chabert* and *La Peau de chagrin.* It argues that Balzac conceives of deep time as both within and beyond history, as both a critical subtext of modern temporality and a model of coherence in a modernity that produces fragments and debris, as well as an aesthetic-literary framework of preservation and reconstitution.

Keywords: modernity, deep time, temporality, *Le Colonel Chabert*, *La Peau de chagrin.*

Dominique BAUER, « *Le temps profond à l'âge des traces chez Balzac. Temporalité moderne dans* Le Colonel Chabert *et* La Peau de chagrin »

Cet essai étudie et contextualise l'idée du temps profond chez Balzac, en se référant surtout au Colonel Chabert *et à* La Peau de chagrin. *Il est soutenu que Balzac conçoit le temps profond comme à la fois dans et au-delà de l'histoire, à la fois sous-texte critique de la temporalité moderne et modèle de cohérence dans une modernité productrice de fragments et de débris, ou encore, un cadre esthético-littéraire de préservation et de reconstitution.*

Mots-clés : modernité, temps profond, temporalité, Le Colonel Chabert, La Peau de chagrin.

Karen QUANDT, "Leaves of Thistle. Paper Ecologies in Balzac's *Illusions perdues*"

In *Illusions perdues*, Balzac portrays a paper-based ecology which, through David Séchard's company, recycles the practice of using local plants. This article explores this botanic vitalism in the context of industrialization and the large-scale production of books.

Keywords: papermaking, botany, plant paper, book production, Chinese papermaking.

Karen QUANDT, « *Feuilles de chardon. Écologies du papier dans* Illusions perdues *de Balzac* »

Dans Illusions perdues, *Balzac représente une écologie du papier qui, à travers l'entreprise de David Séchard, recycle la pratique de l'exploitation des plantes locales. Cet article se propose d'interroger ce vitalisme botanique sous-jacent dans le contexte de l'industrialisation et de la production de livres à grande échelle.*

Mots-clés : fabrication du papier, botanique, papier à plantes, production de livres, papeterie chinoise.

Pierre FORFERT, "Balzac's Poplar Trees. The Economy of Timber in *Eugénie Grandet*"

In conversation with early nineteenth-century agronomists, this article investigates how the environmental cost of intensive tree farming feeds into the narrative economy of *Eugénie Grandet.* The poplars exploited by cooper-turned-speculator Félix Grandet emerge as sense-making cues of a burgeoning capitalist modernity. Using plant tropes to metaphorically capture mechanisms of wealth, Balzac coins a dendrological grammar that interrogates the uncontrollable growth of speculative endeavors.

Keywords: poplar tree, silviculture, misery, economy, speculation.

Pierre FORFERT, « *Les peupliers de Balzac. L'économie sylvicole dans* Eugénie Grandet »

Cet article se propose d'analyser l'économie environnementale de la sylviculture dans Eugénie Grandet, *en montrant la manière dont le roman, par l'intermédiaire de l'exploitation par Félix Grandet de milliers de peupliers, développe une grammaire dendrologique qui interroge l'incontrôlable croissance des entreprises spéculatives et, par-là, la modernité capitaliste naissante.*

Mots-clés : peupliers, sylviculture, avarice, économie, spéculation.

Abigail FIELDS, "Peasants v. Pastoral. Some Uses of Animality in Balzac's *Les Paysans*"

In *Les Paysans* Balzac elucidates, via the proxy of Émile Blondet, a vision of the French countryside that conforms to a bourgeois pastoral. This pastoral relies on the animalization and 'othering' of the peasant, who cannot enter into this scene as fully 'human'. The development of the peasant figure complicates this narrative, however: by manipulating the terms of their own animality, the peasants assert a counter-pastoral, which troubles the Parisian environmental imagination.

Keywords: peasant, pastoral, counter-pastoral, *animalité*, environmental imagination.

Abigail FIELDS, « *Paysans contre pastorale. Quelques usages de l'animalité dans* Les Paysans *de Balzac* »

Dans Les Paysans, *Balzac fait jouer deux visions de la campagne française l'une contre l'autre : d'un côté Blondet déploie une fantaisie pastorale fondée sur l'animalisation des campagnards ; de l'autre, les paysans eux-mêmes imposent une contre-pastorale qui trouble l'imaginaire parisien et complexifie la représentation.*

Mots-clés : paysan, pastoral, contre-pastoral, animalité, imaginaire environnemental.

Christopher ROBISON, "Panthers and Pantheism. Animal Sympathy and Balzac's Mystical Biology"

The present project places Balzac's *Une passion dans le désert* alongside *Séraphîta*, highlighting the manner in which the two texts explore largely analogous interspecies relationships between creatures who occupy different rungs along a hierarchical *échelle des êtres* (human-to-panther in the former, angel-to-human in the latter). In comparing the two, the project points to Balzac's sensitivity to questions surrounding alterity and continuism that continue to inform animal studies scholarship.

Keywords: *Une passion dans le désert*, *Séraphîta*, animals, angels, biology.

Christopher ROBISON, « Panthères et panthéisme. La sympathie animale et la biologie mystique de Balzac »

*Proposant une lecture croisée d'*Une passion dans le désert *et* Séraphîta, *deux œuvres qui représentent des relations interespèces entre des créatures de différentes natures, cet article se propose de mettre en valeur la sensibilité de Balzac aux questions d'altérité et de continuisme, si importantes pour les études animalistes aujourd'hui.*

Mots-clés : Une passion dans le désert, Séraphîta, *animaux, anges, biologie.*

Abbey CARRICO, "The Ecology of Emotions. Exploitation of Nature in Balzac's *Le Lys dans la vallée*"

This article examines the relationship between representation and exploitation through narrative perspective in Balzac's *Le Lys dans la vallée*, arguing that nature exists solely to express the human and for human use despite its romanticized and idealized portrayal. Ultimately, it shows that Balzac's modern ideology and mapping of the social world is replicated within his depiction of the natural world, reinforcing an anthropocentric lens at both the diegetic and extradiegetic levels.

Keywords: exploitation, nature, emotions, landscape, romanticism.

Abbey CARRICO, « *L'écologie des émotions. L'exploitation de la nature dans* Le Lys dans la vallée *de Balzac* »

Cet article propose d'analyser dans une perspective écocritique la manière dont la représentation balzacienne se fonde sur une vision anthropocentrique, tant au niveau diégétique qu'extradiégétique, pour peindre une nature idéalisée et constamment mise au service de l'expression des êtres humains.

Mots-clés : exploitation, nature, émotions, paysage, romantisme.

Charlotte BERKERY, "Night Air. Miasma Theory and *La Cousine Bette*"

This article analyses the connection between nighttime and the cold, humid and muddy landscape which is Balzac's Paris through the prism of *La Cousine Bette* where the motif of nocturnal miasma stands in for contemporary anxieties about social change and urbanisation. By replacing the novel in an ecological context, I advance a new understanding of the relations between Balzac's writing, environmental thought, medical humanities and night studies where night air, contagion and the miasmic city.

Keywords: night, miasma, Paris, *La Cousine Bette*, public health.

Charlotte BERKERY, « *L'air nocturne. La théorie des miasmes et* La Cousine Bette »

Dans La Cousine Bette*, les miasmes nocturnes sont un motif symbolique des angoisses contemporaines liées au changement social et à l'urbanisation. Cet article propose de les analyser dans une perspective écologique qui met l'accent sur les liens entre la pensée environnementale, les humanités médicales et l'écriture de la nuit.*

Mots-clés : nuit, miasmes, Paris, La Cousine Bette*, santé publique.*

Virginie A. DUZER, « *Le Chef-d'œuvre inconnu*, ou la disparition de l'herbe verte »

Dans *Le Chef-d'œuvre inconnu*, tout se passe comme si le paysage ne pouvait pas être représenté. Or la comparaison entre les deux principales versions du texte fait apparaître une disparition curieuse de « l'herbe verte » et de la bucolique Grenadière. Cet article propose ainsi de s'intéresser à cette disparition de la nature, afin de comprendre la nouvelle dans une perspective nouvelle – et oblique.

Mots-clés : *Le Chef-d'œuvre inconnu*, herbe, nature, paysage, oblique.

Virginie A. DUZER, "Le Chef-d'œuvre inconnu*, or the disappearance of l'herbe verte*"

The story of Le Chef-d'œuvre inconnu *seems detached from nature: everything takes place in an almost closed setting in Paris populated by portraits, as if landscape could hardly be represented. Yet, comparing the two main versions of the text reveals*

the strange erasure of "l'herbe verte" *and the bucolic Grenadière. These ellipses invite us to reread the tale from a new angle, perhaps the kind of oblique gaze that should have been cast upon the Belle-Noiseuse to fully see her.*
Keywords: Le Chef-d'œuvre inconnu, l'herbe verte, *nature, landscape, oblique.*

Michele MORSELLI, « Le merveilleux napoléonien dans les romans de jeunesse de Balzac »

Dans les romans de jeunesse de Balzac, la représentation de la légende napoléonienne, associée au merveilleux, peut être pensée comme contre-discours du réalisme de la maturité. Le présent article propose d'examiner les modalités de cette représentation dans trois romans : *Falthurne*, *Le Centenaire* et *Annette et le criminel*.
Mots-clés : légende, Napoléon, *Falthurne*, *Le Centenaire*, Argow.

Michele MORSELLI, "*The 'marvelous' Napoleonic legend in Balzac's early novels*"

In Balzac's early novels, the representation of the Napoleonic legend, associated with marvel, can be considered as a counter-discourse based on a realism of maturity. This article examines aspects of this representation in three novels: Falthurne, Le Centenaire, *and* Annette et le criminel.
Keywords: legend, Napoleon, Falthurne, Le Centenaire, *Argow.*

Tania DUCLOS, « Genèse et effet de l'intertexte balzacien. Autour d'un bal de Lady Dudley »

Le présent article propose de montrer la manière dont Balzac, dans la scène de bal d'*Une fille d'Ève*, emprunte à la nouvelle *Onuphrius* de Gautier : l'étude stylistique et génétique, menée du premier manuscrit jusqu'au Furne corrigé, permet de mettre au jour un jeu intertextuel entièrement mis au service d'une nouvelle visée romanesque.
Mots-clés : plagiat, genèse, Théophile Gautier, intertextualité, réalisme.

Tania DUCLOS, "*The origins and effects of Balzacian intertext. On Lady Dudley's ball*"

This article explores how Balzac, in the ball scene in Une fille d'Ève, *draws on the novella* Onuphrius *by Gautier: A stylistic and genetic study, from the first manuscript to the edition published by Furne, sheds light on an intertextual exchange serving a new novelistic approach.*
Keywords: imitation, origins, Théophile Gautier, intertextuality, realism.

Giuseppe Guizzi, « "Le débiteur est plus fort que le créancier". Balzac, la dette et la morale dans la société post-moderne »

Cet article montre la manière dont Balzac représente et interroge dans son œuvre les relations de débiteur à créancier et la relativisation progressive de la responsabilité patrimoniale. Ce faisant, il anticipe sur la tendance, promue par le droit de l'Union européenne, qui consiste à subvertir la règle du « tu dois » de l'idéologie bourgeoise.
Mots-clés : surendettement, procédures de désendettement, droit et littérature, idéologie bourgeoise, *La Comédie humaine.*

Giuseppe Guizzi, "'*The debtor is stronger than the creditor'. Balzac, debt, and morality in postmodern society*"

This article shows how Balzac's work portrays and examines the relationship between debtor and creditor, and the gradual relativization of patrimonial responsibility. Through this, he anticipated the trend, promoted by European Union law, toward subverting the rule of "you owe" grounded in bourgeois ideology.
Keywords: over-indebtedness, debt relief procedures, law and literature, bourgeois ideology, La Comédie humaine.

REVUE BALZAC

La *Revue Balzac* entend ouvrir de nouvelles perspectives critiques à la recherche balzacienne. Annuelle et bilingue, elle présente un profil résolument international.

Retrouvez tous les numéros de la revue en scannant ce code QR :

Et pour recevoir nos dernières actualités, abonnez-vous ici :

IMPRIM'VERT®

Achevé d'imprimer par Corlet,
Condé-en-Normandie (Calvados),
en Juin 2025
N° d'impression : 188201 - dépôt légal : Juin 2025
Imprimé en France

CLASSIQUES GARNIER

Bulletin d'abonnement revue 2025

Revue Balzac

1 numéro par an

M., Mme :

Adresse :

Code postal : Ville :

Pays :

Téléphone : Fax :

Courriel :

Prix TTC abonnement France, frais de port inclus		Prix HT abonnement étranger, frais de port inclus	
Particulier	Institution	Particulier	Institution
28 €	37 €	36 €	43 €

Cet abonnement concerne les parutions papier du 1er janvier 2025 au 31 décembre 2025.

Les numéros parus avant le 1er janvier 2025 sont disponibles à l'unité (hors abonnement) sur notre site web.

Modalités de règlement (en euros) :

- Par carte bancaire sur notre site web : www.classiques-garnier.com
- Par virement bancaire sur le compte :
  Banque : Société Générale – BIC : SOGEFRPP
  IBAN : FR 76 3000 3018 7700 0208 3910 870
  RIB : 30003 01877 00020839108 70
- Par chèque à l'ordre de Classiques Garnier

Classiques Garnier
6, rue de la Sorbonne – 75005 Paris – France
Téléphone : + 33 1 43 54 00 44
Courriel : revues@classiques-garnier.com

mis à jour le 12/08/2024